Baghdad FC

The national game for over half a century, football is potentially one of the binding forces in Iraq. But such is its power that it is as riven by dishonesty, suspicion, fear and feuds as the nation itself. This is a search for truth about Iraq's astonishing sporting story – a story of brutality, cowardice and heroism.

Through a complex web of characters – including the Arab world's Pelé, an ex-Stasi manager, exiled players and current Baghdad voices, all committed to a game they loved even under the yoke of totalitarianism – Simon Freeman uncovers stories that reveal the compromises that people make in order to survive a tyranny. It is a tale of triumph and tragedy – its climax being the Athens Olympics – and asks the tantalizing question: what is the destiny of Iraq's game in a post-Saddam world, where George W. Bush favours baseball over soccer as his globalizing force, and the US military parks its tanks in the national stadium.

Simon Freeman, a lifelong football fan and former *Sunday Times* Insight journalist, has also written for *The Times*, *Evening Standard*, *Guardian*, *Mail on Sunday*, *Vanity Fair* and *International Herald Tribune*. He has covered two World Cups and two Olympics, lectured on journalism in London, the USA and the Balkans, and consulted for the Institute of War and Peace Reporting. His previous books are *Conspiracy of Silence: The Secret Life of Anthony Blunt*, *Rinkagate: The Rise and Fall of Jeremy Thorpe*, *Sport Behind the Iron Curtain* and *Own Goal: Egotism and Greed in Football*.

Other books by Simon Freeman

Sport Behind the Iron Curtain (with Roger Boyes)

Conspiracy of Silence:
The Secret Life of Anthony Blunt (with Barrie Penrose)

Rinkagate: The Rise and Fall of Jeremy Thorpe

Own Goal: Egotism and Greed in Football

Baghdad FC

Iraq's Football Story

SIMON FREEMAN

JOHN MURRAY

© Simon Freeman 2005

First published in Great Britain in 2005 by John Murray (Publishers)
A division of Hodder Headline

The right of Simon Freeman to be identified as the Author of the Work has been asserted by him
in accordance with the Copyright, Designs and Patents Act 1988.

1

A CIP catalogue record for this title is available from the British Library

ISBN 0 7195 6794 7

Typeset in 11.5/14pt Monotype Bembo

Printed and bound by Clays Ltd, St Ives plc

Hodder Headline policy is to use papers that are natural, renewable and recyclable products and
made from wood grown in sustainable forests. The logging and manufacturing processes are
expected to conform to the environmental regulations of the country of origin.

John Murray (Publishers)
338 Euston Road
London NW1 3BH

For Gillian

Contents

Illustrations		ix
Acknowledgements		xi
Preface		xiii
1.	A German called Stange	1
2.	The television deal that never was	15
3.	The end of Uday	30
4.	Dangers of the Web	41
5.	The legend of Ammo Baba	55
6.	The conspiracy of Penmarc'h	72
7.	Ammo's story	88
8.	The victims speak	105
9.	'The Goodwill Tour' turns sour	119
10.	Horror stories	139
11.	A general, a scholar, Mr Fatfat and a solicitor come to the rescue	157
12.	Ammo changes his mind and the boys do well in Greece	175
13.	The game goes on	199
	Notes	221
	Index	229

Illustrations

1. Bernd Stange, the German who coached Iraq
2. Ammo Baba with Uday Hussein
3. Al-Zawraa fans watching a match against a Qatar team, November 1999
4. Uday, Saddam and Qusay Hussein
5. Arkan Mahmood
6. Samir Kadhum
7. Ahmed Radhi
8. Shakir Mahmood
9. Habib Ja'far
10. The Iraqi Football Association (IFA) headquarters
11. Boys from Shia slums of Baghdad training at Ammo Baba's 'football academy'
12. Ahmed al-Samarrai, president of the Iraqi National Olympic Committee
13. Iraqi football fans in Patras, Greece, during the 2004 Olympics
14. Ammo Baba with his team in Penmarc'h, Brittany in May 2004
15. Ammo in the dug-out with 'Bagdad FC' substitutes
16. Ammo with his son and daughter-in-law
17. A jubilant Iraqi fan after his country's victory over Portugal in the 2004 Olympics
18. Mark Clark with the boxer Najah Ali
19. Bernd Stange with officials from the Iraqi Football Association
20. Furat Ahmed Kadoim in Birmingham, 2004

The author and publishers would like to thank the following for permission to reproduce illustrations: plate 2, Photograph AFP/Getty Images; 3, Karim Sahib/AFP/Getty Images; 4, Reuters/Corbis; 11, 12 and 18, Mark Clark. Photographs 1, 13–17 and 19–20 were taken by the author.

Acknowledgements

I would like to thank John Saddler, my agent at Curtis Brown. Through many set-backs he remained enthusiastic. I am grateful to Gordon Wise at John Murray for his understanding as Iraq disintegrated. Walter Ellis urged me on in hilarious e-mails. Finally, and most importantly, I must thank Gillian Cribbs. Without her this book would not exist.

Preface

If the American President, George W. Bush, and the British Prime
Minister, Tony Blair, had been right about Iraq, this would have been
a different book. The Iraqi army would have surrendered within days
of American and British forces entering the country in March 2003.
The Americans and the British would have found weapons of mass
destruction. Saddam, his sons Uday and Qusay and the other gangsters who had pillaged Iraq since 1979 would have been arrested
quickly. There would have been a few months of ineffective resistance
from Saddam loyalists, who had prospered under him and who had
lost everything when he fell, but the majority of Iraqis – Sunni, Shia,
Kurd and Christian – would have welcomed the invasion.

I would have spent several months in Iraq, talking to footballers past
and present, to coaches, to officials who ran clubs and the Iraqi Football
Association and to fans. I would have visited the great clubs of Baghdad,
the heart of football in Iraq, and toured the country, visiting places such
as Basra, Najaf, Arbil, Kirkuk and Mosul, where football has always
been popular. I would have gone to small towns and villages and seen
children playing on dirt pitches and dreaming of glory. I would have
described the revival of football, symbolizing the emergence of a new
Iraq. Through football I would have explained how the country was
recovering from the depredations of Uday, who had run the game in
Iraq for two decades, terrorizing and torturing players, coaches and
referees. I would have told how football resisted him and survived.

But it was not like that. The Americans and the British were wrong
about almost everything. There were no weapons of mass destruction,
though Saddam had always pretended there were, as much to impress
his own people as to deter potential attackers. The Iraqi army fought

harder, and more cleverly, than anyone expected, by avoiding frontal assaults, in which they would have been obliterated by the invaders' far superior weapons. Instead, they hit the Americans and British from the side and rear. The White House and Downing Street underestimated the resentment of ordinary Iraqis at sanctions, imposed twelve years earlier, after Iraq's invasion of Kuwait. They failed to understand that Iraqis were proud, that they could hate Saddam but also hate the invaders who had come to depose him. Before the invasion experts on the region had predicted that both Sunnis and the Shia majority would be angered by the presence of infidels. In short, the invasion caused as many problems as it solved.

As autumn turned to winter in 2004, Iraq became increasingly violent. Six days before Christmas masked men dragged three Iraqis, working for the electoral commission that was organizing the January 2005 elections, from their cars in central Baghdad in broad daylight and murdered them. The same day bombs killed at least sixty people, and injured scores more, in the Shia cities of Karbala and Najaf, to the south of the capital, adding to fears that Sunni militants were trying to provoke a civil war.

The league in Iraq had been revived in the autumn of 2004 but was soon abandoned because of escalating violence. It spluttered into life again in the new year, a tribute to the Iraqis' passion for the game and the desire of most of them for a normal, peaceful life. Iraqis knew that the worst would be over if they could watch their favourite teams, meet friends on the terraces and argue afterwards in cafés about who had played well and who should be dropped. There was a long way to go. Matches were often cancelled, especially in Baghdad and the surrounding Sunni-dominated areas, where hatred of the Americans, the British and the new Iraqi government was most intense. Crowds were small. But football was happening, which was extraordinary since the world saw Iraq as a permanent bloodbath.

At the end of January 2005 there was an election for a national assembly, which would appoint an interim government and construct a new constitution. The election was far from perfect, but it took place and almost 8½ million Iraqis voted for 111 parties, represented by 7,500 candidates. In the weeks after the election, however, the violence escalated. There was a spate of dreadful suicide bombings, which killed hundreds. There were confirmed cases of brutality towards prisoners by British soldiers, echoing the scandal in 2004 of the abuse of Iraqis by the Americans at Abu Ghraib gaol. Three British soldiers were convicted for their part in this, but in the spring of 2005 it was reported that another fifty British troops, including a member of the revered Special Air Service, could face criminal charges. Human Rights Watch, based in New York and respected around the world, said that the Iraqi security forces routinely beat up or tortured suspects. 'The people of Iraq were promised something better than this after the government of Saddam Hussein fell', said a spokesperson for the organization. 'The Iraqi interim government is not keeping its promises to honour and respect human rights.'

This book examines how football grew in Iraq and how Uday almost destroyed it. It shows how the same men who served him were chosen by the Americans and British to run football after he had gone – because there was no one else. I had hoped to find heroes, who had fought Uday because they wanted to save football. But there were none in Iraq; anyone who had openly defied him was dead. There were a few brave men – former players and even a referee – in exile, who had fled because they could not endure his brutality and corruption. Some had spoken out against Saddam and Uday, which took courage because they knew that they could be targeted by Saddam's security services.

Ordinary footballers, most of them poorly educated Shias from the slums of Baghdad, were the closest people to heroes in Iraq. They had wanted only to play football and were grateful if they had earned enough to live. Many were gaoled and savagely beaten by Uday for no other reason than that he enjoyed inflicting pain. They were heroes in the sense that they remained honest. But the men who had run football for Uday, who had wealth, status and power, were not like that. They had lied, cheated and betrayed, because that was the only way to survive. This book is about football, but I hope it explores a broader theme: what happens to a people when it is ruled by monsters.

Simon Freeman
London, April 2005

I

A German called Stange

On Saturday 5 October 2002 a German called Bernd Stange announced that he had been hired to coach Iraq's football team. Hussein Saeed, secretary-general of Iraq's Olympic committee, told Reuters, the international news agency, that the Iraqi Football Association expected Stange, from Jena in the former East Germany, to lead Iraq to the World Cup finals in Germany in 2006. Stange, who was fifty-four, said, 'I have been out of work for a year, and you don't receive many offers at my age.'[1]

British newspapers are not interested in football in the developing world, and I found the story about Stange on a sport website while I was surfing the Internet. I thought that he was unusually honest. Newly employed football coaches always claimed that it was the fulfilment of a life's dream to take charge of this club or that country, when it was obvious that they cared only about the money. But Stange said that he was just glad of the job. He did not say he had always hoped that, one day, he would move to Baghdad. Nor did he promise that he was going to lead Iraq to unprecedented glory. No, he said that he was happy to be working again. This was unbelievably, wonderfully honest.

Every day the football world shows how amoral it is. One player proclaims undying loyalty to a club while his agent is negotiating a transfer. Another claims, hand on heart, that he has never met the lap dancer who has just sold the story of their sizzling, five-times-a-night 'relationship' to a tabloid, when he has long been a regular client. A manager swears after a match that he did not see the tackle that crippled the opposition's star striker, although he had ordered his defenders at half-time to 'take the bastard out'. A chairman dismisses rumours that he is selling his controlling stake in a club to a property developer who plans to turn the ground into a shopping mall, and the next day he has gone, with a cheque for £30 million.

But apart from his refreshing candour Stange's appointment was a non-story. The media in Britain care only about British sport. The tabloids concentrate on football, mainly the Premiership. They leaven this with cricket, athletics, boxing and tennis, though the latter figures only during Wimbledon fortnight, when they ask why Britain can't produce a champion. The more intelligent popular newspapers, such as the *Daily Mail*, do the same but also cover middle-class sports, such as golf, to cater for their audience. The quality newspapers, which used to be called broadsheets before they shrank to become up-market tabloids, run little stories about minor sports, such as sailing and squash, because they are supposed to be catholic. It should be admitted that newspapers and television stations around the world are equally parochial in their coverage of sport. The *New York Times* runs dozens of stories daily from places that its readers have never been to, or even heard of, but its sports section ignores the European Championship, the most important football tournament outside the World Cup, because football is not a mainstream sport in the USA. However, the same paper carries interminable stories about college basketball in the Midwest or minor league baseball, which no one outside these areas, let alone outside the USA, cares about. *USA Today* is mostly sport (and weather), but its sport is almost entirely American, unlike its weather, which is international. Pick up newspapers in Brazil, France, Germany, India or Japan, and it is the same story: local, regional and national sport, but little from anywhere else. Yet, paradoxically, there has been an explosion in books in Britain about sport, especially football.

It began in 1992 with Nick Hornby's memoir *Fever Pitch*, which charted its author's passion for Arsenal. The book was a best-seller and was turned into a successful film. Before Hornby, a 35-year-old freelance writer and former teacher, it had been assumed that football fans were too stupid to read proper books. Football literature tended to consist of inane ghost-written autobiographies or reference books full of statistics, such as the dimensions of every pitch in the Football

League. Hornby's book showed there was a market for thoughtful books about football. In his wake came works by novelists, poets, academics, politicians and comedians. They spent a season with the best, or worst, club in the country. Some authors investigated, while others dreamed up amusing stunts, such as training with the Mongolians or hitch-hiking around World Cup venues. Players and managers, and even referees – and top referees were celebrities now – confessed their addictions to women, drugs and alcohol to a new breed of ghost-writers. These autobiographies were gritty and revealing, unlike the pap that used to be published. By the time Stange was appointed to the Iraq job there were dozens of first-rate works on football in the average London bookshop.

In October 2002 Iraq were ranked at 51 in the world by the Fédération Internationale de Football Association (FIFA), the Zurich-based organization that has governed world football since 1904. England were 6th, Scotland 55th and Wales 61st. The fact that a country in the Middle East was above the Scots and the Welsh, historic football nations, would probably have surprised people who were not interested in the game. If I had asked someone who did not know the difference between a flat back four and the offside trap which country was stronger at football, Scotland or Iraq, they would probably have gone for the former. But by the new millennium, for many reasons – such as globalization and the emergence of satellite television – developing countries were often stronger than members of the old élite. When Stange signed his deal in Baghdad, Iran was ranked at 33 in the world, Saudi Arabia at 38 and Japan at 27. The USA were ranked 10th. Football was popular among America's white middle classes. Many parents liked football, or 'soccer' as they call it, because it was safer than American football and less exclusive than basketball, which could only be played by giants. The ethnic minorities in the USA, from countries such as Mexico, where football was the national sport, also enjoyed the game, which they preferred to American football and basketball. (They enjoyed baseball too.) Despite this, the mainstream media in the USA treated soccer, the most popular sport on the planet, as if it was of interest to only an eccentric minority.

Players from Africa, the Middle East, North America, the Far East and South America, where many clubs were broke, dreamed of coming to the major leagues of Spain, England, Germany and Italy, where wages were stupendous: £50,000 a week for good players, with a few, such as David Beckham, making £100,000 a week. Even ordinary players in the top leagues made more than £500,000 a year. Footballers, who had once been lucky to earn as much as a bank manager, were the new pop stars. Some, such as Beckham, were global icons, with advertising contracts worth millions of pounds. Fifty years earlier players travelled to matches on buses. Now the car parks at major clubs in Europe gleamed with Ferraris, Porsches, Jaguars, Mercedeses, BMWs and 4x4s. Once players in England had lived in terraced houses and worried about their mortgages; now they owned town houses, country estates and villas in exclusive resorts in Portugal, Spain and the south of France. Once they had been flattered if a reporter wanted to interview them; now they had agents and public relations gurus who demanded a great of money for interviews. Young men who had left school at sixteen with no qualifications employed expensive lawyers and accountants to protect them from prying journalists, predatory women and the taxman. Some might struggle to string together a coherent sentence, but all knew their own value; a few years earlier, when I had been researching another book, players had refused to speak to me because I would not pay them.

Professional footballers in Britain had always been drawn from working-class areas in inner cities, and that was still broadly the case in 2004, except that there were now hundreds of foreigners in the four professional divisions. Most came from Europe, Africa and South America, some from the USA, Australia and the Far East but, interestingly, only a few from the Middle East and Asia. What was new in the third millennium was the fact that the top British players were multimillionaires. This was epitomized by Wayne Rooney, a teenage prodigy who was transferred from Everton, in his home city of Liverpool, to Manchester United in August 2004 for £27 million. United paid Rooney £2.5 million a year, but he remained a formidably simple young man who would probably have been a labourer had he not possessed extraordinary talent as a footballer. In Scandinavia,

Spain, Italy and Germany, which did not have Britain's class system, top-level players were generally better educated and more articulate.

There had always been European coaches like Bernd Stange, journeymen who had been forced to the outposts of football because they could not get jobs at home. Iraq had often employed foreigners to run its national teams. An Englishman called William Cook had coached the military team in the early 1950s. From the 1960s, when Iraq was avowedly socialist, most foreign coaches had come from Communist countries – the Soviet Union, Hungary, Yugoslavia, Poland and East Germany – though there also been Brazilians and a Scot.

Even big-name coaches occasionally went into exile. In 1977, before football became big business, managers' salaries in Europe were modest. The late Don Revie, the former manager of Leeds United, resigned from his job with the England team to take charge of the United Arab Emirates because they offered him so much money. Revie shrugged when the Football Association, the media and the fans condemned him for his 'greed' and 'lack of patriotism'. He said that he had been paid peanuts during a long career and had a right now, in middle age, to earn a decent wage. By the third millennium managers such as Revie, and Stange, were often called coaches because clubs and national associations had adopted the model of the Italians and Spanish. In these countries it had been common for many years for one man to be responsible for training and selection at a club while someone else was in charge of transfers, contracts, budgets and so on. Managers in Britain had resisted this because they felt, rightly, that it would diminish their authority, but it was an irresistible trend. However, since the men who ran national teams, like Iraq, did not buy or sell players or negotiate contracts, it made no difference whether they were called coaches or managers.

This was the first time I had heard of Stange. I knew that sport in Iraq was run by a thoroughly nasty piece of work called Uday Hussein, Saddam's oldest son. Uday was thirty-eight when his father was overthrown, two years older than his almost equally odious brother, Qusay.[2] I knew that footballers and other athletes who had escaped Iraq had complained that they had been tortured by Uday's thugs. I suspected that they were exaggerating. If someone is tortured, they are marked or maimed for life (if they survive), but these men – there were no women – were fit. Some said they had physical and mental scars, but otherwise they seemed fine. I thought they might have been roughed up, but no more than that. I was sure that they had had an unpleasant time under Uday, but doubted their lives had been in danger.

Of course, I knew that Saddam's regime had done terrible things. He had allegedly used poison gas against his own people, most infamously in March 1988, when 5,000 Kurds died in the village of Halabja. His troops had behaved abominably in Kuwait. Human rights groups in the West had dossiers about the unspeakable tortures inflicted on Iraqis. One exile described some of the methods favoured by Saddam's brutes:

> Bottles are thrust up bottoms, so severely that prisoners suffer fatal internal injuries. They are made to sit on gas rings. Electric drills are used on hands and feet. A jaw is broken by wrenching it apart. Limbs are cut off with an axe. Fingernails are torn out with pliers. A person's ears are nailed to a wall while he or she is standing. The only way to rest is to tear them off. People are fed to starving dogs. A man's genitals are hacked with a saw.

A few days later the story about Stange signing for Iraq 'took off' – journalistic shorthand for a routine story becoming 'a row' – when a reporter saw a photograph of him in Baghdad, grinning in front of a portrait of Saddam Hussein. This was foolish but understandable. Stange was a football coach, not an expert in public relations. Saddam's portraits – as soldier, statesman, farmer, warrior, 'The Great Uncle', 'the Lion of Babylon' and 'the Lion of Iraq' – decorated countless walls in Iraq, so the odds were short that Stange would end up near one. Unfortunately for Stange, the Americans and the British were trying at this moment to persuade the rest of the world that Saddam possessed weapons of mass destruction and that something should be done about this, such as removing him from power. This photograph became an issue because it suggested that Stange supported Saddam, which he did not.

Stange's colleagues in football in Germany were swift to condemn him. One German coach commented: 'We should show solidarity with our allies, the United States. I wouldn't coach Iraq for all the money in the world.' Another said: 'It is unfortunate when someone goes to earn money in a country led by someone who is a dictator.' Reuters, which pointed out that its photograph of Stange in Iraq had triggered 'heated protests' in Germany, reported Stange as protesting that he was not 'a mercenary'. This was nonsense since Stange had already said he was only going to Iraq because he could not find a job in a more congenial country.

Stange said that he had signed a four-year contract, with a clause that allowed him to leave Iraq if war broke out. He said that he had heard the rumours that players had been tortured by Uday: 'I made it clear to the Iraqis that this would not happen when I was national coach. But everyone in Iraq told me that the stories were not true and I have to believe them.' He added that he had also told the Iraqis that he would not allow himself to be used for 'propaganda purposes'. His critics pointed out that working for Saddam and Uday was propaganda enough.

He replied: 'I have not met Saddam or Uday. I don't have anything to do with the regime. I believe in the Olympic ideal and regard my mission as being an ambassador of peace. You have to separate sport and politics. My only aim is to get back to work as a coach in a soccer-mad nation – nothing more and nothing less. Iraq is a great sporting challenge.' When he was asked about the offending photograph, he said: 'What could I say? There was one photographer there. He asked me to pose. I couldn't tell them, "Oh no, I am not going to allow any pictures of me with Saddam." But I certainly did not go out of my way to stand in front of his portrait.'

Another German, Winfried Schaefer, had been hired in the autumn of 2001 to coach Cameroon. With the bizarre logic that became his hallmark during his reign as Iraq's coach Stange said this was significant. 'If I was in Cameroon I might get eaten by a lion, and if I was in Australia coaching a team I could be bitten by a poisonous snake. Even here in Germany we have people driving at 130 m.p.h. in 60 m.p.h. zones. So there are dangers all over the world.' Although he was annoyed that the stories about him were so critical, it was obvious that he enjoyed the attention. If he didn't, then he would not have been so available to journalists.

He was born in March 1948, in Gnaschwitz in East Germany. He was a journeyman professional who played for lower-division clubs until he retired in 1970. Great players rarely make good coaches – because they play instinctively, without needing to be taught – while average players, who have to work at their game, often become successful. Sir Alex Ferguson, the Scot who managed Manchester United, and Arsene Wenger, the Frenchman at Arsenal, had been ordinary players but were two of the outstanding managers in the world in the new millennium. Stange had taken a club called FC Carl Zeiss Jena to East German league titles in 1972 and 1975 and won the East German Cup in 1973 and 1974. In 1982 he became East Germany's national coach. Six years later he returned to FC Carl Zeiss Jena, then moved to Hertha Berlin.

In 1994 it emerged that he had been an informer for the East German secret police, the Stasi. His duties had included telling the Stasi what his players thought of the government. After the collapse of the Berlin Wall in November 1989 and the reunification of Germany the following year the Stasi's files slowly became public. The country was shocked by the scale of the betrayals, neighbours spying on neighbours, friends informing on friends out of weakness, vanity, greed or plain fear.

Stange had been a low-level informer, whose comments on his fellow coaches and players were probably not even read before they were filed. Most footballers, whether they play in a democracy or a dictatorship, are not interested in politics and think only about themselves – their fitness, how they played – money, cars and women. His players probably grumbled about their wages and the quality of East German cars and clothes, and regretted that they could not enjoy the bright lights of the West, but it is unlikely they condemned the economic policies of the government or argued for the demolition of the Berlin Wall. But Stange was a high-profile character, and the exposure of his relationship with the Stasi was an unwelcome reminder to Germans of the past. So he was vilified and forced to seek work abroad. He coached in Ukraine and Australia. In 2001 he was hired to coach Oman but was fired after three months. During his spell there Oman beat Iraq, which is what alerted the Iraqis to his potential.

The more I read about Stange, the more I was intrigued. The Stasi revelations aside, there was something endearingly open about his statements. 'There has been a lot of criticism of me about working for the Iraqis, but the fact is that no one else offered me a job. The Iraqis have confidence in me and I am proud of that', he said. Although the more excitable German newspapers described his appointment to the Iraq job as 'the scandal of the year', the story soon died. It was absurd to denounce a football coach for posing in front of a portrait of one of the world's many unpleasant leaders. Stange had not broken any laws. By taking the job he had not strengthened the regime of Saddam Hussein. He was simply trying to earn a living. He set up base in Baghdad's Sheraton Hotel, hoping that his wife, Dorothea, a nurse, would follow. She never did.

In December 2002 Iraqi sport was in the news briefly again. An organization in London called Indict, which investigated alleged crimes by Saddam Hussein's government, submitted a complaint to the International Olympic Committee (IOC) in Lausanne, Switzerland. Indict had been set up in 1996 to campaign for the establishment of an international criminal tribunal to try members of the Iraqi regime for crimes against humanity. The campaign, launched in the House of Commons and the US Senate, had been self-financing until money came from the USA, courtesy of Congress's Iraq Liberation Act, which channelled money to Iraqi opposition groups and anyone else who could damage Saddam. Indict said that the IOC should investigate allegations that athletes were routinely beaten, and worse, on the orders of Uday Hussein, the President of the Iraqi National Olympic Committee (INOC).

Ann Clwyd, the Welsh Labour MP who chaired Indict, said that the IOC must suspend the Iraqis. She said:

> The President of the INOC, Saddam Hussein's son Uday, is a sadistic killer who personally tortures athletes and uses the IOC as a front for smuggling and corruption. Indict has collected signed testimony from Olympic athletes to support these accusations. Many others we've

9

interviewed – even those living in Britain – are still too scared to come forward.

The violations described in this complaint are undoubtedly the most serious breaches of the code and the fundamental principles ever to be brought before the IOC Ethics Commission. They constitute violations of the United Nations Convention against Torture and the laws of every civilized country. It is inconceivable that a national Olympic committee that maintains its own prison and torture chambers could remain a member in good standing of the Olympic movement. The violations committed personally by Uday Hussein are utterly inconsistent with his position as President of the INOC.

The Indict document identified some sources, though it did not reveal these publicly. One was a weightlifter called Raed Ahmed, who had carried the Iraqi flag at the opening ceremony of the Olympics in Atlanta in 1996 and then defected. Indict told the IOC in this submission in 2002 that it was vital that the identities of these sources remained secret. (Their names were released in 2003, after the fall of Saddam.) Indict told the IOC: 'These men and their families have already been threatened with death and grievous bodily harm by agents of the regime.'[3]

Indict said that Uday was 'massively corrupt'. It said he used the Olympic banner as a front for smuggling and 'other illegal activities'. It said it had indisputable evidence that Uday regularly ordered that athletes should be 'beaten, tortured and harrassed'. It said that the discrimination – on the basis of race, sex, ethnic origin, religion and political opinion – that the Olympic movement existed to oppose was rampant in Iraq. 'These constitute crimes against humanity and bring the Olympic movement into the gravest disrepute.'

Three days before Christmas 2002 the American television channel ESPN (formerly the Entertainment and Sports Programming Network) investigated Iraq. The programme was based on the crusading work of Tom Farrey, an ESPN reporter who had broken a string of exclusives about Uday's abuse of sport over the previous months. He had tracked down Iraqi athletes who had fled Iraq after being tortured and persuaded them to talk, using their real names. This was remarkable since they had family and friends back home, who could have suffered as a result. Indeed, one of Farrey's sources, Raed Ahmed, had told Indict a few weeks earlier that he did not want anyone to know he had helped them.

Farrey had started digging after he had read a story about a group of Iraqi exiles in Boston who had collected information about the torture of athletes in Iraq. Those Iraqis put him touch with the athletes. Farrey told me: 'There obviously was no paper trail to document the claims they were making, but I checked reports that had been filed by the United Nations and other organizations. I insisted that these athletes use their faces and names because, although anonymity might protect their families in Iraq, we needed that for the credibility of their stories.'[4]

The programme in December pooled Farrey's output on Iraq but, like the Indict submission, it made little impact. Americans and Europeans were preparing for Christmas. The big news was whether the Americans would invade Iraq. But ESPN told viewers that Saddam Hussein tortured and killed his own people, because they were opposed to him politically or, in the case of Kurds and Shias, because they belonged to the wrong ethnic or religious group. What was less well known, said ESPN, was that Uday terrorized athletes and sports officials.

The testimonies were disturbing. Sharar Haydar had been a defender for Iraq's top clubs and the national team until he fled in 1998. He said that was talking publicly because the world had to understand the evil of Uday, even though he had been warned that Iraqi agents might try to silence him. Haydar said that he had been gaoled and tortured four times and thought himself 'lucky' because other players had suffered far worse. 'Every single day I have been beaten on my feet. Twenty a day. And I am not allowed to eat or drink. Just a glass of water and a piece of bread.' Haydar said he had first been imprisoned in 1993, after Iraq lost 2–0 to Jordan. 'Four of us were in gaol for a week. Why four of us? I mean, where are the rest of the players? Are we being chosen by the coach or by Uday – nobody knows.'

Haydar said that he was gaoled a year later, when he told Uday that he did not want to play for Iraq again. This time he was whipped and dragged through filthy water so that the cuts became infected. Haydar said that he had told FIFA what was happening in Iraq after he fled to the West – but that they had refused to investigate. He laughed when he talked about a visit to Baghdad in 1997 by two FIFA officials, Rustum Baker from Qatar and Paul Mony Samuel from Malaysia, to investigate allegations that Iraqi players had been tortured because they had lost a World Cup match against Kazakhstan. Of course the players denied these reports, said Haydar; if they had told the truth to these FIFA officials, they would have been tortured again or killed.

There was much more. Raed Ahmed, the weightlifter, said that he had been forced to urinate in his pants in prison because the guards would not let him go to the toilet. A boxer called Muhsin Hassan remembered how boxers had had their heads shaved – the ultimate humiliation for Iraqis – before being thrown into gaol for a month after they had displeased Uday. Issam Thamer al-Diwan, who had been a volleyball coach, showed ESPN's viewers the scars on his legs from the time he was shackled in prison. He said he spent three months in prison after disobeying Uday's orders to loot sports equipment from Kuwait after Iraq's invasion in 1990. Thamer said that Uday hated athletes because they were loved by the people. 'Uday cannot stand to think that someone in Iraq is smarter, more famous or more popular in Iraq than him. That is why he hated us and always punished us.'

Perhaps the most telling contribution came from a man called Latif Yahia, who had been Uday's double – a decoy for potential assassins – for five years until he escaped to the West in 1992. Yahia said that Uday was beyond bad: he was evil incarnate. Furthermore the Olympic committee, he said, was just a front for crime. 'The headquarters of the committee is actually the headquarters for Uday's smuggling and extortion. There's a prison in the building. He stores whisky, cigarettes, cars there, all stolen from Kuwait.'

Governments throughout history have used sport for propaganda and have abused athletes when it suited them. With the development of cinema, radio and television in the twentieth century – and, more recently, satellite television and the Internet – sport became a tool for governments, to excite, encourage, distract and discredit. The Nazis recognized the value of sport; hence their fury when Jesse Owens, a black American, exposed their racial theories as wrong as well as obscene when he won four gold medals at the Berlin Olympics in 1936.[5] From 1945 until the collapse of the Soviet empire in the early 1990s sport was the battlefield between West and East, between capitalism and Communism. Communist regimes were ruthless in their selection and training of athletes because they believed victory on the pitch, on the track or in the gym demonstrated the superiority of their way of life.

Meanwhile, the governing bodies of international sport, led by the IOC and FIFA, struggled to prevent rivalries, between capitalism and Communism, rich and poor, north and south, black and white, from destroying sport. Everyone knew that compromises, ignoring unpleasant facts, were part of the game. For example, the IOC could not condemn the Chinese for their treatment of child gymnasts without risking the break-up of the Olympic movement. It was better, argued the IOC and FIFA, for international sport to be imperfect than for it not to exist at all. The governing bodies of sport insisted that they stood for justice, equality and fairness, but they admitted that they also had to be pragmatic because they dealt with the world as it was, not how it should be. Only when countries offended both West and East – as South Africa had done during the days of apartheid – would they act; otherwise they shrugged and said that what to one man was repression was to another the will of the people.

The debate that followed Farrey's report explored these tricky issues. Bob Ctvrtlik, one of three American members of the IOC, had captained the US volleyball team in 1996 in Atlanta. He said: 'The IOC takes these things seriously. What could be a greater atrocity than having some athletes tortured? But at the same time you have to realize the IOC is composed of so many countries, and everyone has different cultural differences and ways they look at things. We're a very slow, methodical body and we have to think carefully before we take action. But these are very serious allegations, and if they're substantiated, we'll definitely take some action.'

Peter Galbraith, a former US ambassador to Croatia and a member of the board of Indict, said: 'The issue here is not the human rights situation in Iraq, which is appalling. There are other countries that have terrible human rights records, though maybe not as bad as Iraq's. The issue here is the conduct of the Iraqi Olympic committee, which is headed by Saddam Hussein's son Uday, who is a drunk, a torturer, a sadist and a serial rapist. And it is the way in which he has behaved toward the athletes and the officials in the Iraqi National Olympic Committee. The prospect of war against Iraq has encouraged some of these athletes to come forward. But they are incredibly brave people who are putting their own lives at risk because the Iraqi secret services have a reach that goes outside of the country.'

David Wallechinsky, a historian of the Olympics, said: 'The IOC banned both South Africa and what was then known as Rhodesia for their racial policies under great pressure from the world. I think that the IOC will look into this, as well they should. I think they should do it cautiously, because once they enter the subject of human rights, it's a whole can of worms. For example, not that far from Iraq are Saudi Arabia, Kuwait, Oman, United Arab Emirates, Qatar, all of whom do not allow women to compete in sports and have never entered a woman in the Olympics. So once you open that can of worms, what you are going to do about these other countries?'

However, the alleged mistreatment of Iraqi athletes was of little interest to a world gripped by the debate over whether Iraq had weapons of mass destruction and, if so, how they should be removed.[6]

2

The television deal that never was

In February 2003, a few weeks before the Americans and British invaded Iraq, Bernd Stange left Baghdad and returned home to Germany. He said that the German authorities had ordered him to go, but this was misleading; it was true that they had advised him to leave, but he was a private individual and could do what he wanted. It was entirely understandable and sensible – he could hardly coach football in the middle of a war – but it was unnecessary to give the wrong impression about the reason. However, it was typical of Stange, as I later discovered, to tinker with the facts if they were embarrassing; he probably did not want to admit that he was scared to stay in Baghdad when war was almost certain, because Iraqis, for whom physical courage is important, would think he was a coward.

At home in Jena, Stange talked about his ambitions, how much Iraqis loved him and why war was not necessary. He had an opinion on everything, from the mentality of footballers in the Arab world to the role of football in promoting peace. He said that Iraqi players were 'good technically' and 'loved the ball'. But he revealed that they were tactically naive and were unfit compared to European players. 'I show them pictures of Oliver Kahn [the veteran German international goalkeeper] and say to them, "Do you think he got these biceps from eating good French cheese? No, they're from training. You have to train harder"', he said.

By mid-March 2003, with an invasion imminent, Stange was close to tears. Like many people around the world, he was saddened that the American and British governments believed that war was the only way to solve the problem of Saddam Hussein. He said: 'The most disappointing aspect of all this is that politicians can't find another solution than bombing my players. Something has gone terribly wrong when these players, the people of Iraq who do not have food, or medicine, are about to be bombed. The world has failed. I only wish that politics had rules as clear as those of football. It's not a coincidence that FIFA has more members than the United Nations.'

He was genuinely fond of his players: 'Every day they ring me and say, "Coach, when are you coming back? We miss you". They are still working to the training programme I gave them. We played five games, won three, drew one and lost one. Our good results made me very popular.' He was generous about the Iraqi people: 'There isn't a stereotypical Iraqi as we in the West portray them. I don't know of any other country in the Middle East that is so hospitable and accepting of other cultures.'

In April 2003, a few days after Baghdad was taken by the Americans, Stange travelled to Dubai, where he hoped to gather his players. 'Football for me represents peace, and that's why we should get back to playing again as soon as possible. I'd like to get my team together. They're professional sportsmen, but they're not getting what's needed there now, lacking water and proper nutrition. It is not possible for them to practise in Baghdad. But we have a good team that plays well together – Kurds, Shias, Sunnis and Christians all play in harmony on the pitch.' He said that he had always opposed the war, but that was in the past; now it was time to rebuild. 'I don't expect much from Americans – they don't have a big attachment to soccer anyway. But I would hope the English Football Association might help get us off the ground again.'

He returned to Baghdad at the end of June 2003. He emphasized that this required great bravery. He pointed out that even with a bodyguard, a large young man called Ziad, he might not survive the 'lawlessness' of Baghdad. He talked like a UN ambassador rather than a mere football coach: 'After the terrible time of war it is now important to work on some positive events for the Iraqi people. However, football is not as important as the children, the destroyed hospitals and infrastructure. Nevertheless, sports should be revived as soon as possible, in order to create a new future for the young players, coaches and fans, and to transmit a positive image of the country.'

He said that he was looking forward in the coming months to

qualifiers for the Olympics, the Asian Cup and the World Cup. Unfortunately, he added, there were so many games that he was handing control of the Olympic team, mostly players aged under twenty-three, to an Iraqi, Adnan Hamad. But he made it clear that he would watch Hamad closely. He was not pleased that the offices of the Iraqi National Olympic Committee had been blown up during the war. 'Here were all my things, video recordings, FIFA documents, my personal equipment, laptop. Everything has gone because I had no time to clear my office.'

He said that he had hoped to take his squad to Spain to play a Catalan team in Barcelona's world-famous Nou Camp stadium. But he added that the Spanish authorities had let him down by refusing to issue visas. This – the fact that the world was not treating him and his team fairly – became a familiar complaint over the coming months. Instead of playing in Spain he took his squad to the north of Iraq to train and to play against local teams. After a month there they travelled to Tehran to take part in a four-sided tournament. They won 1–0 against Iran, then ranked 42nd in the world, ten places above Iraq, and lost in the final 5–2 to Uruguay, ranked 22nd in the world. After the Iran game he said: 'We have had no facilities in Iraq, but the secret to winning this game was fighting hard and running until the end. Football is vital for people in Iraq, and this result will take joy into people's homes in Iraq. No one will pay my wages at the moment, I am here now working voluntarily.'

I thought Stange would make a terrific subject for a television documentary. He spoke fluent English. He was passionate and egotistical. I would follow him and his team as they went around the world, training and trying to qualify for the Asian Cup in China in the early summer of 2004 and the Olympics in August that year. There were also World Cup qualifying matches against Uzbekistan, Palestine and Chinese Taipei (otherwise Taiwan), all ranked below Iraq by FIFA. I could see the television programme already. It would track Stange and his team to exotic locations. There would be drama and tension, triumph and defeat.

A friend put me in touch with a respected independent TV producer in Manchester, who knew his way around television companies.

If I could convince him that it was a good idea, he might be able to sell the project either to a station like Channel 4, or to one of the large independent production companies. I talked about Stange, his players, the abuse of football by Uday, the popularity of the sport in Iraq and how much it would mean to the people if the team did well. He said that it was fascinating, an entirely new 'take' on Iraq, unlike anything that had been broadcast. Sure, he said, there had been saturation coverage of the war and its aftermath, but that had been bloody and grim; our programme would be fun but also informative. He said that nothing was certain in television, but he hoped that he would be able to sell the idea.

I told him that I realized that a programme like this would need 'a name' to present it. This was not shyness or false modesty on my part. This was an expensive project – it would not be cheap to follow Stange around the world – and I knew that a television company would not have any faith in me, a 51-year-old freelance writer. They would want a celebrity, perhaps one of the ex-players now working as a television pundit. That was fine by me. We would have done the interesting work, travelling with Stange and the team, watching them train, play, feud and fret. The 'name' would read our script and might be filmed in a few locations, watching Stange's team train, play and relax, to give the impression that he (I thought it was unlikely that television would want a female presenter) had written the script.

The documentary would be about a man, Stange, searching for redemption. It would be about footballers fighting for a better life. It would explain the real Iraq. It would show the public that not all footballers were louts who spent their huge wages on sports cars, women, champagne and designer drugs. It would be about football, but it would also have intellectual depth. It would describe Iraq before, during and after Saddam. I would examine how a dictatorship such as his grew and survived, and how it affected a nation's psyche.

From Iran, Stange took his players to Bad Woerishofen in Bavaria, southern Germany, for a two-week training camp, paid for by the German Football Federation. There were twenty-one players and a dozen officials. Some of the officials, many of whom wore the

Saddam Hussein moustache and dyed jet-black hair that had been the mark of loyalty in the old regime, appeared to know little about football and apparently were more interested in smoking, drinking and watching pornographic videos, if available, in hotel rooms than in anything to do with the actual game. Stange, who was hard-working and honest, was increasingly irritated by this but said nothing publicly because he did not think that it was his place to criticize the association.

While he was in Germany, Stange was often interviewed by local reporters, who were impressed at first by his passion but who soon realized that he adored melodrama – and the sound of his own voice. He said: 'Even if Bayer Leverkusen called now, I would have to reject them. I feel so connected with the Iraqi people and my team. I could take no other job. It's a dream for us to be here. We haven't been able to train properly for six months. The conditions are dreadful. The grass is high. There are holes in the ground. We have no changing rooms, and there is no water for the showers. Training has to take place after six in the evening because of the heat, but we have to stop at eight, when it gets dark, because it is dangerous to be out after that.'

'When I drove from Amman to Baghdad, I had doubts. Then I got to Baghdad and saw what it was like. I almost decided to ask the Iraqi FA to dismiss me from my contract. There were American tanks parked in the stadium. Thousands of seats had been destroyed by a missile. Then I saw the players and I saw hope in their eyes and I knew I couldn't leave.'

He said the celebratory gunfire in Baghdad after Iraq had beaten Iran had scared the Americans: 'They went on alert because they thought it was the start of an uprising. Now they're seeing how important football is to Iraq.' He thought that the absence of a league in Iraq was an advantage because the Olympic and national teams had effectively become a club squad that was always together.

One of Stange's coaches, Ali Ahmed Mohammed, said that the biggest problem facing the squad was the fear of what was happening back home: 'We are always thinking about Baghdad. The players are counting the days before they'll see their wives and families again,' said

Mohammed. Ahmed Khadim, a 25-year-old defender, said that a bomb planted by insurgents and aimed at Americans had exploded a few days earlier outside the home in Arbil, Kurdistan, of another squad player, Rafid Badraddin. 'The windows of his house and his car were broken. He had big problems contacting his family. Luckily they were OK. And Kurdistan is supposed to be the safest place in Iraq.' He added that the team showed that Iraqis could live together, whatever their religion. 'There are never any problems in the team between the Shias, Sunnis and Christians, not even Jews.'[1]

Other players preferred to talk about Uday instead of religious harmony. The captain, Hussam Fawzi, capped forty times for his country, said: 'If you lost with Uday, you knew you would be punished. This pressure is the reason why Iraq didn't do well in the last ten years.' But in another interview Hussam had second thoughts, probably because he feared that his remarks would irritate hard-line Ba'athists back home. He said that, on reflection, much of what had been said about Uday was exaggerated.

While I researched my programme and waited for news from the television producer in Manchester, Stange showed that he could do more than talk expansively when Iraq qualified for the Asian Cup in China the following summer. The opposition in the qualifying round, Malaysia, Bahrain and Myanmar, had been feeble but it was still a fine achievement, as Stange pointed out: 'The intensive training has paid off. We have gone through many weightlifting sessions and have also worked on the technical side of things. There are big incentives for the players. They know how much it matters to people at home that they win and they also know they will win contracts overseas if they do well. There's no money in Iraqi football at the moment, so that is important.'

I had realized by now that it was pointless to look for consistency from Stange; he said whatever came into his head, meant it passionately at the time and then forgot he had said it. He could contradict himself within minutes, and be unaware that he had done so. It did not mean that he was insincere, just chaotic. Nonetheless there were signs that he was losing patience with the Iraqi Football Association (IFA), which was riven by feuding as Hussein Saeed, the interim president, resisted efforts from rivals to dislodge him. Stange now said that he had only taken the job because it was his last chance to lead a side to the World Cup finals, which was not what he had been saying a few weeks earlier. Then he had talked about his love of Iraq and Iraqis and the role of football in rebuilding the country. Now he said he was in the job purely to satisfy his personal ambition.

The 45-year-old Hussein Saeed, the man who had ostensibly hired Stange, had been one of the greatest players in Iraqi history. Unusually in Saddam's Iraq, where players had been moved at the whim of the regime, he had stayed with one club – al-Talaba, the Students – throughout his career, from 1975 until 1990. He had risked his life in the mid-1980s, when he refused to join al-Rasheed, a club that Uday had set up. Players who were asked to join al-Rasheed usually did so, because they knew that they would probably suffer if they did not. But Saeed was lucky – or had influential contacts who saved him – and was not punished for defying Uday.

He was a brilliant striker and helped al-Talaba to three league titles in the 1980s. He played an estimated 100 times for Iraq at various levels. In 1979, 1982, 1984 and 1988 his goals ensured Iraq won the Gulf Cup. He played in the Olympics in Moscow in 1980, in Los Angeles in 1984 and in Seoul in 1988. He played in the World Cup in Mexico in 1986. He retired in 1990 and was briefly a coach before becoming one of Uday's lieutenants at the IFA. Iraqis agreed that he had been a great player, but many detested him for serving Uday, though Saeed protested after Saddam's fall that he had known nothing of the corruption and torture. No one believed him; Iraqis said that it was impossible to work for Uday for more than a decade and not know what was happening. He was well connected: he was a member of the Asian Football Confederation's executive committee and was close to Sepp Blatter, the president of FIFA.

Saeed, who had never needed to worry about his public image when he was one of Uday's henchmen, launched a public relations offensive towards the end of 2003 as he competed with Stange for the approval of the Iraqi and foreign media. But he was no match for Stange. He was stiff and evasive in interviews. Whenever he was pressed to explain his relationship with Uday, he mumbled that he had known nothing. In one typically unconvincing interview he talked at length about the football association's heroic efforts to reconstruct football but did not address a topic that appalled many Iraqis: the continuing presence of men like him, who had prospered under Uday, in powerful positions in Iraqi sport and government generally.[2]

He said that the association was managing to function, despite the destruction of everything – offices, stadiums, pitches – during the war. He said the association was operating out of three borrowed rooms but hoped to begin building new offices soon. He said: 'We're starting again from scratch, and it's very difficult. We are working hand in hand with players, coaches, referees, clubs and football lovers across Iraq. We are all doing our best. The whole country needs rebuilding, and in that context football is very important. When playing football becomes a normal thing to do, that will mean we're back to normal.' He thought it would take time to organize a league, though he was proud of the fact that the association had staged a cup final in the summer in the Kurdish-controlled north. And he paid tribute to Stange as 'a remarkable man'. He said that Stange had 'a very good overall view of Iraqi football', but he added: 'Our main concern is that we should find the resources to be able to keep him – which is far from easy.'

To people who knew the vicious internal politics of the IFA this was ominous. It was widely known within the Coalition Provisional Authority in Baghdad that Saeed resented Stange's salary – reportedly $10,000 a month – and that he was constantly looking for ways to avoid paying it. Officials in the CPA read Saeed's remarks and speculated that he was preparing to sack Stange, on the grounds that the association could not afford him, and replace him with someone who would do as he was told.

Stange outclassed Saeed again late in 2003, when he launched a series of attacks on the Americans and hinted that he would resign soon if things did not improve, which ensured that the story would be published around the world. Stange said that he was emotionally, physically and financially exhausted. He said that his bodyguard had been shot a few days earlier, that he was funding the team himself and that he had not been paid since January.

All this was tremendous stuff for my television programme. It was emotional, dramatic and riveting because Stange was suggesting that millions of dollars from the CPA, FIFA and other sources which was meant to be spent on developing football was, in fact, being stolen. He said that he was single-handedly keeping Iraqi football alive. He said that he had organized the tours abroad without any help from the Americans or the Iraqi FA. And he was appalled by the indifference of Paul Bremer, the American who ran Iraq. He said that Bremer had not bothered to congratulate him when Iraq qualified for the Asian Cup.

'In a country without any working cinemas or theatres, where people are afraid to go out at night, the successes of our team are a matter of huge national pride. Doesn't Paul Bremer understand this? Take American football away in the United States, and in a year people would become very aggressive and nervous. I know that soccer is not the most important thing in life, but this country has always been crazy about the game and they should understand that our successes are helping boost morale and lift Iraq from the ashes.'

Stange said that without an immediate infusion of money it would be impossible to keep the national team together because many of the best players had signed, or were likely to sign, contracts in the Gulf and Saudi Arabia. He said two players, Haidar Obaid and Younis Mahmoud, had just signed for clubs in the Gulf. His star striker, Razzaq Farhan, was likely to follow soon. His Olympic captain, Abdul-Wahab Abu al-Hail, had moved to Esteghlal Ahvaz in Iran after performing brilliantly for Iraq against Iran in August. Abbas Rahim and Ahmed Khadim played in Syria. Nashat Akram, nineteen years old and one of Iraq's most promising players, had been signed by a club called al-Nasr in Saudi Arabia. Manhal Mashal, Nashwan Ahmed, Faris Abdul-Sattar, Amer Qasim and Safa Adnan were in Syria.

He said that this was what had happened in the early 1990s, when Uday Hussein had allowed players to go abroad, providing that they paid him a chunk of their salaries. Stange said that many top players had left then, seriously weakening football in Iraq. For example, Ahmed Radhi, then a star with al-Zawraa, one of Iraq's leading clubs, had gone to the Gulf. As a result al-Zawraa fell apart. In 1993, in the Asian Cup Winners' Cup, they lost 6–2 to an Indian team called East Bengal. Iraqis were shocked by this, much as fans of Manchester United would be if the team were knocked out of the FA Cup by a non-league club.

Until now, Stange conceded, Iraqi players had not made an impact outside the Middle East, but he said that was changing because clubs in the major European leagues were scouring the world for cheap talent. He thought that clubs in Europe understood now how to nurture young, badly educated men from poor homes who did not speak the language. In the past, Iraqis who had moved to Europe had struggled. Partly this was because of difficulties with language, weather and a totally alien culture, but also standards in Europe were higher. Players were fitter, stronger and more disciplined, though Iraqis could match, and often eclipse, Europeans for skill.

The first Iraqi to play in England was a 21-year-old called Youra Eshaya, an Assyrian and a Christian who had been brought up in the 1930s on an RAF base called Habbaniya, 60 miles west of Baghdad. After being spotted by an RAF officer who was an occasional talent scout for Bristol Rovers he was offered a trial in England. He played a few matches for the Rovers' reserve team but was permanently homesick. He returned to Iraq after the Iraqi embassy in London said that he could join the Air Force, one of Iraq's leading clubs.

In 1961 an Iraqi international, Zia Shawel, another graduate of RAF Habbaniya, played in West Germany. But he only lasted a season. A Kurd called Mohammed Abdul-Majid played in Turkey for six seasons in the 1960s. During the 1980s Shiwan Ahmad Sadiq, a former Iraqi youth international, played for some small Italian clubs after marrying an Italian woman. Other Iraqis toiled in the minor leagues of Scandinavia, France, the Netherlands, Spain, Portugal, Greece and even Iceland.

It was low-grade stuff, yet Iraqis always believed that their top players were as good as any in the world. For example, they said that Ahmed Radhi had been one of the best strikers in the history of football. He had made his début for the Olympic team in 1983, when he was picked by Ammo Baba, a former international who was then

Iraq's top coach. This was the first of 124 games for various national teams, in which Radhi claimed to have scored 86 goals. He said that a Paraguayan club had once tried to sign him for a lot of money but complained that Uday had refused to let him go, though he later spent four seasons in Qatar.

Iraqis also thought that Falah Hassan, who was at his peak in the late 1970s and 1980s, would have been a success in Europe. One Iraqi historian claimed that Derby County wanted to buy him in 1977 and that three years later a club in the Gulf made him a huge offer.[3] He retired in 1986, at the age of thirty-six, and became a coach. He left Iraq in 1991, saying that he was tired of the corruption, and settled in the USA.

Stange said it was essential to prevent a mass exodus of players from Iraq, which was inevitable unless money was injected into the game. Obviously, he said, players had a right to better themselves by signing for foreign clubs, but it was vital that Iraqi football retained a nucleus of good players. He said that he would resign at the end of the year if he was not satisfied that money was coming into the game. Then, with a magnificent dramatic flourish, he added that he hoped, somehow, to take Iraq to the World Cup finals in Germany in 2006. He announced that this would 'boost the spirits of weary citizens' in the same way as West Germany's surprise win over Hungary in the World Cup final in 1954. Stange said this had been a huge boost to the morale of all Germans, though it had, in fact, only emphasized to East Germans what they were missing.

He raged about unfair criticism and disloyal players. 'Coaches who criticize and attack me should go on a coaching course and learn about international rules. To prepare the national team under the circumstances was very difficult, and I am very proud of what we have achieved so far. But I resent the negative criticism.' He said that some players had not turned up for Asian Cup qualification matches in Bahrain. 'I had invited them and bought them air tickets. They promised to come but didn't.' Then the team refused to play a match against Myanmar because they had not received their wages for two months. Stange said he borrowed money from the Iraqi ambassador in Bahrain.[4] 'The players should receive their money, and the worst thing is that no one congratulates them or says some encouraging words, but instead we are faced with negative words and comments, so truly I am on the verge of resigning.'

Having made the headlines again, Stange set off with his team to Australia to a 'training camp'. He had become an accomplished scrounger: by cajoling, begging and pleading he was keeping his team constantly on the road, training in the best facilities and playing friendlies against third-rate teams because the alternative – going back to Iraq – was too dreadful to contemplate. Some experienced players could not go to Australia because their clubs in the Gulf and elsewhere needed them, but Stange did not mind as long as they were available for competitive matches. And, he added, it was good that young, unknown players had the chance to travel and bond. These foreign trips also kept Hussein Saeed happy because his cronies could attach themselves to the squad and enjoy themselves.

On 15 December 2003, the day after Saddam Hussein was captured by the Americans, Stange, accompanied by Hussein Saeed, travelled to Basel, Switzerland, to receive an award from FIFA for his work in Iraq. Without mentioning Saeed and his cronies in the association Stange told the audience: 'The troubles in Iraq are not over yet. The hatred and violence cannot be switched off like a lamp. There are still forces of darkness in Iraq. I don't think everything that's happened can be pinned to one person, Saddam Hussein. It is obviously good that the uncertainty about him is over. I hope his capture makes Iraq a safer place. I hope it won't lead to revenge attacks.' He brooded on the fact that many of his squad were based outside Iraq and that some weren't interested in playing for him.[5] He said that he did not blame them since they were never paid by the IFA. He said it was impossible to organize matches in Iraq because 'every Iraqi has a weapon, and weapons have no place in a football stadium'. He said that he was worried about his own safety. 'I am always nervous in Baghdad. I always make a big detour around American installations. Most of my life in the German Democratic Republic was spent behind walls and barbed wire, and it is happening again. I have the same fears as American soldiers, but I don't have a bulletproof vest. I am a soft target.'

As Christmas approached, the television producer in Manchester who had been so hopeful told me that, sadly, he had failed to sell my programme about Stange and his lads. He said there were many reasons for this. Television companies felt that Iraq was not the stuff of lightish-hearted, fly-on-the-wall documentaries; it was a nasty and complicated news story. He said that there were many documentaries being made, starring 'big names'. These would tackle the 'big issues' – had war been necessary, what had happened during the war, what was the future for Iraq and would these events fuel Islamic fundamentalism? I said I understood and thanked him for his efforts. I asked a friend, a correspondent based in the Middle East for a television station, what he thought. He said that Stange would make a cracking programme and that he was sure he could raise money to back it from his contacts in the Middle East. But a few weeks later he said that he too had failed.

I wondered if the premise was flawed, whether perhaps Stange and his team weren't as interesting as I had thought a few months earlier. After all, there were many teams around the world who were more colourful and more fun than the Iraqis and as significant politically and culturally. I could have suggested a programme about the team from a war-ravaged country, such as Afghanistan, that was trying to find a national identity pride through football. FIFA ranked Afghanistan at 198th out of 205 national associations.[6] The Afghan FA had been founded in 1933 and had affiliated to FIFA in 1948. The country did not play a competitive international match from 1984 until 2002, when it competed at the Asian Games in Busan, Korea. The results were disappointing: Afghanistan lost 10–0 to Iran, 11–0 against Qatar and 11–0 to Lebanon. FIFA commented: 'The country's footballers have relatively little international experience due to the upheaval and disruption provoked by war and political instability in recent times.'

Or I could have chosen Palestine, the team without a country and ranked 125th in the world. It had joined FIFA in 1998. Most of its players did not live in either the West Bank or the Gaza Strip, and half had never even set foot in Israel or these areas. They played their 'home' matches in Doha, Qatar. Despite all this, FIFA said they enjoyed enormous support among Palestinian communities around the world. FIFA said: 'When Palestine score, screams of joy are heard not only in the cafés of the West Bank and Gaza Strip, where people huddle around blinking TV sets, but in Palestinian districts throughout the world from Greece to Chile, where many of the squad were born. While politicians struggle to locate a "Road Map" for peace, footballers from Palestine's own diaspora have found the right path to make a depressed and impoverished people happy.'

Palestine's coach was Alfred Riedl, an Austrian who talked like Bernd Stange: 'It is an extraordinary task to train the team of a non-existent country. It is more than a job; it is a mission. These proud men are making huge personal sacrifices to play for a land they have never touched, only heard about from old relatives and seen through horrific TV images.'

Then there was the worst team in the world: Guam, an island in the Pacific, which was ranked at 205, propping up the FIFA rankings. The team was so bad that it often lost games by twenty or thirty goals to teams such as American Samoa, also ranked near the bottom of the FIFA table. Belize, at 80, would have been steamy. They had only formed a football association in 1980 and were usually thrashed when they played their neighbours in Central America. There was Bhutan, sandwiched between India and China, mysterious, fascinating, ranked at 101 but until recently one of the worst teams in the world. It only joined FIFA in 2000, and archery, not football, was the national sport. Rwanda, at 97 in the world, would have offered insights into a country that had torn itself apart. Rwanda had sensationally beaten the mighty Ghanaians in the qualifying stages for the African Nations Cup in 2002. The Rwandan government said that football had the power to unite the country.

Most of the top fifty teams in the world weren't quirky enough to justify a television documentary. The USA was the exception. It was ranked 11th, which was astonishing since football was a minor sport there, though FIFA gave the impression that the game was on the brink of being taken seriously. FIFA had tried everything since the 1960s in its bid to exploit the huge American market. It had even allowed the Americans to host the World Cup in 1994, which was like moving the World Series of baseball to England. The Americans, however, remained loyal to their own games.

If I could not make a television programme about Stange, then I would write a book. Indeed that would be better, because a book could explain the glorious complexities of Iraq. I realized that it would not be enough to trudge around the world following Stange and his team. Instead I would focus on a club or a player and tell the story of football in Iraq through it, or him. Stange would be an important element but not the dominant one. It was a good plan and I was excited.

3

The end of Uday

By January 2004 it was obvious that the White House and Downing Street had been wrong about Iraq. As I searched for a suitable focus for my book, a club or a player who would help me tell the story of football in the country, I reviewed the previous year. The American and British governments had believed that Iraq would emerge as a civilized nation after they had removed Saddam. They had argued that that most Iraqis hated him but were too frightened to say so and would welcome anyone who overthrew him. But commentators on the Middle East had warned that an invasion would be resented and resisted. And they had been right.

Iraq was artificial, created in the early twentieth century by British bureaucrats who had never been to the region and who had, literally, invented the country by drawing lines on a map. The experts had said that without a dictator holding it together through terror and patronage Iraq could break up into three or more countries – Kurdish, Sunni and Shia – with the likelihood of bloodbaths in the mixed regions of the centre and Baghdad. They had said that Iraq would make the civil wars of the former Yugoslavia seem low-key. They had talked about the relationships that bound Iraq – of clan and religion, between the Ba'ath Party and the country's upper and middle classes and the masses – and warned that anarchy would result if these ties were unravelled.[1] They had said that the invasion would destroy what had been, by the standards of the region, a pragmatic, secular society. They had warned that Muslim fanatics would pour into Iraq, just as they did in Afghanistan when the Soviets invaded, to fight the infidel Westerners.

By the summer of 2003 it was indisputable that these experts, who had been dismissed by the White House and Downing Street as anti-Western defeatists, had been right. There was resistance from Saddam loyalists, Sunnis who had served in the army, police and assorted intelligence services. There was anger among the Shia majority, whose religious leaders told them that the Americans were infidels, sent by the Jews to destroy Islam. There were Sunni radicals, many from outside Iraq, loosely grouped as al-Qaeda, who wanted to destroy everything and establish a pure Islamic world. Many ordinary Iraqis were angry, too, because they saw that people who had prospered under Saddam were still doing well.

Issam Thamer al-Diwan, the former volleyball coach, had gone to Iraq to advise the Americans on how to rebuild sport, the first time he had been to Iraq since fleeing the country in 1991. He was bursting with hope and enthusiasm but was soon on his way back to the USA. He had protested in July, when Don Eberly, a well-meaning 55-year-old American academic who was responsible for rebuilding sport, appointed a man called Abdul Razak al-Taey as his deputy at the sports ministry. Thamer said that al-Taey had headed the volleyball federation under Saddam and had 'a bad history'.

Eberly was out of his depth in Iraq, where he had no understanding of the bitter divisions caused by the Saddam years or of the fact that many Iraqis believed that the only way to survive was by lying and cheating. By August 2003 he was back in Washington, where he was happier dealing with his pet subjects, the importance of children knowing their fathers and the role of business in building society, than grappling with men like al-Taey. After Eberly appointed al-Taey, he said: 'There are those who believe that if you were involved in sport in Iraq, or were seen in the presence of Uday, or even if you had a Baghdad address, then you're an evil person. I have to be firm in saying this is wrong.' Thamer was furious: 'I don't know why the Americans support this guy. This guy worked in sport and the only source of funds was Uday.'[2]

Sharar Haydar, the former international footballer who had lived in London since the late 1990s, was also angry that people who had worked loyally for Uday had reinvented themselves as opponents of the old regime in order to ingratiate themselves with the Americans.

Since his defection from Iraq in 1998 Haydar had campaigned tire-lessly to force the governing bodies of international sport to expel Iraq because of Uday's behaviour. In April 2003, as Saddam's regime was crumbling, he had been elected president of the Free Iraq Olympic Group by several hundred exiled Iraqis at a meeting in Germany. He returned to Iraq soon afterwards, expecting to be invited by the Americans to take up a senior position, perhaps even the presidency, with the national Olympic committee. He said: 'There were the same old faces. The same corruption everywhere. So I left Iraq. But I will be back. I am not going to let those people win.'[3] Iraqis complained that the Americans patronized them by handing out footballs. The Americans certainly meant no harm, but Iraqis did not want gestures like this; they wanted jobs, water, electricity and security.

Journalists based in Iraq usually wrote about serious issues, such as the hunt for Saddam and his sons Uday and Qusay, but sometimes they looked at football, the passion of millions of Iraqis. Officials from the Coalition Provisional Authority said that they would know that Iraq was recovering when there was a football league, with regular matches which people could attend safely. They said that it was important that the national team, which had played competitive games outside Iraq before the invasion because of sanctions and security fears, returned to Baghdad. The buzzword of these officials from the Coalition Provisional Authority was 'normality'.

There had been a flurry of interest in the torture of athletes in April, when journalists found an instrument that they called an 'iron maiden' in the grounds of the destroyed offices of the Iraqi National Olympic Committee, a nine-storey building in the east of the city. *Time* magazine reported that Uday had controlled the Olympic move-ment and football for his private benefit – and amusement. It said that footballers who annoyed Uday were tortured, by, for example, having their toe-nails ripped out. (I doubted this; Uday inflicted pain and humiliation on players but did not cripple them.) *Time* continued:

> We have found what may be the first tangible evidence pointing to torture in Uday's own backyard, the administrative compound of the Iraqi National Olympic Committee in central Baghdad. Hidden in a pile of dead leaves, not 20 yards from the building housing the Iraqi

Football Association, was that must-have appliance of every medieval dungeon: an iron maiden.

Around 7 feet tall, 3 feet across and deep enough to house a grown man, the sarcophagus-shaped device is essentially a large metal closet with long spikes on the inside door which closes to impale its victim. Its name derives from its mummy shape and the beatific woman's face depicted on its headpiece. The one found in Baghdad was clearly worn from use, its nails having lost some of their sharpness. It lay on its side within view of Uday's first-floor offices in the soccer association. Ironically, the torture device was brought to *Time*'s attention by a group of looters who had been stripping the compound of anything of value. They had left behind the iron maiden, believing it to be worthless.[4]

In May 2003 the International Olympic Committee concluded that Iraq's Olympic committee should be dissolved because of persistent abuses by Uday and his cronies. No one was impressed by this decision. The IOC had known for many months that Uday and his accomplices had beaten up athletes and used the Olympic movement as a cover for criminal activities such as smuggling. The IOC had only begun an investigation in January 2003, after Indict, the human rights group, had submitted a formal complaint. Issam Thamer said: 'What happened to the athletes was as much the fault of the IOC as Uday, because they covered up his crimes.' Sharar Haydar was disgusted that the IOC had done so little. 'I want them to admit they didn't do anything to stop Uday', he said. Nor did Charles Forrest, executive director of Indict, think much of the IOC. 'Indict should not have been put in the position of having to make this complaint. The IOC should have investigated on their own. The rumours about torture were significant enough to warrant an investigation', he said.

The IOC claimed that no one had complained to them about Uday until December 2003. This was untrue: in 1996 Amnesty International had reported that Iraqi athletes were being abused. When they were confronted with this evidence, the IOC spokespeople in Switzerland shrugged and said that they were only a sports organization, not an international court. Of course, they were right; the IOC existed to run sport because a world with sport was better than one without it. Even so, it was not a proud moment for the IOC.

A few days later two of Iraq's top clubs, al-Zawraa, supported by the Shias of Sadr City, and al-Shurta, otherwise known as the Police, played a pre-season friendly at al-Zawraa's crumbling stadium in Baghdad. In the days of Saddam the stadium had been dominated by his huge portrait, but that had now been ripped down. The police force in Baghdad no longer existed – the Americans had disbanded it because they thought, mistakenly, that it was run by Saddam fanatics – but the football club had survived.

The stadium was packed with young men wearing cheap imitations of shirts from Europe's great clubs: Liverpool, Manchester United, Real Madrid and Inter Milan. The fans bubbled with excitement that Saddam had gone. But there was an edge, a cynicism to them which suggested that they did not trust anyone, including the Americans. Ed Vulliamy, a journalist with *The Observer*, captured the atmosphere at the game brilliantly:

> Tariq Sala supports Inter Milan because their colours are the same as his domestic side of choice, the University. Tariq insists that 'now all the big players will come from Italy and England to play in Iraq'. How so? 'Of course they will. We are very rich in oil, and for ten years we have lived on the oil-for-food programme. Now Saddam is gone, we can sell our oil for Zidane and Michael Owen!' . . .
>
> Asam Ali, a big fan of Roma, says: 'Football was the only good thing under Saddam Hussein. It was where we could leave all that shit outside the stadium and forget about politics. We watched the games maybe twice a week, on either the Iraqi sports channel or Iranian TV. The Iranian channel was better because on the Iraqi one they kept interrupting the matches if there was an announcement by Saddam Hussein or the government.'
>
> The leader of the al-Zawraa pack, Harda Mohammed, was imprisoned by the regime, and has accordingly lost a few marbles. He now urges the fans to support the resurgent Islamic Party, to which the Police supporters reply with a song: 'Sadja, We Love You!' Sadja is a nickname for Saddam Hussein's wife.

Through the spring and early summer of 2003 there were other matches like this, organized by the Americans and by Iraqi football officials in an attempt to prove that the country was returning to normal. But many Iraqis were uneasy, arguing that the same men who ran the sport under Saddam were still in charge. For example, there was Ahmed Radhi, the only Iraqi player ever to have scored in the World Cup finals (against Belgium in Mexico in 1986), who now ran al-Zawraa. It was widely rumoured that he had been close to Uday, though he denied this: 'I was imprisoned three times: in 1986, 1987 and 1996', he said. 'Sometimes we were punished because we lost; sometimes even after we had won.'

He said that football could educate young Iraqis. 'Sport, and especially football, is a good way of making kids behave and leading them in the right direction. Some of our young players didn't have the financial support to stay in the game and, now that they're out of work because of the war, some of them have begun to do wrong things. I'd like to see infrastructures like they have in Europe. We should be doing things like building youth academy centres in order to start producing top-quality players.'

Muthar Khalif, thirty-two and another former international, said that he had been imprisoned three times by Uday. He said that Uday called the squad on the eve of a World Cup qualifying game against Qatar. The team had done so well in the preliminary rounds of the competition that beating Qatar away in their last match would have seen them progress to the finals of the World Cup (for only the second time in the country's history), to be held in the USA in 1994. Uday 'rang to give us a message: "if you don't win, I will kill you"', Khalif said. Not surprisingly, they lost. Iraq were dumped out of the competition, and on their return Uday punished the team in the usual brutal manner.

Saith Hussein, al-Zawraa's striker, had been the star of the team that played in the 1989 World Youth Cup in Saudi Arabia and which beat Argentina, Spain, Portugal and Norway before losing in the quarter-finals to the USA. It was after that competition, Hussein recalled, that Johan Cruyff, the legendary Dutch player who was coach at Barcelona, tried to recruit him. Hussein said that Saddam would not release him. He said: 'It was frightening to play for Iraq because every mistake you made put you in prison. I can't count how often I was gaoled for a few days at a time. The sentence depended on the mistake – for a defensive error, two or three days; for missing a penalty, maybe three weeks. Uday's thugs would come to the cells to beat you up on his orders, but they were football fans and said to us, "Look, you shout and scream a bit, while we beat the shit out of the furniture."' Hussein added that he would like to stay in Iraq but, at the age of thirty-two, needed to make some money before it was too late: 'I want to build the game in a free Iraq, but every player dreams of going to play abroad.' A club in Turkey is interested in me.'

Paul Bremer, the American head of the Coalition Provisional Authority, popped up to kick off a match – between the youth teams of the Police and al-Karkh – but security was such a problem (he was the ultimate target for insurgents) that he did not do it again. He said: 'Sport is a very good way to bring people together; it is a universal language. It is an important part of what we are trying to work on now, which is to build a civil society in Iraq.'

Unfortunately public relations stunts like this were spoilt by the fact that the Americans had thoughtlessly turned the al-Shaab stadium, the People's National Stadium in Baghdad, built in 1966 and a shrine to Iraq's football fans, into a park for tanks. Ammo Baba, now sixty-nine, regarded by many as Iraq's greatest player and coach, was annoyed because near by was his 'football academy' for poor children. He said that the American presence, which attracted insurgents, meant that parents were not willing to send their children to the academy. Baba said: 'I went to the stadium and told the Americans, "You are destroying our chances to rebuild football. The only thing I want in my life is for you to leave this stadium."' The Americans finally realized their mistake, left the stadium and repaired the pitch in late June. They marked the occasion by playing a team of Iraqi professionals. It was another public relations fiasco. Most 'spectators' at the game were American soldiers. The Iraqis thrashed the Americans 11–0 and complained afterwards that they wanted their country back.

'It doesn't mean anything, it's just a game', said Barakat Mahmoud, also thirty-two, a former star of the Olympic side who was then playing for al-Zawraa. 'They called and asked me if I wanted a game. I accepted. Every night I go home to a neighbourhood where people shoot guns and there is no water or electricity. This was only a game of football.' Don Eberly, the CPA adviser in charge of rebuilding sport, was oblivious to this. He burbled: 'This time next year we want to see an Iraqi team competing internationally again.' He said that the match was a sign that Baghdad was 'finally starting to get back to normal', which was palpably not true.

The British also tried to win hearts and minds by supporting football. They were occupying the Shia south – and football was overwhelmingly a Shia sport, since they were Iraq's working class and football is the game of the masses. Whenever possible, British soldiers staged matches with the locals. For example, in the baking heat of midsummer in a town called Umm Khayyal the Royal Marines were thrashed 9–3 by the local team, watched by a crowd of 1,000, who kept screaming that the soldiers needed help from David Beckham.

The breakthrough that the Americans and British had been waiting for in order to prove to Iraqis that the old regime really had gone, came on Tuesday 22 July, when the Americans announced that Uday, who had celebrated his thirty-ninth birthday a month earlier, Qusay and two others (later identified as Mustafa, Qusay's fourteen-year-old son, and a bodyguard) had been killed by American troops. They had been found in a house in Mosul, in northern Iraq, and had refused to surrender, so the Americans had battered the house with gunfire, shells and rockets, as though there was a large and well-armed force inside the house rather than three lightly armed men and a teenager.

There had been much talk about the brothers since they had vanished in April. Some said that Qusay, who had commanded the Republican Guard, should be blamed for the swift defeat of the regular army when the Americans and British invaded, because he had been inept and afraid. Others said that Uday deserved praise for the way his irregulars, the Fedayeen, had resisted. (The Americans had dismissed the Fedayeen before the invasion as a rabble who would be easily crushed by regular troops.) There were reports that the brothers had argued and split up, that they had tried to reach Syria and found the way blocked, that Uday had offered to give himself up, providing he could escape prosecution for his most serious crimes. There were also a number of versions of what had happened in Mosul. One said that Uday had died last, guns blazing. Another reported that he had shot himself rather than be captured.[5] But they were dead, as the Americans later proved when they displayed the bodies for the television cameras. They argued that they had to do this to convince Iraqis that the men were really dead. However, many decent Iraqis were offended and said it showed the Americans' contempt for their country and for Islam.

Most Iraqis had mixed emotions about Saddam. Some had respected Qusay. But no one, not even his closest friends, mourned Uday, who was either evil or mad. Furat Ahmed Kadoim, a 37-year-old FIFA-registered referee, had fled Iraq in December 2002 after being tortured by Uday for refusing to fix matches. In the summer of 2003 he was living in Birmingham in a home for asylum seekers. It was shabby and seedy, despite Kadoim's efforts to keep it clean and tidy. He was an intelligent and gentle man, who had been an engineer in Iraq and said that he did not wish to see anyone dead, but he told journalists: 'Uday was a killer. He ruined my life. I only wish I was at home in Baghdad with my family today so I could celebrate.'

Despite the heat and the dangers of travelling around the country, 13,000 people watched the Iraqi Cup Final in late August 2003. This was an extraordinary figure, which testified to the Iraqis' passion for football, because the game took place in Arbil, Kurdistan, and did not involve a local side. The two teams – al-Talaba (or Students) and al-Shurta (the Police) – came, in fact, from Baghdad but could not play in the capital because it was too dangerous. Thousands of fans instead made the long and expensive journey to Arbil to see al-Talaba win 1–0. It was like 20,000 Londoners travelling to Aberdeen for a match between Spurs and Arsenal.

The Americans were still obsessed, understandably, with Saddam. They believed that his arrest or death would release the majority from the fear that he might return and convince hard-line Ba'athists that they should forget the past. The events of the following year, 2004, showed that they were mistaken. Hostility to the invasion and the new pro-American Iraqi government was based on patriotism, religion and tribalism rather than loyalty to Saddam. Saddam's last reported public appearance had been on 9 April 2003, at the Adhamiya mosque in northern Baghdad. He told the crowd: 'I salute the Iraqi people and I ask them to defend themselves, their homes, their wives, their children, and their holy shrines. . . . I am fighting alongside you in the same trenches.'

Then he vanished. The Americans and British feared that he had used his immense wealth – they estimated that he had $40 billion in foreign bank accounts as well as $900 million in cash, which he had taken from the Iraqi Central Bank as the Americans neared Baghdad – to buy his escape or to finance resistance in the Sunni heartland around Tikrit. Like the rest of the world, I was intrigued. Where was Saddam? Was he masterminding resistance from some secret bunker? Had he fled Iraq? Perhaps he was dead? In late April *al-Quds al-Arabi*, an Arabic newspaper in London, received a letter from Saddam. On 7 May an Australian journalist in Baghdad was given a tape with a message from Saddam. In June Iraqi politicians said that Saddam had been seen in 'the Sunni triangle' to the north and west of Baghdad and was offering rewards to anyone who killed an American soldier.

One of Saddam's key aides, Abid Hamid Mahmud al-Tikriti, fourth on the US military's most wanted list, was arrested and said that Saddam had fled to Syria and had been expelled. In early July the Americans offered a $25 million reward for information leading to his capture. This was an unimaginable amount of money, and I was sure that someone would betray Saddam, if he was still in Iraq. But still he was not captured.

On 17 September the al-Arabiya television station broadcast this message from Saddam, who was obviously still alive and free: 'We call on you [the USA] to withdraw your forces as soon as possible, and without any conditions, as you cannot bear any more losses, as these losses will be catastrophic for you. Your withdrawal from our country is inevitable, whether it happens today or tomorrow, and tomorrow will come soon.' Finally, on the morning of Sunday 14 December 2003, after one of Saddam's bodyguards broke down under interrogation, the Americans found him, cowering in a hole on a farm near his home town of Tikrit in the Sunni triangle. His first words were: 'I am Saddam Hussein, President of Iraq, and I am willing to negotiate.'

The Iraqi Governing Council said that he would be tried for crimes against humanity. It was reported that he was 'unrepentant and defiant'. An Iraqi politician who visited him in prison said: 'When we told him, "If you go to the streets now, you will see the people celebrating", he answered, "Those are mobs." When we told him about the mass graves, he replied, "Those are thieves." He didn't seem apologetic. He seemed defiant, trying to find excuses for the crimes in the same way he did in the past.' Another visitor said: 'He was not remorseful at all. He is a complete narcissist who is incapable of showing remorse or sympathy to other human beings. He tried to justify his crimes by saying that he was a just but firm ruler.'

The Americans hoped that Saddam's capture would be the beginning of the end of resistance. Hard-line Ba'athists would give up, just as Nazi fanatics had done after Hitler's death. The Americans feared that there would still be problems from Islamic fundamentalists, most of whom, they believed, came from outside Iraq. But they were sure that most Iraqis would applaud Saddam's capture as the end of a nightmare and get on with constructing a prosperous democracy. They were wrong.

4

Dangers of the Web

Bernd Stange had told the audience at the award ceremony in Basel in December 2003 that he might resign at Christmas. I doubted this. I thought that he would miss the attention that came with coaching Iraq. I decided that it was more likely that the Iraqis would dump him. Many senior figures within the Iraqi Football Association had worked under Uday; they would sacrifice anyone to save their own skins. The situation in Iraq was getting worse, not better, and resentment over foreigners was growing. I was sure that the IFA would get rid of him if they felt it would look better for them to employ a local coach.

To my surprise, the IFA stuck with him. In the new year it announced that it had extended his contract to the end of the qualifiers for the 2006 World Cup. It also said that it would pay him $10,000 a month, which a spokesman said would 'put an end to the never-ending debate regarding the inability of the association to pay the coach his wages'. In fact, the only comments about Stange's salary had come from Stange himself. It was not clear whether this $10,000 was his existing wage or represented a pay rise.

Either way, Stange was not impressed. A few days later he attacked again. He said that he wished that he had not taken the job. He said that he did not care that people who had condemned him for taking the job were now congratulating him: 'I did the same thing before the war as I do now – with the same people, the same exercises and the same programme. My goal is to train young people into top performers and to teach them to adhere to a set of rules. I also never attacked those who called me the devil's coach because I knew that I am a soccer coach, nothing more. But the award from

FIFA helped me morally because it is a small, good response to the harsh criticism that I have been subjected to.' He argued that it had been unfair to single him out from among all the football coaches who worked in countries that weren't exactly models of democracy: 'Soccer is not only played in countries following the rules of the Westminster parliamentary democracies but also in countries like Cuba, North Korea, Iraq and the African countries that are on Amnesty International's blacklist. I knew that and drew strength from that fact.'

He confessed he had been hurt by the accusation that he was 'Saddam's coach'. He said: 'People were saying, "Once bad, always bad – he already carries the East Germany burden, a Honecker and Stasi man"; that was the accusation. When I first started my job in Iraq, people associated everything I did with Saddam. But I simply signed a contract with a FIFA member. I also contacted the German embassy to ensure that I wasn't doing anything one should not be doing as a German. I was told that I could do this as a private person, so I signed the contract and started my job.'

He said that he had not met Saddam or Uday: 'I never even saw them from a distance. Everything I know about them I have learned from the media, including the statements of players who were tortured and punished, or the report that players who missed a penalty were beaten or thrown into prison. I noticed nothing of this sort during my work. Whenever I asked who wanted to take a penalty, at least six players volunteered, which made me conclude that these must be things of the past.' But he also made some astute points about the Iraqis' attitude towards the Americans – and all Westerners. While the White House, Downing Street, the new Iraqi authorities and some commentators thought the situation in Iraq would improve dramatically, Stange did not share this optimism.[1]

He said: 'Hatred of the Americans is so deeply rooted among the Iraqis that I don't expect the arrest [of Saddam] to change much. Things will change only when the Americans hand over the reins to the Iraqis. But I suspect that even in ten years' time a McDonald's will still be a terrorist target. I find this hatred difficult to understand because I feel that the Americans' intentions are good. Immediately after the war, when I returned to Iraq, there was a noticeable improvement, especially in street life. But over the past two months I have felt a dramatic increase in violence and lack of security. Fear has caught up with me ever since the aid organizations, the Red Cross and the UN as well as Iraqi police officers have become targets. I have felt relatively lonely over the past weeks and months as everybody has left Iraq.'

He confessed that he was afraid: 'I cannot protect myself. I have a bodyguard, a very tough guy, but he was shot and wounded four weeks ago after he dropped me off. He had two bullets in the thigh, one in the head and one through his hand. Iraqis had stopped and assaulted him; apparently they were after his car. He panicked and started to run away, which is when they shot him.'

He wanted to continue because he was already 'incredibly successful'. He said: 'My great goal is to perform well in the Asia Cup this summer and take part in the World Cup in Germany in 2006. But I must weigh my own safety and the concerns of my family. I do not feel safer because I have played myself into the hearts of the Iraqis through the results of their national team. My growing popularity also lures people who have anything but good intentions. The glorification of my person means that I can no longer take a step without being surrounded by crowds of people, with fans trying to kiss me. That concerns me. It also doesn't help when people tell me that they will murder those who try to hurt me. Revenge is so deeply anchored in Islam, and I find all that very disconcerting.'

He described his life in Baghdad as lonely and terrifying. He had lived in a five-star hotel until it was hit by rockets. Now, he said, he was at 'a secret location'. He was baffled by the Americans' lack of interest in football: 'I am hugely occupied with the reconstruction of Iraqi soccer. Soccer in Iraq is dead. There are no championships, no friendly games and the pitches are destroyed. There are a few meadows where we want to train, and there have been initial attempts to hold friendly games, but we had to call them off because we could not rein in the outburst of violence among the fans. So I am not only a soccer coach, I am also rebuilding Iraqi soccer from scratch – the clubs, the teams, the structures, everything. I cannot fulfil the hopes of the associations and players, who believe that I can get more equipment for them in Germany and provide balls for the youths. I need support for my work, but six months after the war I am not getting any support. The Americans did not even phone to congratulate us on our sensational achievement on making it to the Asia Cup.'

He boasted that he was single-handedly keeping Iraqi football alive. He said: 'I have had to rely solely on personal friendships, which meant, for example, that we could do a three-week training camp in Germany, fully paid. And Jako, a small, family-owned German company, has sponsored our equipment. Personal contacts in Australia, where I was a coach for three years, also helped my team: I organized a training camp, took care of clothing, arranged visas and pocket money. I also went to the British embassy once to ask for support. I had to do it all myself.'

He said that the Americans just did not understand the importance of football in Iraq: 'If you deprived the Americans of basketball and football for a year, they would also feel that they were lacking something. If the Americans had recognized the importance of soccer, they would have long ago given us a grass pitch for training. If you can get tanks weighing several tons to Baghdad, surely you must also be able to take a few rolls of grass along. I can only advise the Americans to pay attention to these things if they want to touch the hearts of the Iraqi people.'

Stange's remarks gave me the key I needed. I knew that there would be many books about the invasion and the fall of Saddam, by journalists, politicians, diplomats, academics, weapons inspectors and soldiers. But mine would be different, the story of Iraq told through football.

There was already an extensive library on Iraq. There were scholarly histories about the great pre-Christian empires, academic studies of British rule after the First World War, descriptions of the evolution of Ba'athism and many biographies of Saddam Hussein. There were specialist books, on archaeology, travel and so on.

A Norwegian journalist, Asne Seierstad, who was in her early thirties, had spent four months with a family in Kabul in 2002 and her book *The Bookseller of Kabul* became a best-seller around the world. The hero was the bookseller of the title, who Seierstad had originally thought was a liberal intellectual, but who turned out to be a bully and chauvinist. Her book described the bookseller and his family as they squabbled, feuded and made up; it was a thoroughly entertaining romp, like a television soap opera.

Then she wrote *A Hundred and One Days: A Baghdad Journal*. This was about her time in Baghdad from January to April 2003. Like *The Bookseller*, it was well written and perceptive, but it was about life as a foreign correspondent rather than about Iraq. Seierstad talked about the adrenaline, the fear, the competitiveness and camaraderie of the journalists who cover wars. She described the mechanics of reporting from countries such as Iraq: the thick wads of hard currency that were needed to bribe officials for visas, pay for drivers, translators and hotel rooms, the satellite phones which ate up money. She wrote about the hierarchy of journalism – at the top the American and European television stations and the major newspapers, at the bottom the freelancers from small countries – and how news is shaped, not just reported, by the media. She described how journalists risked so much, because of the rewards, bigger jobs and book contracts, not because they cared about the people they were writing about. Soldiers fought, she said, because that was their job. Some aid workers did it because they had a conscience. But journalists who covered wars were uniquely perverse, because they required misery to prosper and had to pretend they cared.

In her book were fragments about the Iraqis. At one point she met an Iraqi literary critic, who told her that Iraq was 'a country of schizophrenics and cowards, where people fear their friends, their family, their own children'. She said that Iraq was 'a kingdom of fear', where a single word could lead to gaol, or worse. She heard from Iraqi Christians, who were afraid that Sunni and Shia extremists, whom Saddam had controlled, would turn on them once he had gone. She lamented the behaviour of the American troops, who shot anything that moved. Seierstad herself had been surrounded by Iraqi minders, living in a hotel with other journalists in a city where it was usually impossible to find an Iraqi who would talk openly.

In the days before Nick Hornby's *Fever Pitch* it would have been tricky to sell a book about football in Iraq, because publishers thought that most football fans were louts who could not read. But Hornby had shown that there was a market for respectable books about the game. It was ironic, though, that he had become the bible of the middle classes who were now flocking to matches in England, because he yearned for the days when football was working-class, grubby and noisy, when terraces were so crowded that spectators urinated into bottles, or over each other, because they could not get to the toilets. But those days had gone. The Premiership and European club competitions generated hundreds of millions of pounds in television rights, sponsorship and advertising. Stadiums were now all-seater. Every major ground had expensive executive boxes and restaurants. Football was big business in Europe, and the money was spreading outwards to the developing world, like ripples on a pond. Clubs in Europe sent scouts to Africa and Asia in search of new talent and sought to expand their fan base by opening souvenir shops abroad. The giants – in England, France, Spain, Germany, the Netherlands and Italy – signed deals with clubs to supply them with young talent. In countries such as Iraq the men who ran football sensed a new era, when undreamed-of wealth would pour into their pockets.

I had visions of travelling around Iraq in a jeep, interviewing players, referees and fans, with the pennant of Brighton and Hove Albion, the team I had supported as a boy, tied to the radio aerial, waving at smiling children. I thought it would be fun. As a reporter for the London *Evening Standard*, the *Sunday Times* and the *Sunday Correspondent,* and a consultant to think-tanks, I had been travelling to the Middle East for thirty years. I did not regard myself as an expert on the region – proper experts were people who spoke Arabic and could explain the cultural differences between the Shias of Iran and Iraq – but I hoped I knew enough not to make a fool of myself. As a journalist I had covered two World Cups, in Spain in 1982 and in Italy in 1990. I had played football to a passable level at school and had spent a season as a teenager with the Brighton and Hove Albion youth team, which was not as impressive as it sounded since they would take anyone who could run and kick a ball. I had played into my late thirties, until it became too embarrassing, and painful, to continue. I always read the sports pages before the news in a paper. I had written a football coaching manual for children. I had co-authored an analysis of sport under Communism. Most recently I had written a polemic about football in the new millennium. I knew how football could unite and divide, how it could provide role models, how it could inspire the poor and disadvantaged and how it could be exploited by politicians. A book about football in Iraq, focusing on a club or a player, would not be as much fun as travelling with Stange, listening to him complaining and boasting, but the idea appealed to publishers.

In the days before the Internet it would have been difficult to research an arcane subject such as this. I would have depended on libraries for the basic information and would then have tracked down experts and fans, in the West and in Iraq. It would have been slow work. But the Internet had revolutionized the way that authors operated. No matter what the subject – how the Universe began, how to give up smoking, the role of mercenaries in war or football in Iraq – you could type in key words into a search engine and hundreds, often thousands, of pages would pop up. There was not just information; there was immediacy, because pages were constantly updated, and there was intimacy, because, for example, Iraqi fans in Canada could chat by e-mail or on message boards with fans in Australia.

I began with Iraq, the country. That was easy. There were dozens of websites, covering history, geography, culture, population and so on. I skipped from one to another, from academic sites packed with facts to the politicized ones of the White House and Iraqi opposition groups in the USA and Britain. The Internet made expertise instantly available. Want to know about the Ba'ath Party? Easy: type in the name, and a few seconds later there are hundreds of articles waiting to be read. Too much? No problem. Type 'Ba'ath' again, but add the name 'Saddam Hussein', so that only articles about the party and its leader pop up.

It was a feast of information. A typical session would begin with

'Iraq, history' and end hours later with websites about RAF bases in Iraq in the 1930s.

Having established that there was a huge amount of information on the country, some of it dry and historical, much of it fresh and contentious, I moved to football. The results were astonishing. There were dozens of websites. Some were run by the governing bodies of football, such as FIFA. Others were run by newspapers and magazines. Many were operated by Iraqi exiles in Europe or North America. There was one about the al-Talaba club, though the inter-active functions did not work.

I knew Iraq had been a socialist state since the fall of the monar-chy in 1958. I thought this meant that football in Iraq had been orga-nized on Soviet lines, with football teams being run by state institutions. And this was the drawback of the Internet. Much of the information was wrong. In the days when authors researched in libraries or by interviewing experts it took time to find information, but when you did find it, usually it was accurate. The Internet was indiscriminate, pouring out as much dross as gold. For example, I found sites giving the results of every match played by Iraq and the names of every coach of every national team, from the youth squad to the adult team. But that did not mean this information was accu-rate. I realized that I would have to check everything. I could not believe that Iraq really had beaten Yemen 3–0 in 1985 just because someone had posted a page saying so.

It took many weeks to understand that the appearance of order in Iraqi football was wrong. The sport was not run like it was in England, with governing bodies regulating clubs and leagues; foot-ball in Iraq had been an unregulated shambles. The portrait of the sport on the Internet was unreal and bore no relation to the truth. Iraq had the structures of a modern, civilized society, government ministries, courts, industries, banks and so on, but had been run by gangsters who did what they liked. The Ba'ath Party was an Arab version of Stalin's Communist Party, but there were also tribal ties, unknown in Europe, that bound the élite to Saddam. In terms of brutality – though not organization – Saddam, Uday and the rest of the gang matched anything the Nazis had done.

One website gave the names of the c
Olympic and military teams over the deca
winners of competitions I had never heard of:
Malek Abdullah Cup and the Samdurran Cup
'the Presidents of the National Team', which I
IFA. Uday Hussein was shown as the president fr
which was almost right. (He took over the IFA a
he was also shown leading 'the Olympic team' from
This was wrong since Uday ran the Olympic committ   almost
twenty years. More curious was the list of coaches who had led the
national teams. The dates were a muddle. A Yugoslav who was supposed to have coached the Olympic team in one year was shown
leading a different squad at the same time.

The explanation for this confusion was that Uday and his cronies
had hired and fired, imprisoning and killing. There were no cred-
ible records, nothing to show who had done what and when. A man
could be coach of the Olympic team one day and be given a car or
a house for winning a match, but a bad result a few weeks later might
lead to gaol, even death. Al-Shurta, the police club in Baghdad, was
run by Saddam's son-in-law Jamal Mustafa, but he refused to pay the
youth team, which was subsidized by the coach, Jabah Jaed. If Jaed
had protested, he would have been sacked, perhaps imprisoned and
tortured. He had to hope that Mustafa would occasionally give him
'presents' of money or cars.

Slowly I began to appreciate how football had evolved in Iraq.
Until the early 1960s there had been no formal national leagues.
Instead there had been local and regional cup competitions involving teams from schools, universities, the military and state institutions. One of Iraq's leading clubs, al-Quwa al-Jawiya (otherwise the
Air Force), dated from the 1930s, but the rest had been formed in
the 1960s and 1970s. These included al-Talaba (Students), al-Sinaa
(Industry) and al-Jaish (the Army). There were few reliable records
from these years, but it seemed that the first properly organized
league had been set up in Baghdad in the early 1960s. This had
expanded to include clubs from neighbouring towns, but it was not
until the mid-1970s that there was anything approaching a national

This was dominated, however, by clubs from Baghdad, which subsequently remained the centre of the sport.

With bewildering frequency clubs changed their names, merged with others or simply disappeared. For example, al-Talaba had emerged from a club called al-Jama'a, and the respected al-Naqil (Transport) had vanished without explanation. In 1968 al-Quwa al-Jawiya rebranded itself al-Tayaran (Airlines), but in 1991 it apparently decided that this did not work and reverted to its old name. A club called Baladeyat (Municipalities) dumped that name in 1977 in favour of Amana.

The most useful website was iraqsport.com. Every day it carried stories about teams and clubs in Iraq, about great Iraqi players of the past and investigations. Some stories were in Arabic and some in English. I e-mailed Hassanin Mubarak, the Iraqi who wrote the English stories. I imagined him as elderly, white-haired and distinguished, a professor perhaps at Baghdad University, who had been watching football in Iraq for decades. In fact, he was a young man who lived in London. For reasons I never discovered, he would not meet me or talk on the phone, but he was happy to chat by e-mail. He told me that the site had originally been founded in 1997 by Ghaith Nasrawi, who had been born in London in 1980 and brought up in Baghdad but went to live in Tunisia after the Gulf War of 1991 and then studied in Cairo. He now lived in London, where he worked in computers, as well as being the site's webmaster.

Hassanin was born in Baghdad in 1981, but had lived most of his life in Europe – in Oslo from 1982 and then in London from 1989. He joined iraqsport.com in late 2000 and had done other work on Iraqi soccer for newspapers and magazines such as *Football Asia*. 'My work was even translated in the new daily Iraqi sports newspaper *Sport Today*, which replaced the old Ba'athi *al-Ryadthi* newspaper run by Saddam's eldest son, Uday Saddam', he told me. 'I have done other freelance work, and I may go into professional journalism, but I have not decided yet. I am a football fan first.'

He told me that iraqsport.com had thousands of readers, mostly from outside Iraq. Most of the information on the site came from news agencies and newspapers in Iraq, although accuracy, he added mournfully, was not their strongest suit. He said that records were patchy in the country, which would make my task hard. He said: 'I once read a quote from Ali Khadim, who had been a great striker in the 1970s. He said, "I don't know how many goals I scored for Iraq or how many games I played." Even current players do not know how many games they played or goals they have scored. Nearly every English football fan can tell you that Gary Lineker was a goal away from equalling Bobby Charlton's record of 49 for England, but ask any Iraqi football expert, Iraqi FA official or even a player, who has scored the most goals or played the most games for Iraq, and you will get a blank face. I hope things change.'

He told me that football was important throughout the Middle East, though it was organized differently in each country. In Saudi Arabia and the Gulf states clubs were owned by mega-rich locals. There were privately owned clubs, too, in Lebanon but not in Syria. It was vital, he said, for me to forget the British and European models; football in the Middle East was different. 'The Gulf Cup is a great example of how the governments in the region view football. The tournament holds little importance in the international calendar, but the rulers from Qatar watch to see if their team will beat the Saudis and they don't want to get humiliated. In 1976 the Saudi team played so badly that the whole Saudi football set-up was revamped. Ferenc Puskas [the legendary Hungarian player] was the coach of Saudi Arabia in that tournament; they lost 7–1 to Iraq! The television presenter and former player Jimmy Hill actually became the Saudis' saviour! His company at the time took over the running of Saudi football, with several British managers going to coach in the Kingdom.'

Mubarak urged me to travel widely within Iraq, though Baghdad had always been the centre of football, where the top teams, al-Zawraa, al-Talaba, al-Shurta and al-Quwa al-Jawiya were based. Many of the larger clubs, such as al-Zawraa and al-Talaba, also ran teams in other sports. He said that I should visit cities like Basra and Najaf, because teams there, such as al-Minaa in Basra, were as strong as, if not stronger than, those from

Baghdad. He told me that al–Minaa had won the league in 1978, the first team from outside Baghdad to do so. He said: 'It is the second oldest club in Iraq. In 1992 three people were killed and twenty-five wounded when Iraqi forces opened fire on al–Minaa fans chanting against Saddam and his son Uday after al–Minaa had beaten a team from Baghdad.' He was impressed by Najaf, who were third in the league when the war of 2003 started. He advised me to go to Arbil in the north. 'They don't have a good team, but they are building for the future and have one of the best stadiums in Iraq', he said.

An Iraqi called Nick Ask,[2] a former player who had lived in the USA for many years, explained to me the importance that football has for Iraqis: 'Soccer was the only recreation Iraqis had. Nine out of ten Iraqi kids play three to six hours' soccer every day, seven days a week, from the age of five until going to college. Under Saddam football was an escape from hardship and kept people out of politics.' Ask said that Saddam had understood the importance of the sport. 'He appeared on Iraqi TV for three to five hours a day. He knew Iraqis didn't want to watch him. To force them to watch, Iraqi TV used to show hours of Saddam footage prior to the televised soccer matches. This reminded people that he was in control of their lives even when they were having fun.'

The more I researched football in Iraq, the more I realized that it was also the story of the country. When Saddam Hussein had seized power in 1979, its national team was one of the best teams in Asia, while clubs such as al-Zawraa, al-Shurta and al-Tayaran were among the strongest in the region. By the time he was overthrown, Iraqi football was corrupt, bankrupt and an also-ran in the Middle East.

Saddam had literally given football to his family and friends, to exploit for money or propaganda. He appointed his own bodyguard, a man called Sabah Mirza, to run the Iraq Football Association. The previous incumbent, Faleh Akram, was executed. But running the association was not enough for Sabah. He also took charge of a club called al-Shabab. Then he 'persuaded' top players – through bribery and threats – to join the team. In 1982 it was promoted. But it was easy to fall out of favour in Saddam's Iraq. Mirza, who had lost control at the IFA in 1984, when Uday took over, vanished in the early 1990s. Al-Shabab were promptly relegated.

In 1982 Barzan and Watban Ibrahim, Saddam's half-brothers, took over a club called Salah-al-Deen, situated near Arbil, to the north of the Iraqi leader's birthplace of Tikrit. That season the club, which had never looked like winning anything in its history, won the league title, having bribed and intimidated opponents and referees. Hassanin Mubarak told me about al-Rasheed, the club set up by Uday Hussein in 1983. 'The club were promoted to the first division and went on to win the Iraqi league three times in 1987, 1988 and 1989 and a record three consecutive Arab club championships.'

There had been twenty teams in the first division. The two main teams in the Kurdish-controlled north, Arbil and Duhok, were financed by Kurdish parties, which meant they could compete with teams from Baghdad for the best players, buying players mostly from Baghdad and Basra. Outside the Kurdish north, however, clubs were controlled by Saddam's people. For example, al-Talaba, which won the league and cup before the invasion of 2003, was run by Omar Sabawi, Saddam's nephew.

Football had as much history and produced as much emotion in Iraq as anywhere; indeed, it seemed to me that Iraqis had needed football more than other people because it provided a relief from the horrors of real life. Although the leading clubs belonged to institutions such as the police, the air force and the oil industry, there was no shape to the clubs or the league. Clubs had appeared and vanished at the whim of the ruling élite. I realized that it would be impossible to tell the story of Iraq through a single team.

I needed a man to bring focus to the story. I asked Mubarak if he knew of a great player whose career could be the vehicle for telling the story of the game in Iraq – and the history of the country. He replied immediately. He said that I should talk to Ammo Baba, who lived in Baghdad. 'He was one of the most gifted players of his generation. He was captain of the pan-Arab national team of the 1960s, at the height of Arab nationalism.'

I had to find out more about this Ammo Baba, the man who had told the Americans to leave the national stadium in Baghdad because they were scaring children away from his football academy.

5

The legend of Ammo Baba

Hassanin Mubarak was an authority on Ammo Baba: 'He is a national hero. He is incredible. A great player and a coach. His name is synonymous with Iraqi football. He says he scored more goals than Pelé. During his international début, aged twenty, fans chanted "Ammo Baba . . . Ammo Baba . . ." After the match they carried him to his car on their shoulders! This love and affection has followed him all through his playing career to the present day.'[1]

Mubarak sent me Ammo's c.v. According to this, he had begun his career with the RAF Employees (Assyrian) Club. He had played for the Royal Guards, the Air Force, the Assyrian Sports Club, the Military Academy and the Passenger Transport Department. I told Mubarak that I did not understand why Ammo had moved so often. Was he a professional footballer, a military cadet, a pilot, a Royal Guard (whatever that was) or a train driver? Mubarak agreed: it was puzzling.

Baba's career as a coach after his retirement in 1970 was even more baffling. It was a blur of names and dates. He had led clubs to a string of league titles and cups. He had helped Iraq reach the Olympics in Moscow in 1980, Los Angeles in 1984 and Seoul in 1988, though he had not actually gone to these events, presumably because he had offended Uday or Saddam. He coached most of the major clubs in Iraq and led the national team seven times – from 1978 until 1980, from 1981 to 1984, in 1987, from 1988 to 1989, in 1993 and again in 1996, and finally from 1998 to 2000. I presumed that Ammo had been hired and fired whenever it suited Uday and the other thugs who ran football.

Some facts were beyond dispute. He was born Emmanuel Baba

Dawud in Baghdad on 27 November 1934. Two years later his father, also called Emmanuel, took a job as an electrical engineer on the newly built RAF base of Habbaniya, near Fallujah, 60 miles west of Baghdad on the banks of the Euphrates. He grew up there, known to everyone as Ammo. He was an Assyrian, from one of the ancient Christian peoples who straddled Iran, Turkey, Iran and Iraq, and who spoke neo-Aramaic, similar to the language of Christ. Like other intelligent, cultured minorities – such as German Jews and Ugandan Asians – they had been persecuted. They had scattered around the world. In 2004 it was thought that there were 4 million Assyrians, of whom an estimated 700,000 lived in Iraq, though some experts thought that only 250,000 remained there. There were Assyrian communities in France, Sweden, Italy, the Netherlands, Switzerland, Austria, Turkey, Britain, Russia, the USA, Canada, Australia and New Zealand. Most Assyrians were prosperous professionals.

I found many websites run by Assyrians. All extolled Ammo Baba: 'One of the most fabulous and flamboyant soccer players history has ever created', said one. Another reported:

> In 1951, aged seventeen, Baba appeared for Iraqi Schoolboys against Egypt in Cairo and left journalists and the crowd gasping in admiration at his speed, strength and skill. In January 1955, aged twenty, when he made his senior début in Baghdad, Baba says that he had worried before the game that as an Assyrian who spoke poor Arabic he would not understand his team-mates. Due to his magnificent playing abilities and subtle techniques he maintained his position brilliantly. He was always called to play regularly for the Iraqi national teams.
>
> Ammo Baba had dark hair, a powerful body, and acrobatic skills, and was a great goalscorer. His astonishing kicking power and marvellous speed made him unique and outstanding. He is still revered by generations who never saw him play, was an instinctive out-and-out goalscorer, known for his bicycle kicks, heading ability, defence-splitting pace and the power of his shooting. He had an opportunist's eye for goal but also displayed the magnificent technique and virtuoso skill of a great centre forward.

The Assyrians fitted awkwardly into Iraq's complex history. The British had invaded Iraq, then called Mesopotamia and a part of the

Ottoman empire, in 1914 as Turkey prepared to enter the war on the side of the Germans. After the war the League of Nations gave the British a mandate to run what had been separate provinces. London renamed the area Iraq and imposed a constitutional monarchy in the form of a prince from Saudi Arabia, who became King Faisal I.[2]

Britain experimented on the local people with an array of terrible new weapons. The government, including Winston Churchill, the secretary of state for war and air, calculated that 25,000 British troops and 80,000 Indian soldiers would be needed to control Iraq, so they relied on the RAF. Churchill was keen on chemical weapons. At the time he said: 'I am strongly in favour of using poisoned gas against uncivilized tribes to spread a lively terror.' In 1920 tribes in Iraq rebelled against British rule. The RAF was merciless. It dropped 97 tons of bombs and fired almost 200,000 rounds of ammunition. An estimated 9,000 Iraqis died.

One RAF squadron leader in Iraq said: 'Real bombing means within 45 minutes a full-sized village can be practically wiped out, and a third of its inhabitants killed or injured, by four or five machines which offer them no real target, no opportunity for glory as warriors, no effective means of escape.' The British continued to bomb Iraqis through the 1920s. In 1924 one RAF officer, Air Commodore Lionel Charlton, was so disgusted when he visited a hospital and saw the mutilated civilians that he resigned his commission. But many British were brutish. One RAF ranker wrote: 'Woe betide any native [working for the RAF] who was caught in the act of thieving any article of clothing that might be hanging out to dry. It was the practice to take the offending native into the squadron gymnasium. Here he would be placed in the boxing ring, used as a punch bag by members of the boxing team, and after he had received severe punishment, and was in a very sorry condition, he would be expelled for good, minus his job.'

Throughout the 1920s and 1930s the same problems that beset Iraq during, and after, Saddam had been evident: rivalry between the minority Sunnis, who were the élite in politics, business and the military, and the majority Shias, poor and unskilled; friction between the educated urban élites and the rural masses; and an incompetent and dishonest bureaucracy.

Independence on 13 October 1932 had not satisfied many Iraqis because the British had forced Baghdad to sign a treaty ensuring that Iraq would remain an ally, where London could station troops, aircraft and ships. Britain invaded again in 1941, fearing Iraq would join the Axis. The late 1940s saw more humiliation, with the creation of Israel in 1948 and the rout of Arab troops, including Iraqis. The establishment of Israel provoked a hatred of Zionism throughout the Arab world, often indistinguishable from anti-Semitism. This was especially true in Iraq, where the Muslim majority – Shia, Sunni, Kurd and Turkoman – who make up around 95 per cent of the population feuded among themselves but also distrusted Jews.

Just as in Europe, Iraq's 150,000 Jews were influential in politics, the arts, science and medicine, and were resented for this. During the early years of the Second World War a thousand Jews in Iraq were murdered by pro-Nazi Iraqi nationalists. In 1949 Zionism became a crime, punishable by death. By 1950 Jews were being subjected to the kind of laws, stripping them of property and basic human rights, that had been the hallmark of the Nazis.

Muslims also did not care much for the Assyrians, who were Christians and belonged to four religious groups: Chaldean Catholics, the Church of the East, Syriac Orthodox and Syriac Catholic. There were constant disputes among Assyrians; some claimed that they were from different ethnic groups, though all agreed that they were not Arabs.

This argument about the Assyrians – whether they are one nation divided by religion or different peoples – is not easy to resolve. For example, one website written by academics says: 'The Assyrians divide into five principal ecclesiastically designated religious sects, with their corresponding hierarchies and distinct church governments: namely, Church of the East, Chaldean, Maronite, Syriac Orthodox and Syriac Catholic. These formal divisions had their origin in the 5th century of the Christian Era. The Assyrians have been referred to as Aramaean, Aramaye, Ashuri, Ashureen, Ashuraya, Ashuroyo, Aturaya, Chaldo-Assyrian, Jacobite, Kaldany, Kaldu, Kasdu, Malabar, Maronite,

Maronaya, Nestorian, Nestornaye, Oromoye, Suraya, Syrian, Syriani, Suryoye, Suryoyo and Telkeffee.' But in July 2004 the Associated Press, an international news agency that prides itself on its accurate reporting, said: 'Of the 750,000 Christians in Iraq, the majority are Chaldean Roman Catholic, the rest Syrian Catholic, Syrian Orthodox and Assyrian. Most live in Baghdad and its outskirts and some dwell further to the north.'

In 1915 tens of thousands of Assyrians had been massacred in south-eastern Turkey and north-eastern Iran; survivors fled to Lebanon and to northern Iraq, thus swelling the existing Assyrian communities there. By the 1940s the Assyrians were concentrated in the north, in Mosul and in Baghdad. The British were not interested in the Assyrians' calls for an independent state – the Kurds' pleas for their own homeland were also ignored – but thought the Assyrians would be useful tools to suppress Arab Iraqis. They organized the Assyrians into levies modelled on the Indian Army. Already disliked by Arabs because of their religion and air of superiority, the Assyrians became extremely unpopular.

In the 1950s the gap between rich and poor widened in Iraq; revenues from oil increased but, just as it did under Saddam in the 1980s and 1990s, this money vanished into the pockets of a few. Many Iraqis, who did not care about politics, found consolation in sport. Football had arrived in Iraq in the early twentieth century, imported probably by the British but perhaps by Iraqi students who had been in Europe. The first recorded match was played on 17 March 1918 in Baghdad, between two school teams. In 1923 the first club was established in the city, with the tongue-twisting name of Medan al-Tarbiya.

The British provided organization and expertise. Every military base had strong teams, including men who had played professionally for clubs back home. The British did not discriminate, at least in sport. Iraqis were welcome in their teams, especially Assyrians, who played with the same dedication and enthusiasm they brought to education and work. By the early 1950s Iraqi football was evolving independently of the British. Clubs were attached to industries and institutions, such as the police and the army. Players were officially ordinary employees, though most were paid, albeit modestly, just to play football. In 1948 the Iraqi Football Association was formed. Two years later it affiliated to FIFA, the governing body of world football. In 1951 Iraq played its first official international, against Turkey.

Through the 1920s the main RAF base in Iraq had been on the outskirts of Baghdad, but after Iraq's independence in 1932 the British decided that it would be inappropriate for its main base to be close to the seat of the new, nominally independent government. For its new base the RAF chose a site near Fallujah. The land was flat, and there was a limitless supply of water from the Euphrates, which also offered opportunities for water sports. Construction began in 1934. The base was named RAF Dhibban after a nearby village, but then someone realized this was Arabic for 'flies'. In May 1938 it was renamed RAF Habbaniya, Arabic for 'oleander'. One veteran of the base said this was appropriate: 'Habbaniya truly became a camp of beauty with its shaded avenues of eucalyptus trees, hibiscus and oleander shrubs, rose beds, ornamental gardens and green lawns.'

These veterans talked as if Habbaniya was a multi-racial Utopia: 'The civil cantonment was part of RAF Habbaniya and was a "town within a town" with about 10,000 residents. They were the civilian workers and their families, and the families of the RAF Iraq levies. They were of many races, religions and cultures. There were Indians, Armenians, Assyrians, Russians, Persians, Kurds.'

Gerald Seymour, one of the world's finest thriller writers and a former television journalist whose novels were always underpinned by thorough research, had a different view. In his book *Holding the Zero*, published in 2000, this is how a character describes Habbaniya:

It was ghastly. Of course, there was vegetation alongside the river but where we were we were surrounded by desert dune, flat, horrible, lifeless. There was a single runway of rolled dirt reinforced with perforated metal plate. There were only three permanent buildings: administration, sick quarters and a damn great control tower. Everyone, right up to the CO, lived in tents. We were a little island in hostile territory. The King and his government in Baghdad were marionettes for the British ambassador to play with, and increasingly there was resentment from the civilian population and the younger Iraqi officers

60

about our presence so we stayed in camp. All the food was flown in. We had a swimming-pool of sports, a marquee dropped into a sand scrape, and we had sports pitches – we didn't play the locals; we'd go as far as Nairobi, Aden or Karachi for cricket, hockey and soccer. If we had a few days' leave we would hitch rides to Cyprus or Beirut – few of the officers and none of the men were permitted to travel inside Iraq.

The airfield became operational in October 1938 and remained an RAF base until May 1955, when nominal control was handed to the Iraqis. In July 1958 the RAF finally left the base – and Iraq – after radical army officers overthrew the pro-British monarchy.

I tried to find an address or telephone number for Ammo Baba in Baghdad but made no progress. My e-mails to the Iraqi Football Association bounced back. I asked Iraqi journalists in Baghdad if they could find him, but they were too busy reporting the daily mayhem to have time to search for an elderly football coach. Then Hassanin Mubarak came up with the address and home number of Ammo's younger brother Pnouel. Mubarak thought that Pnouel might know how to reach Ammo.

I called and a soft, almost inaudible, voice answered. He said his name was Pnouel – Tarzan to his friends – and that he would be happy to meet to discuss his brother. He lived in a shabby rented flat in Ealing, west London. He was a former Iraqi international, a fast and skilful winger, who had come to England in 1969 hoping to make his fortune as a player. But he had failed to impress clubs in England and was now a small, frail man who looked older than his sixty years. On the walls of his flat were photographs of Ammo and himself as young men, playing matches, in their team blazers in East Berlin, Moscow and Prague or relaxing at their homes in Iraq.

We met several times and talked for many hours about Ammo. He had piles of newspaper cuttings about his brother and hundreds of photographs. At our last meeting he offered me a selection: Ammo playing, Ammo with his family and Ammo as revered national coach. Pnouel was reserved and shy. He said that he had arthritis in his knees, but I suspected that there were other, more serious problems. He had the sad eyes of a man who had been disappointed too often.

He enjoyed talking about his brother. This was puzzling because they had not seen each other for twenty years and rarely spoke on the phone. I wondered why they had lost touch if they were as close as Pnouel suggested. Ammo's wife, Josephine, was in Canada. His son, Sami, and elder daughter, Mona, lived in France. His other daughter, May, was in Syria and hoped to join her mother in North America. Only Ammo's two sisters, Mariam and Gloria, lived in Baghdad. What had happened to tear the family apart like this? Maybe, I thought, there was a family disagreement that no one wants to talk about. Perhaps, I thought, the family think that Ammo should have joined his wife in Canada instead of working for Uday.

I did not put these questions to Pnouel because I thought that he might be offended. So I let him reminisce: 'Oh, I am not exaggerating when I say that he was better than Pelé or Maradona. He was the fittest player ever. He had everything. Speed. Strength. Skill. People adored him', he said. He insisted that Ammo was a hero to ordinary people because he was honest. 'Ammo was never interested in politics. That is why everyone loved him. He cared so much for his country. Everyone respects that.'

He told me that Ammo had often been sent on holiday – usually to London, which was Ammo's favourite city outside Iraq, but occasionally to the USA and Australia – by successive regimes, including Saddam's. It sounded to me as though Ammo had done well out of Iraq's governments and that this was the reason he had never left. But Pnouel insisted: 'He could have left Iraq and become a rich man. He had offers from all over the world. But he would not leave. He loved Iraq too much.'

Pnouel told me that Ammo had been a marvellous centre forward. 'You have never seen anything like him. Coaches and players from East Germany, the Soviet Union, North Korea, Portugal, said he was the best they had ever seen.'

There is no television footage of Ammo in his pomp in the 1950s and 1960s. To fans brought up on today's saturation coverage by television this is unbelievable. But then there are only grainy newsreel fragments of British and European players from the 1940s and early 1950s. And this was Iraq, a new country in the developing world.

It is tempting to dismiss comparisons with players like Pelé. This would be a mistake. Once fans in London, Rome or Madrid would have laughed at the idea that an Iraqi could possibly have been as good as one of their own greats, but no longer. The top sides in the big money leagues of Britain, Spain, France, Germany and Italy now resemble the United Nations. Fans do not care where a player comes from Africa, the Middle East or the Far East, or whether he is black, brown or yellow, providing he does well for their club (though sadly this does not stop the occasional racial abuse of opposition players).

Pnouel told me that there had been five brothers – George, Younan, Ammo, himself and Albert – and two sisters – Mariam and Gloria. He said that his father's friends had given him the ironic nickname of Tarzan as a boy because he was so small. The family had lived in the avenues of bungalows set aside for the locals who worked at RAF Habbaniya. George, the eldest, had died in Iraq. Younan had emigrated to the USA and had been an engineer. He was also dead. Albert, the youngest, who was in his early fifties, was an accountant in Chicago, home to tens of thousands of Assyrians.

He said that Habbaniya had been a wonderful place to learn football. 'There were always six or seven Assyrians in the base team', he said. 'Assyrians loved football.' We talked about Pnouel's own playing career – with teams run by the air force, army and transport ministry, and trips abroad to play in Communist countries. He said that he had earned £10 extra a month for playing, on top of a basic wage of £20. But that was as much as he wanted to say about his own life, and I did not press him. He was happier talking about Ammo: 'Whenever he won a trophy as a player or a coach, they would ask him, "Where would you like to go for a holiday?" Always he said London. He loved London. He used to stay with me in this flat. The king loved my brother. So did the military, who took over after the king. Saddam had adored Ammo. Uday would like to have killed Ammo. He told Ammo he wanted to kill him but could not because of his father. Saddam said if only he had four Ammos he could achieve so much.'

Pnouel played a video, sent by a friend in Baghdad, of a recent television interview that his brother had given to a television station in the Gulf. Ammo looked like the late Rod Steiger. He was almost seventy and suffered from diabetes but was still a handsome man. He was stocky and had close-cropped grey hair. He was tanned. He smiled and laughed a lot. He had that indefinable quality known as charisma. The interviewer, a young woman, was obviously entranced by him. It looked to me as though Ammo must have been a big hit with women when he was younger.

The interviewer did not ask obvious questions – such as why Ammo had worked for Uday or why his wife lived in Canada – but it was useful for me to see Ammo. He was bright but was also pleased with himself. But, I thought, many great athletes are egotists because self-belief is essential to reach the top and to stay there.

Pnouel translated Ammo's words. 'I suffered a lot for telling the truth', said Ammo, when the young woman asked him about Uday. 'I did not leave because I love Iraq. Uday tried to make me leave. People think I am rich. I am not.' And in response to a question about why he was such a successful coach he said: 'Uday used to complain to me, "You are doing magic." Uday used to call the players before a game and tell me not to use this player or something. I took no notice. He would tell players what would happen to them if we lost. The only time that players were not afraid was when I was in charge because they knew they would win.'

The television station called Ammo's wife, Josephine, at her home in Canada. They patched her through to the studio, where the interviewer asked her what her husband had done for Iraq: 'He loved his family but he was always travelling, working', she said.

Meanwhile, I kept in touch with Bernd Stange. Sometimes he was in Jordan, where Iraq now played its home matches. Or he was at home in Jena, Germany. Often he was with his team at 'training camps' at pleasant locations outside Iraq. He was always emotional, always on the brink, always in crisis. In February 2004, speaking from Tashkent, Uzbekistan, where Iraq were beginning their campaign to qualify for the 2006 World Cup (they drew 1–1), he told me: 'If I don't get support, I will die. Clubs will not release my players. I am so alone. My players are not being paid by the association. What can I do? Baghdad is too dangerous for me.' In March he was in Qatar, preparing for the World Cup game against Palestine (a disappointing 1–1 draw). 'Simon, I am exhausted. Everything is on my shoulders. I tell you, I am really through. I have no support. Everyone in Iraq is doing everything for their own benefit.'

I said that I was hoping to meet Ammo Baba. He said: 'You must be careful of Ammo Baba. He talks rubbish. He makes trouble for the football association. He criticizes them for employing foreign coaches like me. I believe he is a good man at heart, but sometimes he lies. He is very involved in all the political fights in football. He blames the Americans for everything.'

I asked him if Iraqis thought Ammo had been too close to Uday. 'The problem is that he worked for Uday. Now he says he opposed Uday. People say he should be quiet now. Everyone has to make compromises. I know what it is like to live in a country like that. You want to survive. But he should have a role to rebuild football. He should be advising. He is too old to be the national coach but maybe he coach the coaches. Maybe he could be an ambassador for Iraqi football because he is so famous. The association should use him because he is a great man.'

Sharar Haydar, the former international who had fled Iraq in 1998 and become an articulate critic of the regime, also counselled caution.[3] He told me: 'Ammo made a lot of money from the old regime. Saddam looked after him. Ammo cries now that he was poor. It was not true. Saddam gave him a pension of 500 dinars a month, which was an incredible sum (about $1,700). My father earned 35 dinars a month and he was a well-known theatre director.'

Haydar fizzed with contempt for Ammo – and others like him, who had worked for Saddam and Uday and now claimed that, actually, they had opposed them all along and stood up for what was right. Haydar said that they would be dead if that was true. He said: 'Ammo had to work for Uday; he had no choice. But as a result, players were terrified of Ammo, for fear of being reported to Uday. The assistant coaches were no more than waiters. They just hung around, giving him food when he wanted it.' Nor did Haydar think much of Ammo as a coach. 'He was a disaster', he said. 'Iraq had a lot of great players and that was why he had good results. As a coach he was old-fashioned and had no ideas.'

My head was spinning. Who was right? I knew that Stange was inconsistent, but he was not malicious. Haydar had always seemed sensible. What was the truth about Ammo Baba? It was clear to me that one of the many unfortunate legacies of Saddam had been the erosion of trust and generosity; Iraq seethed with suspicion and jealousy. People who were friends one day would be enemies the next for no apparent reason.

In late April, Stange announced that he was leaving Baghdad because it was too dangerous, though it must be said he had not spent much time there recently. 'The German embassy there told me I must go. You don't know who are the bad people any more. I'm only back in Germany temporarily. I'm going back as soon as possible.' He insisted that he was not worried about his safety in Iraq, although many foreigners had been kidnapped since the new year. 'I didn't feel danger. The people with black masks sometimes stopped my car, but when they saw my face they said things like "you're one of us" and let me pass. I didn't have any problems directly. The situation was indeed deteriorating, but I'm not going to let my players down.' He said that he would decide what to do in July. Obviously, he said, he could not remain as Iraq's coach if he could not live in the country.

A few days later the Olympic team, coached by Adnan Hamad, whom Stange had supplanted when the Iraqis hired him, qualified for the Olympic Games when they beat Saudi Arabia in Amman, Jordan. Back in Baghdad the Americans tried to make the team pose for photographs at the al-Shaab stadium with a new Iraqi flag, proposed by the Governing Council. Instead, the players carried the old flag, singing: 'This is our flag, not Saddam's, and we are proud of it.'

The Governing Council had already modified its original design for a new flag after protests that it resembled that of Israel, the country that Iraqis hated. The new design had two blue stripes along the bottom, with a yellow stripe between them and a crescent above them in a white field. However, many Iraqis saw the new flag as a symbol of American domination and said that the old Saddam-era flag – a red, black and green banner emblazoned with the words

'God is great' – should not be changed 'because it carries the name of God'. A spokesman for the Governing Council said: 'We cannot raise the flag of a party that committed many crimes against Iraqi people.' But the new design was never adopted. They kept the old flag, though they tinkered with the style of the motto, *Allahu Akbar* ('God is great'), because the handwriting was supposed to be Saddam's.

Newspapers described the scene in the stadium:

Paul Bremer arrived by Black Hawk helicopter and landed on the famous pitch to greet the team. He ran out, trademark blue blazer and white pocket square flapping in the gusts created by the rotors. Six armed bodyguards were beside him. 'Iraq is back', he shouted triumphantly as cameras rolled and reporters scribbled. He shouted again and again.

The stadium was empty apart from the media, Bremer and his bodyguards and the Iraqi football squad because the Americans could not risk someone taking a shot at their top man in Iraq. Ahmed Ali Jaber [a player] said: 'They did not allow our families to come for fear someone would kill Bremer.'

There was also squabbling about money. This was another feature of life in the new Iraq: rows about who was making the most from the Americans. It was starting to look to me as though Iraqis had become inured to corruption, to cheating generally, because that had been the only way to survive under Saddam. It was not an attractive quality. One newspaper reported:

The players gave Bremer an Iraqi shirt, but they were angry when he did not give them the bonuses they had been promised for reaching the Olympics. Mounzer Fatfat, a Lebanese-American and Bremer's adviser to the Ministry of Youth and Sport, told the players it was 'a misunderstanding' and said he was sure they would be paid by someone. But, if they weren't, he said he would pay them from his own pocket. The players shrugged. They were used to broken promises and not being paid. Afterwards they said that it was like the era of Uday, only now there were lots of thieves controlling the sport, not just one.

Stange was not going to let squabbles about flags and bonuses upset him. He told me that he was excited by the coming months. First, there was a 'Goodwill Tour' of England, where his team would train and play friendly matches against Bristol Rovers, the club where Youra Eshaya had once played in the 1950s, Trinidad and Tobago, and, best of all, an All-Star XI, featuring players from the Premiership. I said this sounded terrific, though I doubted the latter would happen. Premiership players are valuable commodities, and it seemed unlikely that their clubs would allow them to turn out against a team like Iraq. After the tour of England, Stange told me that he would take his team to play Italy in Florence.

Stange said he owed all this to Tony Blair and the Italian Prime Minister, Silvio Berlusconi. 'I wrote to them and they didn't just write back – they made things happen. This is the sort of international assistance I was hoping for ten months ago. I wrote emotional letters everywhere saying football can do a lot more than diplomats believe. I reminded them we need good news from Iraq and not just bad news. But the Americans have done nothing for us. They don't know how important soccer is.' After Italy he would fly to Chinese Taipei for a World Cup qualifier on 9 June. In August he would take the full national squad to China for the Asian Cup. Then he would watch Iraq play at the Olympics in Greece, though strictly speaking they were Hamad's boys. (In fact, most of the Olympic team were also in the full national team, so Stange was entitled to view them as his team.)

Pnouel had given me Ammo's telephone number in Baghdad. After many unsuccessful attempts to get through, eventually there was an answer. It was Ammo. He said that he had been away. I said that I was writing a book about football in Iraq and would like to meet him. He said he would be delighted to help and said that I would be a welcome guest at his home in Baghdad. 'Do not worry', he said. 'You will be safe with me. I am loved. I am surrounded by people who want to shake my hand whenever I walk in the streets. I will take you to Najaf and to Karbala, and you will see how people adore me. If I go to a mosque they will kiss my hand, though I am a Christian.'

In England a man like Ammo would have been surrounded by agents and lawyers, who would have demanded large amounts of money for an interview with him. But he was accessible and did not ask to be paid for his views. He talked to me as if we had known each other for years: 'I saw Josephine [Ammo's wife] in Chicago four years ago. We spent three months together. I do not want her to come back, and she is afraid to come. I miss her. She is beautiful. She was a preacher and they put her in gaol when I was away with the national team. I love her very much.'

He did not think much of Stange. 'He is a cunning man. He is not a coach. He stayed a few days in Baghdad and then ran away before the war. He gives nothing to the players. They complain about him. I never had the money he has. I worked for nothing. I had tight discipline. Players knew I would send them home if they were one minute late for training.' Nor was he impressed by the Americans and Paul Bremer. 'The Americans take our oil, our money. The Americans give us nothing. Not a cent. Many times I have spoken against Bremer. He should come and see me and ask what I want. They say he is busy. Busy? Busy killing people is what I say. It is part of his job to see me. If one American dies, they kill five or six Iraqis. The Americans are mercenaries, killers.'

He believed that Iraq needed to be ruled firmly. 'Iraq needs a strong man like Saddam. As soon as the Americans and British go, the Ba'ath Party will come back because they have experience running the country. Before there was law and order. Now anyone can say anything about me. People are kidnapped every day. Every day people call me and say, "Sir, please help me my child has been taken."'

He said his health was suffering. 'I have diabetes. I take injections. I need someone to look after me. To clean, cook. If I get soup, steak, it is only by chance. I am tired. I get angry and nervous. I sit at home. I sleep a lot. Good people, doctors, educated people, are running away because they are afraid. People tell me I should have guards at my house. I say, no. I am safe. People like me.'

This was wonderful stuff. He was frank about his personal and professional life. But I was also a little uneasy. He was not a simple Mr Nice Guy. He was dismissive or downright rude about most people.

He hated the Americans and liked Saddam. But he was elderly and had been through a lot. I hoped that he would emerge as a softer, more sympathetic character when we met. What was encouraging was his assurance that I would be safe with him. This contradicted what I had been told by friends who were reporting for newspapers and television from Baghdad. They said that after the fall of Saddam they had roamed the country, interviewing, investigating, analysing. Although it had always been clear to them that many Iraqis did not welcome the invasion, this was not the same as saying that most Iraqis had supported Saddam.

Journalists, however, had not felt threatened, and many moved out of the claustrophobic hotels in the Green Zone, the area of central Baghdad where officials of the Coalition Provisional Authority worked and lived behind blast-proof walls, and into large houses in the city proper, where they could relax in swimming-pools and gardens instead of sweltering in stuffy hotels. Journalists told each other that they were getting to grips with the real Iraq and were contemptuous of CPA officials who refused to leave the Green Zone except in convoys of armed bodyguards.

Then journalists became targets, to kill or kidnap. They thought this was not fair, that they were doing an important job, describing what was happening in Iraq. They were right, but it did not matter. Journalists, whether they were reporting the Crimean War for *The Times*, the D-Day landings for the *New York Times* or the Vietnam War for NBC, had often been viewed as the enemy. Bullets do not weave around a person because he or she is a reporter. Rebels, terrorists, insurgents, dissidents, however they are described, had realized that by terrifying journalists in Iraq they could also terrify the West. Reporters returned reluctantly to the fortified, sandbagged hotels of the Green Zone. If they left to cover a story in the city or in the countryside, they were accompanied by armed bodyguards.

A few weeks later I learned that Ammo was taking a team of children from his football academy to a tournament in Brittany. I called him again and we agreed to meet there. I was relieved about this; we could chat in France, over a glass of wine, rather than in Baghdad. I still planned to go to Iraq, to see Ammo with his adoring fans, to talk to other players, coaches and officials about Uday's abuse of football and to take Ammo with me on a tour of clubs in cities like Basra. But France meant that I would not need to stay as long as I had originally planned. Thanks to Ammo, who would protect me, I would gain unique insights into Iraq.

6

The conspiracy of Penmarc'h

It was a glorious morning in late May 2004 on the wild, rocky Atlantic coast of Brittany. I was in the Penmarc'h peninsula, in the south-west of the department of Finisterre, which translates as 'The End of the World'.

It was the start of a four-day football tournament for boys, called Le Mondial Pupilles de Plomelin. There were seventy teams from around the world, divided into eight groups playing – and staying with local families – in villages around the regional centre of Quimper, the sort of bustling, cobblestoned town, with churches, cafés and chic shops, that features on television programmes about Britons making a new life in France. The final of the tournament would be played in Plomelin, a few miles south-west of Quimper.

I had arrived the previous night, having flown to Dinard, on the Channel coast, and driven south-west through Brittany. I found a small, cheap hotel and read my notes on Ammo. I was excited by the prospect of meeting a legend, Iraq's Pelé, the man who had defied Uday and, remarkably, lived to tell the tale.

The tournament had been running since 1986, and many young-sters who had taken part had gone on to great things. Arsenal's Thierry Henry, from France, arguably the best striker in the world in 2004, played for Monaco here in 1991. In May 2004 there were teams from major European clubs such as Dinamo Kiev and Anderlecht. There were also teams from Germany, Belgium, Bulgaria, Spain, Croatia, England, Wales, Italy, Poland, the Czech Republic, Russia, Romania, Jersey, Slovakia, the Ukraine, Madagascar and Canada. There were teams from the Brittany villages hosting the event. And there was Ammo's team from his football academy in Baghdad.

There were also the boys from Maccabi Haifa of Israel, who were playing in Plomelin. I wondered what would happen if Ammo's team was drawn against the Israelis in a later round. No Iraqi team had ever played Israelis, and it was inconceivable that Ammo would allow his youngsters to face them. Although Iraq was agnostic compared to many countries in the region, such as Iran and Saudi Arabia, it had a long and dishonourable history of anti-Semitism and had always been implacably hostile to Israel. But the tournament organizers had been shrewd and had ensured that Ammo's team and the Israelis could not meet before the final.

Ammo's boys faced some strong sides in their group in Penmarc'h. There were four from France, including one from Lille that was attached to a professional club and one from Namur, Belgium, also attached to a professional club. The Madagascans, who had been delayed, were reputedly excellent. Only a side from a Roman Catholic school in Slovakia looked easy.

The pitch in the municipal stadium in Penmarc'h was as good as anything in the English Premiership. It was a manicured, like a bowling green. There was a grandstand, beneath which were changing rooms and offices. There were two training pitches, where teams could warm up. There were refreshment stands, selling hot dogs, sandwiches, soft drinks and beer. There was bunting. There were at least 1,000 spectators for the opening game. It felt like a professional match, not a tournament for boys.

There was a glossy programme, full of advertisements and profiles of the teams. It talked about football uniting the world, teaching young people that taking part matters more than winning, that cheating is wrong, that multiculturalism is healthy, that violence solves nothing. Ammo's side was described as 'Bagdad FC'. Later I decided that the missing 'h' symbolized the hosts' lack of understanding of Ammo, his team and his country.

I recognized Ammo immediately: a powerful man with clipped white hair, wearing sun-glasses, a tweed jacket and slacks. He was watching his team warming up. I was struck by their size – they were tiny – and by their kit, which was new and expensive. A middle-aged Iraqi in a track suit, who was obviously the coach, was yelling instructions as they jogged, passed balls and sprinted. They looked like miniature professionals. Ammo's boys weren't much bigger than the balls they were kicking. Their opponents were almost young men, apart from the team from Slovakia, who were also very small.

I introduced myself, and Ammo smiled. 'Welcome, welcome', he said. We exchanged pleasantries. Then he said that the French charity that had brought them to Penmarc'h, Enfants du Monde, or Children of the World, were 'bastards'. I nodded. It seemed that Ammo in the flesh was as grumpy as the Ammo in Baghdad to whom I had spoken over the phone. But it was a lovely morning, and I thought that he was probably nervous because this was the first match. I hoped he would be less aggressive later.

We chatted, and I asked him what would happen if his team was drawn against the Israelis. 'I want to be frank. I respect all human beings. But if we played a team from Israel, I would have a problem when I went home. Every Arab, every Muslim, every Palestinian, hates Israel. They say we should not play them. I would like to play them and beat them, but it is not possible. It is very difficult. Football is about bringing people together, not hating.'

A young woman approached him and said that she was a reporter from a newspaper in Brest, the large port to the north. She said that she wanted to talk to him about Iraq and what it meant for the boys to come to this tournament. Ammo beamed, pleased that a journalist realized that he was not just an old man hanging around a boys' football team. He glanced at me and smiled, indicating that he expected many more interviews like this.

This vanity was a constant factor over the next four days, as reporters from regional newspapers and television came in search of an inspiring story about Iraq that also brought credit to France. Interviewer and interviewee always misunderstood each other. Partly this was the language barrier. Ammo did not speak French, and the reporters did not know Arabic or his native language, neo-Aramaic. His English was clumsy. Often he did not understand questions but was too proud to say so. Thus his answers often had nothing to with the questions. Sometimes what he said was not what he meant. The most serious problem, however, was the ignorance of the journalists.

A few knew that Ammo had been a great player and an outstanding coach, but many had no idea who he was. Most thought that he had opposed Saddam. They had gleaned this from American government websites, which quoted him selectively, as if he had hated Saddam and had welcomed the invasion. In fact, he had admired Saddam, though he had hated Uday. He had opposed the invasion and thought that the Americans were destroying his country. But the Americans had taken bits of quotes and spliced them together so that Ammo sounded like a member of the George W. Bush fan club, which he certainly was not. These nuances confused reporters. They wanted him to gush thanks to Enfants du Monde, to the families in Brittany who were looking after the boys and possibly to the Americans, though this was optional since the French government had opposed the invasion.

Unlike these journalists, I did not have a pressing deadline. I had the time to make sure he understood me. I taped our conversations and every night transcribed them in my hotel room, cleaning up his English without changing the meaning or the mood. If I had quoted him word for word in this book, he would have sounded an idiot, which he was not.

The following, however, is a verbatim extract from the interview with the French journalist. It is typical of the conversations that Ammo had with the media over the next four days. It illustrates the scale of the misunderstandings that were a feature of Penmarc'h.

AMMO: Children. The first time. We have a school training them. I make school.

JOURNALIST: When did you make it?

AMMO: National stadium.

JOURNALIST: When?

AMMO: I started before four years. We bring players. A little good with talent. We try to bring it high. But it is very difficult in Iraq. Twelve years body is small. If you compare for Europe you can very high, body good. This is our problem.

JOURNALIST: Because of the embargo?

AMMO: No, before like this. Now worse. Before Ministry of Youth used to help us with shoes, balls, food, transport, many things. Now we miss all this because American doesn't give freedom for people to work. No money. They not look after children. They think these are animals. I am sorry to say that. I feel it like this. No one attend. I ask many times to come and visit these children. Because I want to keep children in football. This is the game for all Iraqis. You see a thousand people come and want to bring their children to the school. I want to make nearly a hundred school in all Iraq. OK? We need money.

JOURNALIST: You say bodies of boys are smaller than before?

AMMO: Because of food. This is one of the things. If they have money they can eat. OK? Now they come here and they see food they never see. I used to give them three times in a week a hamburger, an orange and a banana. Now no one helps them. Myself I am a volunteer. I cannot spend. Twenty other coaches and three doctors. We all work. We make the ground. We cut the grass. I go here and there and ask people to help us. We buy them balls. We buy them good. Nobody look after them. Every time I speak in the papers and TV I say, why, does Americans not care about children. They don't give them food. They don't look after them. I am sorry I can see everything is good looking here. America they destroy every-thing. Some Arabs, with Iraqis, they stole everything we have. So I am rebuilding the ground and the goals. This has cost me. A hundred thousand. A lot.

JOURNALIST: You don't have any more goals? They have been destroyed?

AMMO: I repair it. Because I came and saw Americans in the stadium . . . putting ladies, I am sorry to say, clothes. They broke it. Home-made goals. We make it. Not like this [thumping a goal post with his hand]. OK? And the armoured cars crush it all.

JOURNALIST: How many boys do you have in your school?

AMMO: I used to have 350 boys before the war. Very big stores. Plenty of good. Not from Uday. Uday doesn't like these players or I make school. He hate specially Shia. He used to tell me, cancel the school. I say no, I insist to stay with the children.

JOURNALIST: Who told you that?

AMMO: Uday. Uday. Saddam.

JOURNALIST: You are Shia?

AMMO: I am Christian. I Christian. I run all the sports in Iraq. They like me. All my friends are Muslim and they respect me.

JOURNALIST: I am sorry, I don't follow you on the Shia problem.

AMMO: Because I am popular. Since '59, I went to Egypt as a player. I represent all Arab, all Muslim countries as a player captain team. I was a good player you know.

JOURNALIST: Did you play in Egypt?

AMMO: I play many times in Egypt. We want to make Arab team in Egypt. I represent Iraq. We train every day. For two months we could not make a team. Anyone not playing go home. They want all of them, eleven players. So I become after I retire, 1979, retire as a player I become a coach. I get good results for the country. Gulf tournament four times. Win. Arab tournament one time. Asia, all Asia tournament one time. Worldwide to Olympics three times. Qualify to World Cup Mexico one time. I have two players here sick. They remember family, they cry. I never follow twelve-year-old player. He cry. He want his father, his mother.

JOURNALIST: Don't you think, when you are twelve years old and if you are used to being with your family for seven days but for them it is the first time, leaving a country at war, don't you think it is more difficult?

AMMO: Yes, I know, yeah. I know. We have fathers call them twice in a day. They want to know how are the children.

JOURNALIST: They are worried?

AMMO: Yeah, they want to know what happened to them. Where are they.

JOURNALIST: Are you proud?

AMMO: I like that. Although I am old now I have experience enough to run sports, to train children. It's not difficult for me. I know it will happen this. These childrens we train them good, very good. We have 350 children, but now more than 100 children not coming. Why? Because no transport. When they want to arrive to the school they are afraid. In the streets bombs, you know.

The journalist then asked one of Ammo's boys what he thought: 'It is very green here. Very nice. We are glad we are representing the children of Iraq. I want to win to make my parents proud. The Americans occupy Iraq. We need security.' The reporter trotted off to interview the French charity and the organizers of the tournament. Ammo was not happy. He said that he was disappointed she had known so little about him: 'Journalists should know me. In Iraq people call me all the time. They like my ideas. I want to be friends with everyone but I also must be frank', he said.

'Bagdad FC' trotted out in a smart green kit to face the Belgians from Namur. Ammo nodded approvingly. 'I bought all the kit. I gave the boys pocket money. $210 each for the week', he said. I wondered if this was true. By the coach's feet were bags containing spare strips. How could Ammo, who had no money, have bought all this? I could see already that the more he dissembled, the more his English fell apart. If he was telling the truth, he was crisp and decisive; if he was fibbing, he sheltered behind ungrammatical *non sequiturs*. But I decided that I did not have the right to judge a great player like Ammo. If he had been born half a century later and in a different country, he would have been earning millions of pounds a year and would never have talked to someone like me.

'Bagdad FC' did their best but were thrashed by the Belgians, who were older and bigger. It was a grotesque mismatch, heavyweight against flyweight, which, luckily for the Iraqis, only lasted twenty minutes. The score was 2–0 but could easily have been 10–0. I suspected that the Belgian coach had told his boys to go easy on the Iraqis.

Ammo was standing by the dug-out. He was furious with the charity. 'They are using us as an advertisement. They talk about us on television. They say, "Look, we have brought poor little Iraqi children to France." They don't care about the results of the games.' He reflected that the game against Namur had taught him a valuable lesson. 'We don't have boys like this in Iraq, big and strong. Without power you cannot be a good player.'

It was true that the charity did not think it mattered if 'Bagdad FC' were hammered in every match. As far as they were concerned, it was enough that the Iraqis were there, enjoying the hospitality of the French, seeing how much the world cared about Iraq. The charity had been founded in 1984 by a French priest called Yves Buannic. (By coincidence he had been born in Penmarc'h.) It had been operating in Iraq since 1995, employed eighty people there, mostly locals, and concentrated, as its name suggested, on helping children. They had spent £10,000 bringing the team to France, a considerable sum for a charity. They had flown the team from Baghdad to Jordan, because the roads were unsafe, and from Amman to Paris. They had spent a day there and flown to Brittany. One member of the team from Air Serv International, the humanitarian airline that had flown them from Iraq, described the journey from Baghdad: 'I could feel the children's awe and mischief. It was their first time on a plane and each one was nervous. We talked about France and what they expected to see and the tournament and the fact they will play against the French. . . . The plane to them was like riding a roller-coaster – some laughed and some prayed.'[1]

Buannic was elderly and had retired, but he remained the charity's figurehead. He was small and grizzled. Despite his age and an obviously limited knowledge of football, he was keen that the Iraqis should do well and constantly bellowed advice in French, which the Iraqis did not understand. During the Iraqis' next match, later that morning – another thrashing, 3–0, this time by a French side – Buannic hopped up and down on the touchline, waving his arms and shouting instructions in a rasping, smoker's voice. He meant no harm, and it was hard to see why Ammo was so offended. After all, this was a tournament for boys, not the Olympics or the World Cup.

Ammo had retreated to the stand and was glowering. He had taken a violent dislike to Buannic, who, it must be admitted, smelt as if he did not bathe regularly. Ammo raged: 'He is dirty. He is filthy. He doesn't wash or change his clothes. Why am I here? I would like to take my team home.' He was incensed that four others from the charity – Alexandre Boskowitz, the vice-president, who was based in Paris, two male staff from Baghdad and a female translator from Lebanon – were also on the touchline, obscuring the vision of the team coach and the substitutes in the dug-out. 'Look, look at that', Ammo said. 'Why are they there? It is not professional. If I was the coach, they would not dare come near me. If they did I would punish them.'

Although it was undeniable they meant well and did fine work in Iraq, they did not understand that Ammo, and his team, wanted to win. On the other hand, I thought he was going too far, that he could have made his point in a more restrained manner. Boskowitz, the charity's vice-president, told me over lunch – in a school canteen, with Ammo fuming in a corner – that the team from Baghdad consisted of Sunnis and Shias, though I knew there was only one Sunni. I presumed that he said this because he was trying to project Ammo's academy as fashionably multi-religious. Everyone in Iraq knew that most boys at the school came from poor Shia families from Sadr City, the vast Shia slum to the north-east of central Baghdad.

The results did not matter, said Boskowitz. 'The boys are enjoying it. Losing is not important. What is important is to play. They are being spoiled by the families they are staying with. They are getting so many gifts.' He said that Ammo had known that his boys would be smaller than the other teams. 'Iraqi children are not strong. It is because of sanctions.'

In the afternoon I sat with Ammo in the grandstand and asked him about his football academy. He told me about the importance of instilling the right habits into players when they were young. He told me again how much he was loved by everyone. As he talked, I realized that I had misunderstood; it was not an academy in the sense of having buildings and a permanent staff and children who attended every day. Ammo's academy consisted of him and some volunteers coaching children a few times a week, security permitting.

The first match in the afternoon, against a team from Penmarc'h, was another defeat, 2–0. But the game against Lille was much worse: 'Bagdad FC' lost 7–0. By now his boys were demoralized and exhausted from playing teams who were so much stronger than them. Ammo was sure there had been a conspiracy to humiliate him. He told me that had been forced to stay with a family in the village, instead of in a proper hotel. He said that a man of his age and reputation should not have been treated like this; it was disrespectful. He said: 'Mine is the only football school in Iraq. If we get good results, people at home will back me and say there should be other schools like it. Iraq needs to win in sport. We need to win here.'

The next day he told me how he had been deceived. He explained that the charity had insisted that the tournament organizers had specified that the boys must be born after a certain date. 'It is all about the price of plane tickets. Boys below a certain age travel for half-price', he said. 'At first the charity said the boys could be thirteen and four-teen years old. Then they said that boys had to be born after 1 May 1992. Other teams here have boys born on or after January 1991. My boys are playing against boys who are thirteen, nearly fourteen. There's a big difference. A twelve-year-old is small and weak. A four-teen-year-old is big and strong. If they had told me the truth, I would have bought the tickets myself. The Iraqi people will blame me. People in Iraq are interested in this tournament because I am here. They expect us to do well.'

He said that the French charity was still cheating him. 'I buy soft drinks for the boys, but they buy nothing. They don't pay for any-thing. They put us with French families and are making good money out of us. A rich French man told me that he would give the charity money for the boys, but the charity have given us nothing.'

He brooded on the ticket scandal for the rest of the day. I suspected he was talking rubbish, but I spoke to the tournament organizers and he was right: the charity had misled him in order to save money on tickets. I asked Alexandre Boskowitz why they had done this, and he smiled and repeated that taking part was all that counted. It was under-standable – the charity had limited resources – but misguided because Ammo was furious, and his team became increasingly frustrated that they were playing boys who were bigger than them.

Ammo and the Iraqis who worked for the charity took action next day. They photographed their team with their opponents to prove to the people back home that they had been cheated by the French charity. Ammo said: 'The Iraqi people will blame me. The French charity say my team are just kids and don't care they are losing. But they want to get results.' Ammo said. 'The French don't understand how to treat the children. The French are very bad, all of them.'

After losing two more games – conceding eight goals and scoring none against teams from France and Madagascar, who had arrived late after their flights were delayed – he calmed down, probably because he had expended so much nervous energy. He said: 'My boys ask me, "Why are we losing?" They say, "Are they much better than us?" I say, "This is football. You must appreciate there are better players than you." I am a leader in football in Iraq. People believe what I say. I will go home and say we were good losers. I will say, we must think how to build, how to make our children stronger. I will look at schools, clubs and offer advice. The boys here understand. I have told them that I often got angry with the national team. But I have said they are doing OK. I have said, "You are doing your best."'

He settled into a routine. He watched games from the stand, stared at Buannic, talked about the conspiracy to humiliate him and bemoaned the fact that his team was so small. He would pick at the simple lunches in school canteens provided by the French hosts and then go back to the house where he was staying for a short rest. He resented all this. He felt it was *small*. He had been a great player. He had been a great coach. He had been world-class. Now he was watching children play football in a village and was staying with a family. He should have been watching the best players in the world. He should have been in a five-star hotel. He did not articulate this and might have denied it, but I was sure this was how he felt.

We talked for many hours over the following days. He spoke about his life as a player and as a coach, about Saddam and Uday, about the legendary England manager Alf Ramsey, about Don Revie and the great Portuguese player Eusebio. He guffawed when he heard that an ex-Iraqi international called Ahmed Radhi, the former vice-president of the Iraq Football Association, who had played for him when he coached Iraq, had been arrested on suspicion of throwing a hand grenade at the home of Hussein Saeed, president of the Iraqi FA, who had just sacked Radhi. 'I have bad memories of him. Radhi said bad things about me. He said that I was paid $50,000 by Uday. He is wrong. He said that Saddam's bodyguards used to give me everything I wanted. A house. Four jobs. Things like that. Now they are playing hell with him', he said.

On the third day his boys, who were treated with a mixture of kindness and pity by the French families with whom they lodged, stopped behaving like plucky no-hopers. They spat at and kicked opponents. One Iraqi was booked by the referee, a symbolic gesture since the boy would never play again in France.

Ammo was distracted briefly when his son Sami and his wife,

Wassila, arrived. They had not met for four years and hugged and kissed each other with obvious affection. Sami was thirty-six and was a mechanic in the south of France. He had deserted from the Iraqi army in 1991 and found his way to France. He was chubby and smiled a lot. But he did not want to talk to me. He simply said: 'We love our father.'

After they left, Ammo returned to the attack. He told me that the 'Bagdad FC' coach, Moufaq Zaidang, had cheated him, just as the charity had done. He accused Zaidang of taking bribes from parents who wanted their sons to come to France. 'I will punish him', said Ammo. 'He gave me the names of the boys he wanted to come to France. Perhaps he had been bribed by the fathers of boys. I could have found better players. When I suspected this had happened, I told the charity that I was going to change the team but they said it was too late.'

There was a pattern. He saw conspiracies everywhere. He thought most people were crooks. Sometimes I liked him, at other moments I thought that was a spiteful egomaniac. I guessed that, like veteran athletes in former Communist countries, the previous regime had given him a generous pension for serving the state well. I imagined that he was struggling in the post-Saddam, dollar-based economy. In Saddam's Iraq the patronage of the governing élite brought a comfortable lifestyle; contacts and influence were as important as money. In the new Iraq only hard currency, preferably dollars, mattered. And I doubted Ammo had much of that.

He kept insisting that he had never been paid by Saddam and Uday. 'I am a decent man, a Christian. I never steal. I am straight. I speak the truth. I talk for the benefit of sport, the country. I used to give money to poor people. People think I have millions of dollars. They should know I am a poor man.' He kept returning to the subject of money, though he never even hinted that he wanted me to pay him. 'Uday used to employ foreign coaches. But he gave me nothing. I never had much money. People used to come and ask me for help. I gave them what I had. I did that a lot. They appreciated it.'

I suspected that, like all Iraqis who had prospered under Saddam, he had made more compromises than he was admitting now. Perhaps

that was why he told me again and again that he had been so generous to people. Had he really defied Uday? Had he looked away when
his players were dragged off to prison? Surely it could not be true that
he was never paid? How he had brought up his family? How had he
paid for his house, his cars, his clothes. Despite his age and his diabetes, he looked like he had always lived well, unlike his brother
Pnouel, whose entire demeanour – posture, eyes, skin – suggested a
life of struggle. If Ammo had co-operated with Uday, then I could
not blame him: I had no doubt that I would have flattered and fawned
to survive. Ammo was obviously not a hero, but many Iraqis thought
that he was because they needed to believe in someone.

He told me that he was proud of his school. 'Uday was against my
school. He didn't want it. He hated it because most of the children
are Shia. Why did I set it up? Because I wanted to be remembered in
fifty years. Two months before the war the Iraqi Football Association
insisted that I close it because they knew that was what Uday wanted.
I told them, "If anyone comes to my school, I will kill them." They
said, "Please Ammo, do as he wants." This school is all my money.
The Americans give us nothing. Not a cent. Most boys are Shia, from
poor homes in Sadr City. Sunnis are richer and don't come to the
school. Only four or five boys in the school come from richer homes.'

As we talked, it was clear that he regretted the fall of Saddam, not
because he approved of the way Saddam ran the country – he was not
interested in politics – but because he, Ammo Baba, had prospered
under Saddam. He had been young and successful under Saddam;
now he was old and only had his memories – and his boasts. 'Scouts
from clubs come to my school all the time. I can tell who will make
a good player, from the way he moves. I have created many good
players. In Africa everyone wants to be a footballer. It's good money
now. They are strong and fast. Japan and Korea are producing good
players too. But you must feed the children properly.'

He said that his wife, Josephine, whom he had married in 1960, had
fled Iraq in 1994. 'She had been gaoled once by Uday when I was away
with the national team. When I came back I had her released. In 1994
she went to France for Sami's wedding. I could not go because I was
with the team in Bulgaria. Then I had to go back to Iraq to play Jordan

and India. Josephine called me from France and said she was going to Canada to her sister, who was sick. I said I loved her but could not leave Iraq. She asked me many times to come but I always refused. She is a beautiful and I miss her.'

He said that he pitied Pnouel. 'In Baghdad there are always people around me. I live in a nice house in the officers' pensions district. They come to my house. We sit and drink. This makes me happy. I don't want to be like Pnouel. He sits alone in a small house. Nobody attends to him. I pity him.'

He worried that Iraqi society, which had always respected men like him, who had served their country, was becoming Westernized. 'When I arrived in America in 2001 to see Josephine, hundreds of people welcomed me. When I left six months later, I was alone. In Baghdad hundreds of people surround me in the street. "Ammo, Ammo", they say. I am used to this. But here, in France, I am alone. In America you meet someone once and never again. Everyone is busy. No one had time to sit with me. In Baghdad people come to my house and make me tea, coffee. What would I do here in France? I would sit alone and watch TV. In Baghdad people sleep in my house. When I was young I could adapt, but I am seventy years old now and I can't.'

He said he found solace in the Bible, but that he had no time for organized religion. 'I used to go to church. But not now. The church made trouble for my family. A priest at Habbaniya accused my father and eldest brother, George, of being Communists. Because my father knew he went with women and stole money from the church. The English gaoled them on the basis of the priest's accusation. Their health suffered in gaol. That is why I hate the church. But I am always reading the Bible. I knew more now than the priest ever did. Jesus did not talk about building churches. He said your heart is the church of God. Churches are where people go to talk about making money. Pnouel loves the church. That is a problem with the family. They don't like the fact that my wife and I read the Bible but don't go to church.'

He told me a long and confused story about the deaths in April 2003 of his brother-in-law James and James' children Nicola and

Eddie, who were killed, he said, by the Americans. 'They were staying in my house and after eleven days decided to go because the fighting was close. They took one of my cars – I have two Mercedes and a Toyota – and my money, $130,000. The car was destroyed by the Americans, and they were killed and all my money was stolen. People thought I had been killed because it was my car. Many came to my house to see if I was alive.'

I was puzzled by this. If Ammo was poor, how could he own two cars, one of them a Mercedes? Where did $130,000 come from? It was clear from everything he said – that people were always visiting or staying with him – that he owned a large house in an up-market neighbourhood. How had he bought this? I could have asked him, but he would have been offended. And, anyway, I suspected that he had not told the whole truth about his relationship with the previous regime.

He said it was a consolation that he commanded such respect among the football community in Iraq. He said: 'The new minister of sport is making a statue of me. Journalists ask me all the time, will I take this job or that job? But everyone today wants to get a job, a position. My students take power. Like Hussein Saeed, whom I knew as a player. Both sides at the Iraqi FA, those with Hussein and those against, like me. That is why I don't want a position there. People say to me, form a group to run the association. I tell them I want to remain alone, not to be for or against anyone. Hussein Saeed came to my house and said I could have anything I wanted.'

He said he was worried that the religious extremists were winning. 'Shia clerics come to my school and talk about religion. I wanted to make a branch for women, but that is difficult. Iraq is the headquarters of killers, people who want to shoot Americans. They don't want us to do anything, like having a drink in a bar.'

His coach, Moufaq Zaidang, had not heard, or perhaps did not care about, Ammo's allegations that he had taken bribes from parents to select their boys. As his team trudged off the pitch after their final game, a 4–1 defeat to a French team, Zaidang said that he was disappointed that they had only managed to win one point, from a 0–0 draw with the Slovaks. 'If we had a team of the same age as the others then we could do better, maybe win it', he said. But he said it had been a privilege to work with Ammo. 'Everyone loves and respects him. He has much to give to football. People still call him by his names, the Flying Player, the Hunter Player, the Shooter Player.'

Mohammed al-Jbir, an Iraqi who worked for Enfants du Monde, said: 'All Iraqis like him. He is a good man. He is the best coach ever in Arab countries.' Waleeb Oraibi, who also worked for the charity in Iraq, said: 'Everyone loves him. He is a special personality. He gets angry because he is serious.'

Ammo, meanwhile, was looking forward to his next trip abroad – taking an under-19 team to the Gothia Cup, an international tournament for teenagers in Gothenburg, Sweden, in July. But this time, he smiled, his boys would be the same age as their opponents. And he would be staying in a proper hotel.

7

Ammo's story

Ammo Baba told me that he had been a natural athlete when he was growing up at RAF Habbaniya in the 1930s and '40s . He said: 'I was lazy in the classroom, but I loved sport. I was good at everything. Best of all was football. I trained with a ball for six hours a day because I knew that practice makes perfect.'

By his mid-teens he was playing for the RAF Employees' (Assyrian) Club, having been recruited from Assyrians employed on the Habbaniya base. It was one of the strongest teams in Iraq and, he insisted, would have troubled many professional English teams. In 1951, aged seventeen, he played for Iraqi Schoolboys against Egypt in Cairo. He said: 'I was better than the players playing today. I was very strong. I was a centre forward but could play anywhere. I have to say, and it gives me no pleasure to say it, that I was in better shape than players today. I used to run 42 kilometres in one go. I practised all the time.'

He played for the RAF Employees' team until 1955, when he moved to Baghdad and joined a team known as the Royal Iraqi Guards. In the late 1950s a Scotsman called Frank Hill, who had once coached the Iraqi Military team, and who had become manager of Notts. County, a club that was then in the Second Division, offered Ammo a contract. Ammo wanted to prove himself against British players. Money was not a major factor. He said that he was badly paid in Iraq – $100 a month – and would not have earned much more in England, where players at that time were not allowed to earn more than £20 a week.[1] But another part of him could not bear to leave Iraq. He told me: 'I don't know why I did not leave Iraq. Sometimes I screamed aloud, "Why God, why did you make me love Iraq so much? Why?"'

There were compensations. The king was a football fan and admired Ammo. He sent him on frequent trips abroad, for medical treatment or to relax. Ammo usually chose London. He was in London on 14 July 1958, when two army officers, Brigadier Abd al Karim Qasim and Colonel Abd as Salaam Arif, overthrew the monarchy. King Faisal II and many members of the royal family were executed. The British embassy in Baghdad was attacked and damaged by a mob who loathed the king's British friends.

Ammo said he had been approached in London by Fulham, Liverpool and Celtic, who wanted to sign him, though, it must be said, this would not have been easy since this was many years before overseas players were common in the British game. Then the Iraqi embassy in London told Ammo that Qasim wanted him to return to Iraq. A few days later he was back in Baghdad.

He said: 'The king liked me a lot. In 1958 he sent me to England for a check-up. I was staying in London with friends. They dealt with the English clubs who wanted to sign me. Notts. County had already written to me when I was in Baghdad. I still have the letter. They wanted me to sign for them. Then Celtic were interested. And Fulham and Liverpool. I had always wanted to be a great player for Iraq, but I also wanted to play in England. I was confused and did not know what to do. After the revolution in the summer of 1958 the Iraqi embassy in London came to me and said I had to go back. They said, "You will have a good job, a good salary." I was worried about my family. So I went home. Every time I decide to do something important I change my mind again. My life is about missed opportunities.'

Because Iraq was so closely linked to Moscow, Ammo's opportunities to play internationally were limited. In 1959 he became the first Iraqi to score in an Olympic qualifying match, against Lebanon. Most internationals were against Iraq's neighbours or Communist states such as North Korea and Czechoslovakia. In the West he was unknown; but within Iraq he was a hero.

In Britain football clubs grew out of the Industrial Revolution. They were usually set up by local self-made businessmen. Some genuinely wanted to help the community, but many wanted the status of owning a football club, where factory workers would go on Saturday afternoon after their morning shift. Even in the advanced capitalist economies of western Europe there were important differences between the way that clubs were organized and financed in say, England and Spain. In the 1960s and '70s clubs in the England were owned by local worthies, men who owned shops or factories. In Spain clubs were extensions of regional pride, epitomized by Real Madrid, representing the centralism of Franco, and Barcelona, standing for Catalan separatism. In Italy clubs evoked memories of the time when the country was a patchwork of warring city-states. Football in a developing country such as Iraq could not be based around privately owned clubs. It was too poor. It had an agricultural economy. Its social and political texture, even under the pro-British monarchy, was Arab, not Western.

I pressed Ammo hard for details of his career as a player. He did his best to remember, but it was a long time ago and players in Iraq had moved frequently, without contracts or transfer fees. One season they would be with a club that was attached to the police; the next season they would be turning out for one that was run by the Ministry of Transport. In 1959, aged twenty-five, Ammo became player–coach of the Assyrian Sports Club and led them to victory against the Air Force, his former club, in the Iraqi Cup Final. In 1961 the government closed the Assyrian club, because the team was drawn exclusively from an unpopular minority, and he rejoined the Air Force. Two years later they won the league and cup.

Games often ended in mass brawls, he said, because 'Iraqis have hot heads'. But there were other reasons: football was an outlet for the frustrations of a people who felt they had been betrayed by their government. The two senior members of the military government, Qasim and Arif, had little in common apart from their hatred of the monarchy. Arif, the junior in the partnership, favoured closer ties with Egypt's Gamul Abdul Nasser and was sympathetic to the Ba'ath Party, which had a pan-Arab agenda. Qasim, meanwhile, looked to Iraq's powerful Communist Party for support. He was also considered to be a social inferior by the Sunni-dominated officer class of the army because he was of mixed Shia–Sunni parentage and had been born in south-eastern Iraq, rather than in the Sunni heartland to the north-west of the capital. Qasim prevailed. Arif was arrested a year later and sentenced to death. (He was pardoned in 1962.)

Qasim developed close ties with Moscow, alienated conservative neighbours such as Iran and Kuwait with territorial claims and worried the West, who regarded him as a dangerous mix of nationalist and Communist. The Ba'ath Party also hated him and, using a 22-year-old activist called Saddam Hussein, tried to assassinate him in 1959. Qasim was injured but survived. Saddam fled to Syria and then to Egypt, where he studied law and waited for his chance to return to Iraq. In February 1963, hemmed in by regional enemies and facing Kurdish insurrection in the north and a growing nationalist movement at home, Qasim was overthrown and killed by army officers, some of whom were associated with the Ba'ath Party.

Apart from a few months in 1963, military officers ruled Iraq for the next five years. They toyed with establishing a pan-Arab state, with Egypt and Syria. Some professed to support Ba'ath principles – 'socialism, freedom and Arab unity' – but family and tribal loyalties were more important than ideology. In the summer of 1968 there was another coup, this time by young army officers. The Ba'ath Party immediately overthrew them.

In 1964, aged thirty, Ammo was appointed a lieutenant in the Air Force. However, he was soon thrown out of the service, and the football club, because he refused to join the Ba'ath Party. This was brave. The approval of the party – Ba'ath is Arabic for 'rebirth' – was usually essential for survival.[2] The party could excommunicate people from society, leaving them ineligible for food rations, bank accounts or houses, which was crueller than arresting them. At street level, party activists issued orders and watched each other, and everyone else, for 'irregularities'. Higher up the party ladder were committees that had wide-ranging powers, including the right to arrest people. There were party groups for students, farmers and young people. Military officers, though not the rank-and-file conscripts, had to be party members. Meanwhile, the party's assorted security agencies spied on everyone and on each other. As they climbed the party ladder, members won privileges that made life more comfortable. But the higher an Iraqi rose, the more compromised morally he (or she) became.

Iraqis became inured to this. Promotion required them to demon-strate loyalty to the party by informing on friends, even family. If you were not a good party member, your children had no chance of going to university and would struggle to get respectable work. Even Shias in southern Iraq, many of whom loathed Saddam and his Sunni élite, became party members because they wanted to live reasonably. Over the years the party inculcated pettiness, spite and brutality into the national psyche as qualities to be valued.

Ammo moved to a team in Baghdad called the Military Academy. He was still a great player. He scored twice against the North Korean team who later performed heroically in the World Cup in England in 1966. In 1967 he joined the Passenger Transport Department. The following season he was back with the Military Academy.

But he was growing old. In 1966 he had been injured playing for Iraq against South Yemen in the opening match of the Pan-Arab Games in Cairo. He travelled to London for surgery. The operation was successful, and he returned to Iraq. However the pace, the agility and upper body strength were fading. On 12 March 1967 he played his last international, against Libya in Tripoli. In 1970, aged thirty-six, he retired: 'We were playing the Police Machinery team and thought we would win, but we lost 5–0. After that I give up playing', he said.

He now had to support his wife, Josephine, the teacher whom he had married in 1960, a daughter, Mona, and a son, Sami. (He later had another daughter, May.) If he had lived in England, he would have opened a pub or become a newspaper columnist; if he had retired in 2004, he would have been a multimillionaire with homes in London, the south of France and the Caribbean. But he was an Iraqi in the 1960s. So he became a full-time coach. 'I started coaching the army team. I coached the national team twice. We were always travelling. I was straight and honest. I was never paid. I was very popular. The papers were always talking about me.'

Many Assyrians, who felt uncomfortable in the radical, aggressively Arab Iraq, moved abroad, especially to the USA, in the coming decade, but Ammo refused to leave, to the irritation of his wife, who felt he had given too much to a country that did not value him. His brother Pnouel emigrated in 1969 to Britain, where he tried, and failed, to make a new life as a professional footballer.

From 1970 until 1974 Ammo coached the Military Academy in Baghdad. Then he moved to the Army Club and in 1975 to the Kirkut-based Youth Ministry team, where he won the league title in 1976. In 1971 he took charge of the Iraqi Military team. In 1978 he was appointed coach of the full national squad. The following year he led them to victory in the Gulf Cup, a biennial tournament.

Iraq was not a poor country, but its football team was starved of cash. In 1973 the national squad spent three days travelling to Melbourne for a World Cup qualifying match against Australia because the IFA had bought cheap tickets. The journey began with a ten-hour bus trip to Kuwait City. They waited ten hours for a flight to India, spent ten hours more in an airport there, flew to Bangkok, where they spent another ten hours, before catching a plane to Sydney and then on to Melbourne. Not surprisingly they lost 3–1 and missed qualifying for the next round by one point.

Nick Ask, the Iraqi who had left Iraq in 1985 and now lived in Michigan, told me how the players lived. 'In 1976 four players from Basra – Rahim Karim, Jalil Hanoon, Hadi Ahmed and Ala Ahmed – were chosen to play for Iraq in a Olympic qualifier in Baghdad. They played for al-Minaa, the club of the Iraq Port Authorities, and were paid 60 dinars – about $190 – a month. They had to make their own way, and at their own expense, to Baghdad. They stayed in a hotel that charged them 1 dinar each, though they had to share a room with four other people.' Ask said that the IFA was 'hopeless and corrupt' before Saddam and Uday came to power. He said: 'The association would not build decent facilities for the national team or the leading clubs. It had no budget. Players were not paid properly. Everything was a mess. The cup competition often did not happen. Sometimes the league programme was not completed. Injured players often did not receive proper treatment and had to retire.'

Despite this, football thrived. By now the game was played mainly by the Shia majority, who were traditionally the poorest and worst-educated people in Iraq. Every village had a football pitch. Every boy dreamed of turning out for one of the major clubs in Baghdad, the centre of football. Thousands of people used to watch games between rival villages.

Life, though, became increasingly difficult for Iraqis. The Ba'ath Party had its own intelligence network, the precursor of the terror machine that Saddam used to control the country in the 1980s and '90s. Its ideology was a muddle of socialism, nationalism and pan-Arabism; family and tribal loyalties, rather than ideas, bound its leadership. However, it was ruthless and dedicated to one thing: the maintenance of power. 'If you kept away from politics, you would probably be OK', said Ask. 'But the spying apparatus was everywhere. You could be executed if one of your friends said anything against the government.'

General Ahmed Hasan-al-Bakr, who led the party, came from Tikrit, like most leading members of the party, including his deputy, Saddam Hussein. Saddam was three years younger than Ammo Baba. He was born on 28 April 1937 in al-Auja, just outside Tikrit. He moved to Baghdad when he was ten, after his father died and his mother remarried. His uncle Khayrallah Tulfah, an anti-Western, anti-Semitic army officer, brought him up. In 1963 Saddam married his cousin Sajida, with whom he had two sons, Uday and Qusay, and three daughters, Raghad, Rana and Hala. This did not mellow him; on the contrary, he became even more determined to eliminate rivals to his destiny – the leadership of Iraq.

Pan-Arabism had died in the wake of the disastrous Arab war against Israel in 1967, and Iraq squabbled with Iran and Kuwait over borders. Saddam used the money from booming oil prices to build a network of spies. His thugs murdered his opponents, real and imagined. On 16 July 1979 Saddam forced his friend and patron General al-Bakr to resign. At the age of forty-two Saddam became head of state.

Ammo thought Saddam would be neither better nor worse than all the others who had had ruled. He did not care about politics, but if he believed anything, it was that Iraq needed a strong ruler, like Saddam. He was loyal to his country, not to the people in power. When I pressed him for an opinion on Saddam, he said that he had been the most effective ruler in Iraq's history, better certainly than the monarchy or the military, because Iraq had been stable.

Like top sportsmen in Communist countries, Ammo led a privileged life. Money was less important than connections and status. People knew that Saddam liked him, which meant that he was safe. He had supreme confidence in his abilities as a coach. He believed that fitness, strength and power were essential and put his teams through gruelling training sessions that were unprecedented in the Arab world, where players looked for inspiration to South America, known for its languid and skilful players, rather than to Europe, where they thought football was all about fitness and brute force.

He told me that Sir Alf Ramsey, who had won the World Cup for England in 1966, once visited Baghdad and watched him training his players. He said: 'Alf Ramsey said his players would have to be as fit as mine if they were going to win the World Cup again in 1970. When I was a player, I used to run the 100 metres 120 times. When I was a coach I had tough interval training. Two 880 metres. Then six 440 metres. Then eight 220 metres. Then twelve 100 metres and then fourteen 50 metres. After that short, sharp bursts. I believe in conditioning, Many Iraqis did not approve. They said that all I cared about was fitness.'

He boasted that his team had played – and thrashed – the UAE team managed by Don Revie, the former Leeds United and England manager. 'Revie asked me, "How do you get these Arabs so fit?" I took boys when they were fifteen, sixteen and seventeen years old and turned them into players. I worked them hard. I had four principles: power, endurance, speed, technique. Players must have good muscles, endurance, speed of reaction and good technique. When they have that, then you can tell them what they should do on a pitch. Not until then. I don't like isometric exercises. I prefer players to run, to move, not to remain still lifting weights. My players were trained to play in matches. Everything was geared to that. So I made them zigzag when they ran. I built speed and flexibility.'

Ammo said that Saddam and the IFA did little to help football. But he told me that he was determined that lack of resources would not hold back his teams. So he used to hire trucks and load them with earth so he could improve pitches. He maintained his record of taking his clubs to major honours. In 1981 he led al-Talaba, the top Baghdad team, to the league title.

On 23 September 1980 Iraq invaded Iran, nominally because of a long-standing dispute over control of the Shatt Al-Arab waterway. In reality Saddam feared that Iran, an Islamic republic since the fall of the Shah in February the previous year, would provoke Iraq's Shia population and that the radicals in Tehran would undermine his claim to be the natural leader of the Arab world. Everything in Iraq was subordinated to the war effort, and Saddam's portrait, as soldier, statesman and philosopher, stared out from every street; Iraq was a country out of George Orwell's *1984*.

The Iranian revolution and the subsequent war had an immediate impact on football. Afraid that Iraqi Shias would turn to fundamentalism, as the Shias of Iran had done, Saddam poured money into football from 1978 until 1980. 'In each town or village new fields were constructed, kits and other supplies were distributed at no cost to all Iraq amateur teams at all age levels. They even started televising the league matches and the best of the international competitions, inviting foreign clubs and national teams', said Ask.

The war with Iran meant this boom in football was undermined almost the moment that it began because war required men and money. In the early years fighting was a long-distance affair, conducted by artillery. In 1982, however, the Iranians switched tactics and began using human waves of troops to try to break the Iraqi defences. As a result the Iraqi army increased in size from 100,000 in 1982 to 1 million by 1985. Most of these troops were young Shias. At the same time football pitches throughout the country were taken over by the military.

In the 1984–5 season, when the Iraqi army was suffering defeat after defeat at the hands of their Iranians, Saddam's son in-law Hussein Kamil told the president of the IFA, Sabah Mirza, Saddam's ex-bodyguard, that it was imperative for national morale that the Army club win its first league title. In a game against al-Talaba the Army was losing 1–2 after 90 minutes. The referee played another half-hour and then awarded the Army a penalty, from which they scored. Against the Trade Club the referee played an extra thirteen minutes until the Army scored the only goal of the game. Then he blew for full-time. In the final, crucial game of the season the Army had to beat the Air Force to win the league. After the Air Force scored two goals in the first half the referee was told at half-time that his life depended on the right result. In the first few minutes of the second half he sent off two Air Force players.

Clubs were run by Saddam's relatives or by people with strong ties to him. Matches were fixed. Players were transferred at the whim of the people in power. The government often cheated at international tournaments. In 1989 Iraq sent over-age players to compete in an under-19 tournament. FIFA found out and suspended them for two years.

Nick Ask had tracked all these developments from the West. He said that it had been incredibly depressing to watch football being destroyed by Saddam and his cronies. 'In 1982 the under-19 players had to sign an affidavit. It said they agreed to be executed if they met Iran in the competition and did not win. Friends on the team told me they deliberately lost in the first round so they would not have to play Iran.'

Meanwhile Ammo thrived. He was a football coach, not a politician. He was only interested in the game, not the people who ran the clubs or the country. He told himself that he was doing his best in an imperfect world. Most Iraqis thought that he was a brilliant coach. They pointed to the country's record: Iraq qualified for the World Cup in 1986 and for the Olympics in 1980, 1984 and 1988. It won the Gulf Cup three times in five attempts. It also won the Asian Cup, the Arab Cup and the Pan-Arab Games. Whenever the team played European sides, it did well. Iraq also drew with Turkey 0–0 in 1975, with Finland and with East Germany, as well as defeating East Germany 1–0 in 1979. The country had a surfeit of top-class strikers, such as al-Talaba's Hussein Saeed and al-Zawraa's Falah Hassan.

But Ask was not impressed. He said: 'Ammo devoted his life to football in Iraq. He was dedicated and hard-working. I met him twice while playing amateur soccer in my youth. In both cases he gave me good advice. But he was the worst coach in Iraq's history. The tournaments we won were because of our players not because of him. All he knew was fitness, fitness, fitness. It was like he was preparing horses, not a football team. Under his coaching our play was predictable. It was always the same tactics, the same style, the same line-up.

Year after year he stuck with the same style of play, long crosses, the style of English football in the 1960s. Even the English abandoned this by the early 1970s. But Ammo stuck with it.'

The lives of Ammo Baba, the fifty-year-old football legend, and Uday Hussein, the twenty-year-old son of Saddam, who was possibly mad but definitely evil, became inextricably intertwined in 1984. It was then that Saddam handed control of sport to Uday, when he appointed him to run the Iraqi Football Association and the Iraqi National Olympic Committee.

Ammo told me: 'After the Americans captured Saddam in 2003, people asked me what I thought about this. I said that I never thought I would see this happen. Saddam the Great ending up in a hole in the ground. People said, "Aren't you going to attack him?" I said, "No. He was good to me." But I said that I had many complaints about Uday.'

Ammo could still remember the day, thirty years earlier, when he first met Uday: 'I was training the army team. An officer told me that Uday wanted to see me. So I went. It was the first time I had met Uday. He called photographers, and we posed for them. I still have the picture. I am wearing a track suit. Uday told me to prepare a good team. I said, "Yes, I can find new, unknown players." He said, "No I want top players."'[3]

Uday was talking about a Baghdad club called al-Karkh, which he had just taken over and renamed al-Rasheed. Ammo told Uday that the leading clubs would not let him take their best players. 'He said he would take care of it. I gave him a list of the best players. He got all but two. Hussein Saeed (then a 26-year-old striker with al-Talaba) and Raad Hammoudi (a brilliant goalkeeper with al-Shurta) would not join al-Rasheed. But the team was unpopular. People always jeered it. Eventually Saddam had had enough and told Uday to disband the team.'

Uday was born on 18 June 1964. As a boy, he had been taken by his father with his younger brother, Qusay, on a tour of the Baghdad torture chambers. Uday enjoyed the experience and became an expert on the best methods of inflicting pain without killing the victim. He joined the Ba'ath Party when he was twelve and was educated at a school run by his mother, Sajida. He always came first in every subject, though he never did any work. He defied the school's dress code by wearing jeans and T-shirts.

In his teens he cruised Baghdad with his bodyguards in a white BMW looking for young women to kidnap and rape. He was a regular at a disco on the top floor of the Mansour Melia Hotel. Everyone dreaded his arrival. Women feared that he would kidnap them. Men were also terrified, in case he was offended by their clothes or just the way they looked at him.

Uday arrived at the FA and the Olympic committee after graduating from the University of Baghdad College of Engineering with a literally unbelievable 98.5 per cent in his final exams. Any teacher who had dared to grade him honestly in the past had been executed, so staff at the university sensibly gave him fantastic marks.

Ammo's voice shook with rage and residual fear when he talked about Uday. 'He used to call players before games and threaten them. Sometimes he telephoned the dressing room at half-time. He talked nonsense. I told him to go to hell. I said he knew nothing about football. How did I survive? Because the people loved me. Uday's security people always told me, "Sir, please don't say anything bad about Mr Uday."'

I knew that he was not exaggerating Uday's sadism and greed, but I wondered, as I had done when he had met in Brittany at the football tournament, if he had compromised more than he was willing to admit. Ammo insisted that he had rarely been paid by Uday, but I doubted that. I guessed that he had never received a regular salary, like an ordinary Iraqi, a policeman or a civil servant, but I knew that people like him, who did important and glamorous jobs in Saddam's Iraq, were given large amounts of cash, always in US dollars, houses and cars when the regime was pleased with them. Often I asked Ammo how he had lived without money, but he ignored the question or repeated: 'I am a poor man. I have no money. People say I am rich but I am not.'

He said that Uday had stopped him going to the World Cup in Mexico in 1986 because he 'lacked experience'. Ammo told me: 'Uday said that I wasn't good enough, that I didn't deserve the job.'

He said that Uday often threatened the Iraqi team. 'Before games he told the players they would be punished if they lost. They cried and trembled with fear.' He recalled the day in 1988 when Iraq returned from South Korea after being eliminated from the Olympics. 'We did not taxi to the terminal. The plane stopped short. They told us to walk to the terminal. The players got off and ran away. I walked to the terminal and was met by the secret police. They put a gun to my head and stomach and dragged me away.'

That November, Ammo had a respite from the madness when Uday shot and killed Hama Jajou, one of Saddam's senior bodyguards, who also tasted his food in case it was poisoned. Uday was furious because Jajou had introduced his father to a woman called Samira, who became Saddam's second wife and bore him a son. So he killed Jajou at a party in Baghdad in front of hundreds of people, including Suzanne Mubarak, the wife of the Egyptian President, Hosni Mubarak. Saddam was not pleased and sent Uday to Switzerland as punishment. But the Swiss authorities did not care for Uday and asked him to leave after he threatened to kill a man in a restaurant.

Ammo said: 'Uday did not know the meaning of the word mercy. I don't know why Saddam didn't stop him behaving like this.' This was a telling remark because it revealed that, like many Iraqis, Ammo regarded Saddam as a stern but fair ruler rather than as a thug. He said: 'Uday did things that even Hitler could not imagine doing. He beat us with cables. He made players play with a concrete ball. He used to watch and laugh when they kicked it.'

Once, he said, he was watching television with Uday. A female newsreader appeared. Uday told Ammo that she was also a Christian. He said that he would bring her to Ammo so they could have sex in front of him. Ammo refused and told Uday that he would rather kill himself. On another occasion he said that Uday injected him with an unknown substance so that he 'screamed for three days'.

Uday would explode when Ammo ignored an instruction to pick a player whom he liked or to adopt a formation that he had suggested. Ammo told me: 'Once Uday said, "I will kill you for that. I will hang you. I will cut your tongue out." I said, "I don't care. I am doing my job well. You are no better than me"', recalled Ammo. He said that he always fought Uday: 'Once, in the 1990s, I was coaching al-Zawraa and the referee disallowed two goals, because that was what Uday wanted. There was a crowd of 60,000. The referee apologized to me. I told him that he had no choice. Then Uday handed out the cup and the medals. I stood there, in the middle of the pitch. I did not care what happened to me. I would not shake his hand. I think the crowd were surprised that I did this. The crowd did not cheer Uday's team. They stayed silent. But later people cheered me.'

Without Saddam's protection he said that Uday would have killed him. 'Saddam told me that I was the most honest man in the country. Everyone knew that Saddam liked me. He once asked Uday, "Why do you always complain about Ammo?" Uday told Saddam that I was speaking against him. They called me to see them. Uday said, "Hello, troublemaker." I said, "Now look here, Mr Uday, there's one thing I want to tell you. I am Iraqi, Christian, Assyrian. You know what Jesus Christ said in the Bible. He said, respect your government. I respect you, but you do not respect me. I am older than your father. You criticize me. I have done only good for you, for the country. You want me to say that you are getting these good results and not me. People would laugh if I said that, because they know it's not true." He said, "I have told my father you speak against us." I said, "Yes, I speak against you but not your father."'

'I told Saddam, "Uday wants me to say that it is he who gets good results for the team. But people will laugh if they say that, because it is not true." Anyhow we kissed after this. Three days later he sacked me from my job again. In all he sacked me nineteen times from jobs coaching the national team and clubs. Often after the national team had lost, he would call and tell me that I had to come back. He used to send one of his private planes for me. God help me, but I got good results for him.'

He said: 'I often used bad language to Uday. I spoke against him. I told people that I would always tell the truth because I was loyal to my country. Uday's security chief came to me once and said, "Please, Mr Ammo, we like you, but what can we do if Uday orders us to do this or that?" I was the only person who told Uday that he was wrong. I told him he couldn't send players to gaol for two weeks or longer if they lost a game. He used to order them to be beaten up. I told him "You must do not do this." I don't want to pretend that I am some sort of hero. I was afraid of Uday. His security people often came to me and said, "Please, Mr Ammo, do what he wants."'

He thought that he did his best in an impossible situation. 'People understood my position and approved of the way I used to deal with Uday. Now people come to me and say, "Say something about Uday." I say, "No. I said enough when he was alive. Let other people speak."'

Others who criticized Uday, in far milder terms than Baba, were not so lucky. Tariq Abdul Wahab, a journalist for Shahab, said that Uday's thugs eavesdropped on his telephone conversation with an Iraqi footballer who lived abroad. Wahab said that he told the player that he was not entirely happy with the way that sport was being run in Iraq. That was enough for Uday's men, who dragged him off to prison. They held him for a month and beat him repeatedly. His right arm, which had held the telephone, was smashed with a sledge-hammer. His right ear, which he used to make the call, was mutilated. His right leg was broken.

Ammo told me that he turned down lucrative offers to work abroad. But many of the country's best players did leave Iraq, which Uday allowed from 1993, providing they paid him a chunk of their salaries. He warned them that their families in Iraq would disappear if they failed to do so. Iraqi football continued to disintegrate. Uday did not care because the game had helped make him hugely wealthy. By the early 1990s he ran newspapers and television and radio stations, owned football clubs and smuggled oil and cigarettes. His father allowed him to found a paramilitary force.

He had so many enemies that an attempt on his life was inevitable. In 1996, while he was driving to a party in Baghdad, his car was raked with bullets. He was hit seventeen times and spent six months in hospital. He never fully recovered. He became even more unpredictable and violent because, it was rumoured, the shooting had left him impotent. Within a month of being discharged from hospital he had killed a bodyguard who had annoyed him. Then he murdered a young woman who resisted his advances.

According to medical reports found after the invasion of 2003, and backed up by interviews with his servants, he had suffered terrible injuries and become obsessed with finding cures.[4] The shooting had caused a stroke, damaged his brain and torn apart his left leg. He had 'clawing' toes on his left foot, which made walking difficult. He suffered from seizures and spastic reactions in his left leg. His servants had to push him around his houses in a wheelchair. He used a bedpan at night. He slept in a hospital bed. He screamed in pain when his staff dressed him.

He used acupuncture, Chinese herbal medicines and sleeping pills. Once, it was reported, he ordered his aides to bring him a woman who had just given birth. He sucked her nipples for what he believed would be vitamin-rich milk. The pain made him even more sadistic. When he heard that a friend, who knew of his many crimes, was planning to leave Iraq, he invited him to his thirty-seventh birthday party. His bodyguards sliced off the man's tongue with a scalpel so he could not talk.

Ammo said he was still battling Uday in the late 1990s, though he had not had a regular job since 1993. He said: 'In 1997 I went to the Kurdish north and met an influential local leader. He said how much he had admired me as a player. He kept talking about my bicycle kicks, which I was famous for. Uday saw me with this man on the television and asked me why I had spoken to him. I was gaoled for three days because of that. They wanted to shave my head.[5] I told them that if anyone touched my head, I would throw myself against the wall and kill myself. I had left a letter in my house, saying that I had been taken away by Uday. Then they would have known what had happened to me if I had died.'

Meanwhile, Saddam lost patience and made it clear that Qusay, not Uday, would succeed him. Uday was furious and tried to convince his father – and the country – that he was a changed man. In 2000 he was elected to parliament with 99.9 per cent of the vote in a Baghdad constituency. The following year he converted from Sunni, the religion of the ruling élite, to Shia, the religion of the majority.

In 2000 Ammo founded his football academy in Baghdad. Furat Ahmed Kadoim, the Iraqi referee who fled to England in December 2002, said that he had felt sorry for Ammo in the late 1990s. 'Saddam lost interest in him. Ammo had been very well paid, but then the money stopped. Everyone knew that Uday hated Ammo. So no one wanted to go near him. That was the way it was in Iraq. If people thought you had problems with Uday, they wouldn't be seen with you. I don't blame Ammo for working for Saddam and Uday. He had to live.'[6]

Dr Basil Abdul Mahdi, a veteran sports bureaucrat, said: 'For many years Ammo was the highest-paid coach in Iraq. He travelled abroad many times, to England, the USA, Australia. He had six, maybe seven cars. It was so silly for him to say that this was not true. He was never an opponent of the regime. There is a difference between Ammo the legend and Ammo the man. Saddam and Uday did not treat him well in their final years, but that is not the same as being an opponent. No one could openly oppose Saddam and Uday and live. Ammo told me that he was gaoled by Uday but I don't believe it. Uday did not like him, but that is all.'

8

The victims speak

By the early 1990s the world had heard a great deal about Uday, from diplomats, politicians, journalists, spies and Iraqi exiles who had contacts back home. But it seemed impossible that anyone could be as evil as these stories suggested. Then an Iraqi called Latif Yahia turned up in the spring of 1992 in Vienna and began talking about the three years he had spent as Uday's *fiday* or double. Latif said he had been much more than a diversion to confuse assassins. He said: 'A *fiday* is not just a double. A *fiday* is everything. It means a disciple, a fighter and a partisan. A serf who must always be prepared to give up his life for his master.'[1]

Yahia wrote his first account of his time as Uday's *fiday* in 1994, published under the title *I Was Saddam's Son*. He wrote a new version in 2003, called *The Devil's Double*. He said that he had wanted to expose the evil that was Saddam Hussein. 'By bringing this story to the attention of the Western media, I put myself in the spotlight. If I disappear, people will ask questions. If I had not written this book, I could have easily found myself in a diplomatic box on my way back to Baghdad, which is a well-used method of transport by the Iraqi Intelligence.' He said that it was important that people in the West understood how their governments had supported Saddam. He said: 'Remember, in 1992 Saddam was still a friend of the West. In my first book I had written about the mass graves that are now being found in Iraq. But this material was taken out by the publisher.' Yahia claimed, and there was no way to prove or disprove this, that the Iraqis tried to kill him four times after publication of his first memoir.

Everything that Yahia said — about Uday's torture of athletes, the serial rapes of teenage girls, his greed, his passion for cars — was confirmed, first by a handful of Iraqis who escaped Iraq before Saddam fell and then by others, talking publicly for the first time after the invasion of 2003. There were minor discrepancies over dates and names, but it was clear that he had been telling the truth.

Yahia was born in Baghdad on 14 June 1964, four days before Uday. The son of a millionaire businessman, he went to the same school as Uday, Baghdad High School for Boys, which was reserved for the sons of the élite of Iraq society – the governing clan from Tikrit, Saddam's home town, senior Ba'ath Party members and the merely rich, like Yahia. As a teenager Uday was already a sadist. He swaggered around the city with his bodyguards, selecting girls and then raping – and sometimes killing – them. He was lazy and not very bright. He liked power, Italian suits, Cuban cigars, alcohol, cars, women and, best of all, inflicting pain. Yahia said that Iraq under Saddam was about privilege, the few exploiting the many, and violence. He said: 'That's what Saddam taught us. In our school we were Iraq's poster boys, the young tip of a system in which the privileged enjoyed every conceivable advantage. It was a complete inversion of socialism.' It was also about violence: 'In Iraq it's customary for all men to carry guns. If you don't own one, you are not a man.'

Like many Iraqis, including Ammo Baba, Yahia approved of Saddam: 'Admittedly he executed lots of people, but he also declared war on illiteracy, gave women rights and pushed up oil production, for the benefit of everyone. When he came to power, everyone celebrated. My father said that Iraq would become the leading Arab nation. Later, after I had met Saddam, I thought he was impressive. He was charismatic and had a captivating manner. He did not seem cruel.' A few months after Saddam became president in 1979, Uday brought a young woman into the classroom at school. The teacher objected. Next day he had vanished. Yahia said that no one mentioned the man again. He had never existed.

Yahia lost touch with Uday after school, and was glad of it because anyone who was too close to Uday was in constant danger from his savage and unpredictable temper. In September 1987 he was recalled from the front line in the war against Iran, where he was an officer in the army, and told that he had been selected to be Uday's double. He was reluctant, so he was imprisoned and psychologically tortured.

(Uday did not want to risk their remarkable physical similarity by beating up Yahia.) Yahia broke down and agreed to become Uday's double. For months he was tutored to *become* Uday. Saddam's personal dentist turned his normal front teeth into Uday's protruding teeth. He studied videos of Uday, walking, talking, holding a cigar, eating. He studied videos of people being tortured horribly, which Uday watched for fun. He had to learn to smile as people's eyes were gouged out or had their limbs shattered with hammers or severed with axes. He practised staring with Uday's arrogance.

Uday spent much of his time at the offices of the Iraqi National Olympic Committee on Palestine Avenue in Baghdad. This was the headquarters of his business empire, of smuggling, theft and extortion. In the basement were his Ferraris, BMWs, Mercedeses, Porsches, Rolls-Royces, Jaguars and Lamborghinis. Many had been customized, with extra-powerful engines or armour. They were worth tens of millions of dollars. On the first floor, behind a 300-seat meeting room, was his private prison, with fifteen small cells. This was where he flung footballers who irritated him; anyone who really angered him was sent to al-Radwaniyah prison, 15 miles outside Baghdad. On the second floor were the offices of the Fedayeen, otherwise 'Saddam's Revolutionary Fighters', Uday's personal security force. Uday's bodyguards also had offices here. The third floor was for Uday's public relations, financial and computer staff. The fourth floor was his office. The fifth floor housed his sports newspaper, *al-Ba'ath*. The sixth floor had once belonged to the sport federations, but Uday had moved them to another building since he did not think they were important enough to justify space in his building. The seventh floor was reserved for Uday's 'parties', at which he drank himself senseless, raped women and ordered guests to stage orgies.

Yahia said: 'People weren't important in Iraq. There was violence everywhere. Thousands were executed every year. It was normal, and no one noticed.' He said that sport was useful for Uday because it gave him a high public profile. 'But he knew nothing about sport. I doubt he even knew how many players were in a football team. He did not even know when the Olympics were held.' In 1988, Yahia said, he doubled for Uday at a match between Iraq and a European club. 'Iraq

lost. A scandal! How can that be! Uday returned from a trip abroad –
where he had lost millions of dollars gambling – and was furious when
he heard the result. He ranted. He lost control. He hit me. I spent two
weeks in a cell at the Olympic building.' Once, Yahia said, Uday shot
and killed a man in his office after the man had come to complain that
Uday had raped his daughter.

In 1989 the Iraqi boxing team returned from a competition in the
Gulf. Yahia said that that Uday was upset at the performance of one
man. 'Uday jumped out of his chair and started punching him in the
face. "This is how you box!" And then he shaved his head, as he
usually does with athletes, and put him down in a cell in the Olympic
building.'

Yahia said he often felt as if he had lost his soul, but he admitted
there were rewards. As Uday's double he had the best clothes and
food. He lived splendidly, surrounded by servants who knew that
Yahia could dispatch them to hell if he wanted. When he retired as
a *fiday*, Uday gave him an import–export business, a house and
land, a car and money. He also told Yahia that he could use suites at
Baghdad's best hotels whenever he wanted. This was how everyone
lived who was close to Uday, at least until they displeased him.
Ammo always denied that he had been given gifts like Yahia, but
this was hard to believe. I wondered why Ammo would not talk
about this: was it shame or fear that his 'fans' in Iraq would turn on
him?

In 1999 came another account of Uday's abuse of footballers.
Sharar Haydar was a big, strong defender who had played forty times
for Iraq, including appearances at the Olympics in Seoul in 1988. In
April 1998, aged thirty, he had bribed officials in Baghdad to let him
cross from Iraq into Jordan. From there he had gone to Lebanon,
where he spent three months. He moved to Egypt, hoping a club
would sign him, and then returned to Jordan. After six months there
he went to Morocco. In August 1999 he decided to tell the world
what was happening to footballers and other athletes in Iraq. It was a
momentous decision: 'I knew that my family and friends would
probably suffer, but I had to do it. Someone had to tell the truth', he
said later.[2]

That August he said that footballers were routinely imprisoned and tortured by Uday. He said that Iraq regularly cheated by entering over-age players in football tournaments. He dismissed the FIFA investigation two years earlier into the alleged mistreatment of footballers – after they had lost a match against Kazakhstan that cost them a place in the World Cup Finals in 1998 – as a whitewash by the 'Mafia' who ran international football. He said: 'I remember the FIFA investigation. It was naive to think it could find out what was going on in Iraq by asking questions there. No one dared tell the truth. If they had, they would have been killed.'

He said that he had been gaoled four times. 'I was tortured for the first time in 1993, after the Iraqi national team lost 2–0 to Jordan in the finals of a tournament. I was brought to the Olympic prison, where I joined three other players. Why the four of us? What did we do wrong? Nobody knows but Uday. But from there we were taken to another prison on the outskirts of Baghdad, al-Radwaniyah, where many Iraqis were tortured. We were beaten for four days, sleeping for no more than thirty minutes at a time on a hard floor with no blankets or pillows. The guards terrorized us in many ways. One time they woke us up and told us, "We want you to catch a fly, and we want it to be male, not female." Well, one of my team-mates, Habib Ja'far, one of the best Iraqi players, caught the fly and showed it to the torturers, who said, "No, that's male. It needs to be female." So they beat him. Then they told him to catch the same fly he had just released.'

The third occasion, in 1994, was worse. He had just returned from a trip with the national team to Sofia. He decided that he had had enough of the bullying, abuse and fear of prison. He told me: 'I decided to retire from the national team. I said to myself, "Why should I be beaten and put in prison for playing the game I love?" I couldn't handle it. I said, "What's the point in playing for my country?" I went to the football association and told them I would not play for Iraq again. They said, "Are you mad? We will have to tell Uday. Do you know what will happen to you? You have to play."

'I said no. I went home. I stayed there for two days. Uday's body-guards came to my house at 2.30 in the morning of the third day and took me from my bed. My parents started crying because in Iraq, if they come take you from your house, you're never going to come back. They drove me to the Olympic headquarters, where one of his bodyguards handed me a walkie-talkie. Uday was on the other end. He said: "So, why don't you like to play for the great Iraq?" I said: "Well, I've been playing for the Iraq national team for five years now, but I don't feel very well. I've got an ulcer – a bleeding ulcer – so I can't continue." I tell you, I was terrified. Uday told me to return to practice the next day because at the time the 1994 World Cup in the United States was looming, and it was very important that we qualified. (We didn't.) I said: "Well, let your doctor examine me, and if he says I am able to play, I will. If he says no, I can't." Uday responded: "I will show you what you can and can't do."'

'He took me to the Olympic prison, where the guards whipped my feet – a traditional Arab punishment called *falaqa* – twenty times a day for three days. They gave me nothing to eat or drink other than a daily glass of water and a slice of bread. Then they sent me to al-Radwaniyah again, and this time I got the full treatment. I was greeted with what is known as "The Reception". They took my clothes off, laid me down on my back and dragged me by my legs across hot pavement until my back was a bloody mess. Then they made me roll in the sand. And just to make sure that the wounds got infected, I had to climb a 15-foot ladder and jump repeatedly into a pit of sewage water filled with blood and who knows what else. When they tortured you, they really wanted to hurt you, to make sure you'd never say no to Uday again.'

After a month he was released. Then one of Uday's thugs told Haydar that Uday had banned him from playing or watching football for life. In the late 1990s Haydar moved to London, where he became a journalist on an Arabic newspaper, in between taking coaching courses, which he hoped would lead to a job in football in England or Europe. His family and friends were constantly interrogated but, surprisingly, were not gaoled or tortured. Haydar said: 'I was always writing about Uday. He hated it. Uday sent me messages, saying I should come back, that I would be welcome, that I would have a big job in Iraq. If I didn't want to do that, they said I would have salary in London if I stopped writing about Uday. I would not. I am proud of what I did. I was the first one to speak against Uday.'

Sharar Haydar was not a typical footballer. He came from a middle-class family. His father was a Sunni, his mother a Shia. He had five brothers, all of whom were bright and well educated. He said: 'Poor kids play in the streets all the time. But not the middle classes. Football had a bad reputation then. People thought that the coaches wanted to have sex with the players. I loved football. I combined it with my education. I wanted to go to university and play football at the highest level. I used to go to school and then go training and then come home and do my homework.' He joined al-Rasheed, Uday's club, and was on the fringes of the first team as he approached his seventeenth birthday. He said that he remembered his first meeting with Uday: 'He seemed like a decent person, like a normal Iraqi. I thought to myself, he is nothing like his father. He certainly seemed to think highly of me. I was just a kid, still in high school, but Uday was asking me to join the first team on his personal soccer club, whose members included most of the Iraqi national team. The soccer people told him I was too young, that I couldn't cut it. But Uday was insistent. "Next year I want to see him on the first team", he told them. I was in the first team the following year.'

Haydar became a regular in the side but also went to Baghdad University, where he studied journalism. He said that al-Rasheed was the most unpopular club in the country. 'Uday hand-picked the best players from other clubs around the country, which made us very hated. Every single game we played, all of the fans were against us – 40,000 or 50,000 people shouting profanities. We couldn't even walk in the streets without everybody swearing at us. Uday put huge pressure on us to win. We were the champions and one of the best club teams in Asia, but we were always being punished. If we lost, he would take players to his prison at the Iraqi Olympic committee headquarters for several days. Sometimes longer. The first time it happened to me, after we lost a league game 1–0, I was locked up for four or five days with other players and the coach.

'Uday liked to play mind games with us. Twice during my career – in 1988, when I was with the junior national team, and again in

1990, before a game against Iran – he threatened to blow up the plane on our return flight if we did not win. Nothing happened, but we could never be sure when dealing with Uday. Sometimes he would keep us four hours after a game, letting us think we were going to be punished, then at midnight tell us, "No, go home now. But I won't forget. I will watch your next game."'

'Uday usually watched us play on television. For the big international games, he had a telephone with a speaker set up in the locker room so he could tell us what to do at half-time. It didn't matter what the coaches thought. Uday would tell us to play this or that way and scream at us. Uday treated us as his property. He used to summon us at 2 a.m. to the field at his palace because he wanted to play a game of football against Iraq's best players. Of course, Uday wasn't any good – he had funny legs – but everybody was terrified of tackling him.'

Haydar said that it was difficult for people in Europe to understand what life was like for a footballer under Uday. 'Everything became corrupt. Players and referees were bribed. If you played well for Uday, you'd get maybe a sheep. We didn't get paid much. Most players depended on gifts from supporters. But I never took money from them. Uday decided everything, which clubs you played for, everything. You kept your mouth shut or you were killed. You trusted no one. You said nothing bad about the government, not even at home. You had to be in the Ba'ath Party if you wanted to have a decent life.' Haydar stayed with the club until 1993, by which time it had been renamed al-Karkh. Haydar said: 'Iraqis loved abusing al-Rasheed. They couldn't tell Uday what they thought of him so they yelled at his team. Saddam did not like that, so he told Uday to shut down the club.'

After he had been imprisoned and tortured in 1994, Haydar spent ten months at home, unable to play football. He trained secretly every morning, until Uday found out and ordered him to stop. By now Haydar was desperate and agreed to apologize to Uday, though he hated himself for doing so. He played for al-Talaba, the Students. But he was soon in trouble again. 'I went to the Hungarian embassy in Baghdad', he said. 'I wanted to get out, to go to Hungary. But Uday found out, and I was put in prison again. But only for four days.' After

Bernd Stange, the German who coached Iraq, grafted European discipline and fitness training on to the team's natural flair. Under him, Iraq became a world-class team

Ammo Baba with Uday Hussein. Ammo hated Uday and claimed to have defied him on several occasions. But he also admitted that he was scared of Uday, who was evil and possibly mad. Ammo believed that he survived only because Saddam liked him

Al-Zawraa fans watching a match against a team from Qatar in November 1999. Football was an escape for people under Saddam: they could shout and scream without fear of arrest by one of Iraq's many intelligence agencies

Uday and Saddam Hussein with Qusay, Saddam's younger son. Although released by the Iraqi government in December 1996, this photograph was not necessarily taken then. Uday is in civilian clothes because he did not hold an official military rank

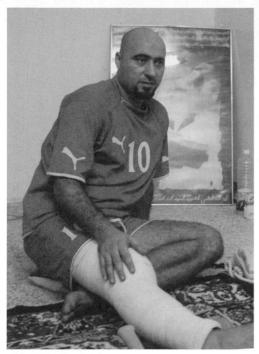

Arkan Mahmood

If they had been in their prime today, these former players would have been on lucrative contracts in the Middle East or elsewhere. Under Saddam many players were gaoled and tortured because they displeased Uday

Samir Kadhum

Ahmed Radhi

Shakir Mahmood

Habib Ja'far

Left: The Iraqi Football Association (IFA) headquarters in Baghdad. Uday Hussein dominated the IFA from 1984. To the disgust of many Iraqis, Hussein Saeed – who had run the association for Uday – became the association's president after the fall of Saddam

Below right: Ahmed al-Samarrai, a former general in Saddam's army, became president of the new Iraqi National Olympic Committee in January 2004. He had lived in London since fleeing Iraq in 1983

Above left: Boys from the Shia slums of Baghdad training at Ammo Baba's 'football academy' outside the al-Shaab national stadium. Ammo founded the school in 2000 despite opposition from Uday, who despised the Shia majority. Security problems after the invasion meant training sessions were sporadic and badly attended

Fans in Patras, Greece, during the 2004 Olympics. Most Iraqi fans lived in Greece or elsewhere in Western Europe, and were young and hysterically patriotic. They behaved like football fans everywhere – drinking heavily and screaming abuse at the opposition and referee. This shocked Olympic officials, who were used to more genteel crowds

Ammo Baba (far right) with his team in Penmarc'h, Brittany, in May 2004, for the Mondial Pupilles de Plomelin, a tournament for boys that attracted teams from around the world. Most of the Iraqis, called 'Bagdad FC' by the French hosts, came from poor Shia homes

Ammo Baba sits in the dug-out with 'Bagdad FC' substitutes in Brittany, in May 2004. He said that his boys did not have a chance of winning any of their matches because they were younger and smaller than the other teams. He claimed this was a conspiracy by a French charity to humiliate him

Ammo with his son Sami and daughter-in-law Wassila, who had driven overnight from their home in the south of France to Penmarc'h. Ammo had not seen his son for four years and was shocked that he had put on so much weight

A jubilant Iraqi fan holds his son in triumph at the stadium in Patras. Iraq confounded the experts' predictions by beating Portugal's stars in the opening match. Iraq eventually lost to Paraguay in the semi-finals

Mark Clark (right), a Scottish solicitor who specialized in sports law, went to Iraq in the summer of 2003, expecting to serve as an officer in the Territorial Army. Instead he ended up masterminding the reconstruction of sport in Iraq. He is pictured in Athens with Najah Ali, Iraq's only boxer at the 2004 Olympics

Bernd Stange (second from right), the German who had coached Iraq brilliantly after the fall of Saddam, with officials from the Iraqi Football Association at the team's hotel in Greece during the 2004 Olympics. From left to right: Yassem Saleh, assistant coach; Hussein Saeed, the president of the IFA; Adnan Hamad, who had succeeded Stange a few weeks earlier; Stange; and Abdul Khaliq, the IFA treasurer

Furat Ahmed Kadoim, who had been the top referee in Iraq, in Birmingham in 2004, waiting to learn if he would be granted political asylum. His application was refused, and he had to return to Baghdad

a spell with al–Quwa al–Jawiya, the Air Force, he moved to Algeria, though, like everyone who played abroad, he had to give 40 per cent of his salary to Uday.

He was in Algeria for two years. Towards the end of his time there Ammo Baba, who was coaching Iraq, asked Haydar if he would play for him. Haydar said: 'I met Ammo in Jordan. He asked me if I would play for Iraq, and I said I would not as long as Uday was in charge. He was shocked.' Haydar returned to Iraq, where he played for the Air Force again. Ammo was sacked, and Haydar agreed to play for the new coach but only appeared twice, in friendlies, before fleeing in the spring of 1997.

The next Iraqi footballer to talk publicly about Uday was Saad Qeis, who fled Iraq in 2001.[3] He was an experienced international, who had played in the 1988 Olympics in Seoul. He said that Uday totally dominated sport in Iraq. 'He uses sports, Iraqis' last resort to entertain themselves, as a tool to stamp his mark on life in Iraq. He bullies, humiliates and tortures players. Before him the team was one of the Middle East's strongest. Now it is nothing. Uday always gets away with his crimes and can do anything he wants with impunity. He has established himself as a ruthless lord of the black market, with a finger in every pie from the media to football. He heads a fearsome commando force, whose members can gaol, maim, torture and kill to indulge his every whim. He sends anyone he is unhappy with to one of his gaols. His gaol wardens, called "teachers", sometimes administer horrendous torture methods, like branding and amputation.'

He said that he had been beaten up in 1997. 'Uday was furious with me because the referee sent me off after an argument during a match against Turkmenistan, which we lost 4–0. When we got back to Iraq, I was driven to the headquarters of the Olympic committee. Then I was sent to the prison of al-Radwaniyah. There they put me in a room with an array of canes mounted on shelves on the wall. They ordered me to strip to the waist and lie on the ground. They flogged me. I bled profusely and fainted.'

'I had my head shaved. I was there a month. Since I was a boy kicking a ball in the streets of Baghdad, football has been my life. Uday ruined it for me. I had to find the courage to leave. I was there when

the FIFA investigators came to Baghdad. They asked athletes questions about whether they were tortured or not. None of us could have
admitted to torture and stayed alive. Nobody dares to tell the truth
while he is still in Iraq. Another team-mate, Radhi Shnishel, then our
captain, was thrashed after the team lost a match against Kazakhstan
that denied it a place in 1988 World Cup finals in France.'

Issam Thamer al-Diwan played for Iraq's volleyball team from 1974
until 1987. He coached at al-Rasheed, Uday's club, and took charge of
the national team briefly in 1989. He fled with his wife and two daughters in 1991.[4] He talked publicly for the first time late in 2002: 'Being
a well-known athlete can get you killed. Dozens of athletes and leaders
in the Iraqi sports movement have been executed. Many of them were
framed under the pretext of political reasons – you need only to criticize the government – but the fact is, Uday cannot stand to think that
someone in Iraq could be smarter or more famous than him.'

'Many of the executed athletes lost their lives following the 1991
uprising, when Iraqi citizens in the southern part of the country failed
to oust Saddam after US-led forces defeated his army in Kuwait. I also
know of a popular weightlifter, Saleh Mahdi, who was driven to take
his own life. He heard that security forces were coming to arrest him.
He was afraid they were going to rape his wife in front of him to make
him confess – a normal practice in these situations. So he killed his
wife, his children and himself, and left a taped message that many athletes know about in Iraq. He said, "You bunch of dogs will not take
my honour!"'

'I was imprisoned twice. The first time was in 1986, when I was
still playing, after our Iraqi national team came third in the Arab
championships. Uday's bodyguards picked all twenty-one of us up at
the airport in vehicles that looked like school buses, except they were
green with tinted glass, and took us to a special prison at the old
Presidential Palace, in the Karradat Maryam district. We were held
together for about ten to fourteen days, in a room so small that all of
us could not lie down at the same time. We slept in shifts.'

'The second time was in the autumn of 1990, after the Iraqi military had invaded and quickly seized control of Kuwait. The government formed special committees to take, or rather steal, equipment

that belonged to different establishments in Kuwait. The Iraqi Olympic committee created a delegation from all the clubs and federations with instructions to go to Kuwait and gather all the sports equipment, plus any cars parked at the Kuwait sports federations and Olympic committee. I, like other athletes who had good relations with our Kuwaiti peers, was opposed to this idea. I refused to go. After the delegation came back from Kuwait with its loot, a young man named Hilal al-Rawi met me outside Uday's office at the Iraqi Olympic committee. He handed me a piece of paper the size of a cigarette packet and told me it was from Uday. The only thing written on it was my name, under which I could read, "Must be gaoled".'

'I was sent back to the old Presidential Palace prison, where I was forced to stand in a cell in a painful position. My ankles were shackled to the wall, and my arms were tied together behind my back and raised high by a rope connected to the ceiling. I stood in this hunched position, with my head angled forward and leaning against the wall, for three days. I begged the guard to let me sit down, because my left knee was weak from an old volleyball injury. Instead, he just kicked me there.'

Raed Ahmed, the Iraqi champion in the 99-kilogram weightlifting category from 1984 to 1996, had defected while competing at the Atlanta Olympics in 1996. He had lived quietly in the USA since then, having smuggled his wife out of Iraq. In December 2002 he also talked for the first time. He said: 'After my defection Iraqi television immediately reported that I had been sentenced to death *in absentia*, and that I was to be executed if I was apprehended. Uday ordered my wife to divorce me. My whole family – my father, mother, sisters and brothers – was rounded up at 3 a.m. in our hometown of Basra, in southern Iraq, and driven seven hours to the Olympic headquarters in Baghdad. They even interrogated my little sister, who was just nine at the time.'

'My parents were transferred to the national security headquarters and spent two weeks in prison. They were allowed to return to Basra, but they still cannot leave town without notifying the authorities. Some people told me not to talk because they want me to protect my family from retribution. But I'm willing to speak out about Saddam and Uday because the public cannot imagine how brutal these guys are. Before every international competition we are interviewed by one of Uday's assistants and asked how we expect to fare. If, for example, you say you are going to finish in the top three, then you become committed to bringing this result back home. If you come in fourth place, you have to expect that your head will be shaved and that you'll be thrown in gaol – until Uday wants to let you out. You will also have to pay back the government for the money it spent on you for the trip.'

'If you're from a poor family, where do you find the cash? Certainly not from the prize money or fees you earned as an athlete. Uday steals it. For participating in the Atlanta Olympics each Iraqi athlete was supposed to receive $8,000 as a reward. The head of our delegation had the cheques in his hands but told us he didn't have the authority to cash them because he was under orders to give the money to Uday. I avoided problems with Uday by letting him think ahead of time I was hurt. I would get a doctor's note saying I suffered from a leg or shoulder injury, for example, and that I had no chance to win. That's what I did for Atlanta. That way, I could participate but wasn't forced to win. If travelling meant being forced to win, I would not go.'

'Other times, nothing more than good fortune kept from me being tortured. In 1990 I was unable to travel to the former Soviet Union for an Iraqi training camp because university exams were held at the same time. While there, some members of the team acquired steroids and tried to bring them back to Baghdad. Uday heard about it and had the whole thirteen-member delegation picked up at the airport. Their heads were shaved and they were sent to al-Radwaniyah prison, where they were beaten for an entire month. Uday is fine with athletes taking steroids. As long as it doesn't hurt his reputation.'

Furat Ahmed Kadoim, the Iraqi Kurd who had been Iraq's top referee, also talked about his defection in December 2002. In February 2003, with his wife and two sons safely in the Kurdish north, he said that he had fled after being gaoled and tortured by Uday for refusing to fix matches. He was born in 1965 in Baghdad. His father and mother were Kurds.[5] They were prosperous and middle-class. His father was an engineer at the airport. Kadoim had three brothers and three sisters. He liked the idea of becoming a full-time player but knew that it would be more sensible to go to university.

In 1979 his sister Wasila, then aged eighteen, was seized by police at school during the wave of arrests that took place after Saddam became president. The family never saw her again. 'We were too scared to ask about her', he said. 'We did not know why she had been arrested. Maybe they thought she was a Communist. One of my brothers was a Communist, and he was also arrested. But they let him go after he signed a piece of paper saying he would give it up.' In 1987 the police told the family that Wasila had died in prison. They did not know when or how she had died.

Kadoim played football for the Police club while he was studying engineering at university. In 1984, the year Uday took control of football in Iraq, he went on a refereeing course out of curiosity. He did well and enjoyed it. By 1997 he was a FIFA-recognized referee, the highest ranking for an official, and was able to take charge of any match. He had been refereeing top club games in Iraq since 1993. He was only paid $7 per match but liked travelling around the country and was proud that he was regarded as the best referee in Iraq.

There had been interference in football under Saddam, but Uday's arrival changed everything. Referees were regularly told how a match should end. 'No one knew which club Uday supported. I think it was always about gambling. He needed a certain result to win money', said Kadoim. He had met Uday at the annual conference for referees. 'Sometimes he was normal, nice. Sometimes he was terrible', he said.

In 2000 Uday's bodyguards told him that al-Zawraa had to beat the Police in a match that he was refereeing. The Police team, al-Shurta, was run by Watban Ibrahim, Saddam's half-brother. Uday had shot him in 1995. He had lost a leg as a result. But Kadoim did not think that had anything to with the demand. 'It was probably about money', he said. The game ended in a 2–2 draw because Kadoim refused to cheat. This was out of pride, that he was respected as an honest referee, and courage, but subconsciously he did not believe anything would happen to him.

'His bodyguards came to my house that night', said Kadoim. They said, "Why did you do that? He is the son of the president. Why did you refuse his order?" They took me to al-Radwaniyah prison. For ten days they beat me up, every day, hitting my feet with sticks. They would make me run and run in the 50° heat. They made me crawl through a pool of filthy water. They burned my feet with cigarettes. I still have the scars. They shaved my head, which was humiliating. They were Uday's bodyguards. Brutes. They enjoyed it, really.' He was released after ten days. 'Everyone knew what had happened to me. They saw my head. No one said anything.'

Six months later Uday's men again told Kadoim that he had to fix a match, between al-Karkh (formerly al-Rasheed) and al-Zawraa. 'They wanted al-Zawraa to win. Who knows why? A bet maybe', said Kadoim. But al-Zawraa lost 1–0. 'I could not do what they wanted. I would have lost my reputation', he said. He was arrested again and spent a week in prison, enduring the same tortures. 'One guy was beating me with a stick and counting up to 100. He used to get to 98 and say, "Oh, I forget where I am so I must start again." And then he laughed.'

Kadoim was shattered now. 'Iraqis had no compassion because of Saddam. After all the wars and the arrests they were only interested in violence and death. Everyone knew I had been tortured. Everyone knew Uday was unhappy with me. The people at the football association told me I could no longer be a FIFA referee. When I asked them why, they said it was their opinion. It was not true. They were afraid of Uday and wanted to show him they did not want me.'

In the summer of 2002 he told his wife to take the children to the Kurdish north. Then he went to Syria and, using a false passport, slipped away to Turkey, then Belgium and Britain. He said: 'They destroyed my life. I had a home, a family, a good job. I loved refereeing.'

9

The 'Goodwill Tour' turns sour

The 'Goodwill Tour' of England by Bernd Stange and his team in the last fortnight of May 2004 disintegrated into a bad-tempered fiasco within hours of their arrival. They thought they would be staying at a hotel near Bisham Abbey, the world-famous sports centre on the banks of the Thames 34 miles west of London, where they would be training. Instead they went east from Heathrow into central London. They were furious when they saw their hotel near Hyde Park. They said it was cramped and seedy and did not have the facilities worthy of a top football team, such as a sauna, jacuzzi and swimming-pool.

After protesting to Yamam Nabeel, the 28-year-old London-based Iraqi who had organized the tour, to the Foreign Office, to the Football Association and to the Coalition Provisional Authority in Baghdad, they moved a few days later to a Holiday Inn near Bisham Abbey. But the tone of the visit had been set. Some members of the group were associates of the IFA's interim president, Hussein Saeed, and to some of the other members of the group they appeared to have no function other than to eat, drink, smoke and be rude to people. They seemed to treat the tour as an expenses-paid holiday. One had come because he wanted to visit a Harley Street dentist. He vanished after his appointment and was not seen again. These 'officials' often screamed abuse at hotel staff, Stange and Nabeel.

I was not surprised by the chaos. I had first met the man behind the tour, Yamam Nabeel, in the new year. He wanted to help football in Iraq recover from the depredations of Uday and had conceived the visit after interviewing Stange in Germany in April 2003 for a television station. But he had no experience of sports sponsorship. He thought that the men who controlled the IFA, such as Hussein Saeed, were decent people who cared about football as much as him, when basic research should have told him that they had worked for Uday and were unlikely to be saintly. He once told me: 'Hussein Saeed is a friend of my uncle and was not a Ba'athist. He was a rebel and would not play for al-Rasheed, which was Uday's club, as you know.'

Nabeel had been born in Iraq. He had left when he was three years old after his father, Nabeel Yasin, an acclaimed writer and poet, fled when Saddam Hussein came to power.[1] Yamam was brought up in Hungary, where his father worked as a journalist and translator. He said that he had been a fine footballer, an attacking midfielder, but had been judged too small to make it as a professional. He went to secondary school in England and to Bradford University but dropped out before finishing his degree. He drifted into freelance journalism, helped by the fact that he spoke fluent Arabic, German, English, Hungarian and Russian. By now his father had also moved to Britain.

Nabeel set up a company, AKB Media, to give himself credibility in his new incarnation as a television producer and organizer of money-spinning sports events, the first of which would be the 'Goodwill Tour'. But the company consisted of just him, operating out of a flat in Hammersmith, west London. He was a likeable, clean-cut young man and cared deeply about Iraq. But I thought that he was out of his depth. He issued many press releases over the coming months. In one he said that the tour would 'help the Iraqi national team prepare for competitions with much-needed first-class facilities, help the Iraqi FA financially, establish and strengthen the goodwill relationship between the UK and Iraq and between the West and Iraq, and raise money for several charities working in Iraq'.

His publicity material was pompous and vague, presumably because he thought that was how successful businessmen talked:

> This is an AKB Media project, devised, initiated and run by the Chief Event Organizer. Our strategic partners are Truce International (Patron Sven Goran Eriksson, Chairman Nancy Dell'Olio).[2] Plans are being drawn up to implement ideas at all levels. We need to structure the grassroots level development in Iraq, but the Iraqi league and the Iraq national side need urgent help as well. So we are trying to bring

together a team of experts in the field of development, marketing, media and PR to help structure the rebuilding process. CARE International are our charity partners. They are currently the biggest aid agency in Iraq. We also have official support from the FA and FIFA.

AKB Media was founded my me in 1998 as a television production company, producing mainly Sport and Entertainment items and programmes for CNN, Canal +, Sky News, Sky Sports, Sky Sports News, Channel 4, MBC, ANN as well as for Gillette World Cup Special and Western Union World Football Show. It has evolved since, and we work on cross-media packages, but since September 2003 I have mainly concentrated on developing projects for Iraqi football, to help it get back on its feet.

When I read this, I was very surprised. I knew Nabeel had done some freelance journalism, mainly low-grade work, such as fixing interviews for television stations. But that was it, as far as I was aware. His press releases were packed with the gobbledegook of public relations. He talked as if he ran a successful company with a turnover of millions, which had deals with major sports organizations around the world. I admired his determination, positive thinking and self-belief – all necessary qualities if he wanted to make progress in a competitive world – but this was dangerous fantasy. Football was a multi-million pound global industry run by accountants, lawyers, marketing experts, public relations wizards and agents. They were slick and ruthless people, dedicated to making money for their clients – and themselves. Nabeel seemed to think that he could crash in and take over the potential goldmine that was Iraqi football.

I asked him how he intended to raise money for football in Iraq. Did he think that Western companies would sponsor the national team or the bigger clubs? But surely, I said, Iraq would have to be stable and peaceful for that to happen? Or did he think that Arab or Iraqi companies would pay to have their names splattered across players' shirts and on hoardings around stadiums? He frowned, as if I was being negative, and mumbled that 'oil companies' would stump up the money.

He said that, apart from training at Bisham Abbey, the Iraqis would play three games in England: in Bristol, against Bristol Rovers, where

Youra Eshaya had been the first Iraqi to play in England half a century earlier, against Trinidad and Tobago[3] at West Bromwich Albion's ground in the Midlands and, best of all, against a team made up of stars from the Premiership.

I was alarmed when he sent me the press release about this last game, due to be played at Macclesfield, south of Manchester. He had chosen this unlikely location because one of the directors of Macclesfield Town FC, Bashar Alkadhi, was also a director of a mobile phone company that was sponsoring the tour. This is what Yamam sent me:

IRAQ V. PREMIERSHIP / LEAGUE ALL-STARS
Hosted by Macclesfield Town, Moss Rose Stadium.

Possible managers

Bryan Robson
Peter Reid
Gordon Strachan
Kevin Keegan
Mark Hughes
Steve Bruce

Possible players

Goalkeepers: Peter Schmeichel (retired), David Seaman (retired), Brad Friedel (Blackburn Rovers), Richard Wright (Everton), Jerzy Dudek (Liverpool), Mark Schwarzer (Middlesbrough), Shaka Hisplop [*sic*] (Portsmouth).

Defenders: Lee Dixon (retired), Tony Adams (retired), Dennis Irwin (Wolves), Celestine Babayaro, Marcel Desailly (Chelsea), Bruno N'Gotty (Bolton), Ibrahim Ba (Bolton), Lucas Radebe (Leeds), Mark Fish (Charlton), Martin Keown (Arsenal), Lorenzo Amoruso (Blackburn), John Arne Riise (Liverpool), Graeme Le Saux (Southampton), Chris Powell (Charlton), Steffen Freund (Leicester).

Midfielders: Paul Gascoigne (retired), Gavin Peacock (retired), Paul Ince (Wolves), Gary Speed (Newcastle), Steve McManaman (Manchester City), Ryan Giggs, Quintin Fortune (Manchester United), Youri Djorkaeff, Jay-Jay Okocha (Bolton), Harry Kewell (Liverpool) Juninho (Middlesbrough), Dennis Bergkamp (Arsenal), Brett Emerton (Blackburn), Jonathan Greening (Middlebrough), Robbie Savage (Birmingham), David Batty (Leeds), Nolberto Solano (Aston Villa), Jamie Redknapp, Darren Anderton (Tottenham), Nigel Quashie (Portsmouth).

Forwards: Niall Quinn (retired), Les Ferdinand (Leicester), Alan Shearer (Newcastle), Ole Gunnar Solskjaer (Manchester United), Mark Viduka (Leeds), Dwight Yorke, Andy Cole (Blackburn), Tomasz Radzinski (Everton), Nwankwo Kanu (Arsenal), Dion Dublin (Aston Villa), Paolo Di Canio, Shaun Bartlett (Charlton), Freddy Kanouté (Tottenham), Teddy Sheringham (Portsmouth), Kevin Phillips (Southampton).

I was amazed when I read this. There was no chance that most, or indeed any, of these people would turn out for Yamam Nabeel, of AKB Media of Hammersmith. The managers who had jobs with clubs would be too busy; those that didn't were always on television or writing columns for newspapers. The men who were still playing were worth millions to their clubs, who would never allow them to play in an exhibition game like this, even if the players wanted to do so. The players who had retired were millionaires who spent their time playing golf or commentating on television and the radio. All these people had agents and lawyers who negotiated personal appearances, usually for a big fee. Many did charity work, but they chose carefully because there were so many demands on their time. But Nabeel was not a charity. The tour by the Iraqis was a commercial exercise, to raise money for the development of football in Iraq. I asked him if he believed that these people would take part in a match against Iraq, and he mumbled that the list was 'provisional'.

Before the Iraqis arrived in England, there was bad news when Bristol Rovers cancelled the fixture, which Nabeel had said would be one of the highlights of the tour. He tried to put a positive spin on this set-back: 'This is a blessing in disguise. It allows us to concentrate on Iraq's first international game on British soil, against Trinidad and Tobago. Now that game, deservedly, will become the first ever game of Iraq's Goodwill Tour. It will also increase the attendance at the game and will push the game's already high profile. And I believe this will increase revenue for the charities and the Iraqi FA.' Later, however, he told me that the Rovers had double-crossed him by refusing at the last minute to pay for policing.

To fill the gap he organized an alternative, a match in London against a team of Members of Parliament. It was an inspired decision because this was what the media called a 'fun' story: middle-aged politicians trying to keep up with fit young footballers from war-torn Iraq. Later he said that he had wanted Iraqis to know that politicians were ordinary people. 'The match showed people in Iraq that the people who rule in a place like England are approachable. Iraqis cannot imagine their leaders playing football in public.'

The game, at the Royal Hospital, Chelsea, on the Thames Embankment, home of the Chelsea Pensioners, the army veterans whose red uniform appears on countless postcards, was the only time the national press in Britain covered the tour. This was a typical report:

> When the two football teams ran on to the pitch at the start of the match, it was obvious, as the song goes, who had eaten all the pies. On one side was the Iraqi national team; young men glowing with fitness, not a paunch among them, parading their silky soccer skills. On the other was the British Parliamentary team.
>
> After an 11–0 drubbing, Tony Clarke, the Labour member for Northampton South, who was taken off after 43 minutes to save him further punishment, was magnanimous in defeat. 'They were quick, young, organized and skilful. We are old and fat and disorganized. For the first ten minutes we could not get the ball and for the rest it seemed we didn't want it.'
>
> The mismatch had been arranged by Truce International, set up by Sven Goran Eriksson and his partner, Nancy Dell'Olio, to help provide sports fields and therapy programmes for children whose lives have been devastated by trauma.
>
> The Iraqi national squad is ranked 44th in the world, and it showed.

Normally, the parliamentary team plays MPs from other countries or journalists with similar dietary habits. 'This is the first time we have played a national team', said Dr Ian Gibson, the joint manager. Jim Murphy, the Labour MP for Eastwood, said: 'When I accepted the challenge to play them, I thought it was a group of Iraqi politicians, not the national side.'

The Iraqi goalkeeper did not have a shot to save and touched the ball only twice, more than some of the MPs. Bernd Stange, Iraq's coach, said: 'I don't even know the score. 11–0? Well, that's really 1–0, because I told them to imagine the MPs started ten goals ahead. What really matters is that after so many horrible events in Iraq, we can come and play football. That brings a good message to the world.'[4]

After the match the Iraqis changed into blazers and slacks, which had been donated by well-wishers, and went to a government reception at Lancaster House, near Buckingham Palace. But the players did not want to be photographed with British politicians such as Jack Straw, the Foreign Secretary, who had backed the invasion of their country. Iraq's captain, Hussam Fawzi, talked about torture under Uday: 'It was horrible. Athletes should not be treated like that', he said. 'In the West players might have their wages taken away, but they would not be tortured.' But he made it clear that this did not mean he approved of the invasion. Stange also moved away from the photographers, muttering that he would be 'a dead man' if he was pictured with Straw.

The next game, against Trinidad and Tobago at the Hawthorns, West Bromwich Albion's ground in the Midlands, was a disaster. Iraq lost 2–0, which was surprising as they were ranked 44th in the world and their opponents were 75th, but worse was the tiny crowd of 1,564 and the fact that the national media ignored the game.

After the match Stange was furious: 'We made horrible mistakes. You should not see such mistakes at international level – never, never, never. Our passing was nice to watch, but these skills are not enough if you want to win at international level. Too often we make good chances but the players do not have strong enough shots to score goals.'

It did not seem that things could get worse, but they did. The final match of the tour at the Moss Rose stadium, home of Macclesfield

Town FC, was a disaster. Instead of the Premiership team of Nabeel's dreams, Iraq met players from non-league clubs such as Woking, Worcester and Morecambe. Like the entire tour, there was an air of unreality about the event. In the programme Tony Blair – or rather Blair's aides – wrote that the match 'demonstrates how football can unite countries'. Richard Caborn, the sports minister, also welcomed the team. Then there was a press release from Yamam Nabeel, in which he talked about the exciting commercial deals that he was about to clinch, which, of course, never happened. There was also a confused description of football in Iraq. According to the programme, there had not been a league in Iraq from 1992 to 1996. But other, usually reliable, sources, such as the Asian Football Confederation, contradicted this and listed the clubs who had won the league in those years. The programme also listed the winners of the Iraqi league from 1974 until 1991, but these did not tally with other sources. It seemed fitting to me that many of these programmes had been stapled together incorrectly so that the last pages were at the front, because the information inside was such a shambles.

Just over 2,500 people watched the match in Macclesfield, though the size of the crowd was irrelevant as admission was free. Iraq won 5–1, which was predictable as they were playing has-beens and never-wases. The following evening I went to 'the exclusive Paragon Lounge in Mayfair, London', where Nabeel had told me he was staging 'a gala fund-raising dinner' from eight until midnight. He said this was a chance to spend 'an unforgettable evening' with the Iraqi team. Since only 120 tickets were on sale, he advised me to arrive early. He said that there would be a three-course dinner, a raffle and the opportunity to buy tour memorabilia.

Wearing my best suit, I arrived at the Paragon at 7.45. It was deserted. I asked the barman about the Iraqis. He said he did not know anything about them. I telephoned Nabeel, and he said that the dinner had been cancelled. 'The tour is over, finished', he said, sounding like a man who has just found his wife in bed with another man. I asked him what had had happened. Where was the team? 'Most have gone', he said. What about the reception at the Paragon? What about all the tickets he had sold? He muttered that 'they' had not wanted the reception to take place and said that he was not well and had to go. That was the last time he mentioned the Paragon. It was evident that he felt that someone – the Iraqi FA, the Foreign Office, persons unknown – had sabotaged him. The tour had taken place, which was laudable, but it had generated no money and little publicity. Once again Iraqis had fought among themselves and, as a result, everyone had suffered.

The players scattered, with some returning to clubs outside Iraq, many going home to Baghdad and other cities, where life was uncertain and dangerous. Qusay Munir, a 22-year-old who played in midfield, found that the house in Baghdad where he lived with his parents had been hit by a mortar. He said he was not pleased to be back. 'I am frightened. It is difficult for me to get to the stadium to train.'

Tom Farrey, the indefatigable ESPN reporter who had exposed Uday's abuse of footballers and other athletes, had taken a close interest in Hussein Saeed and his friends at the IFA during the visit to England. Farrey had spent time with the team at their hotel near Bisham Abbey and concluded that Saeed was not the right man to lead the organization: 'The players hate him because he was the right-hand man to Uday. The Iraqis need to bring in someone with unquestioned integrity and with no ties to the old regime.'

Farrey blamed the Americans for allowing Saeed to remain in power. He thought that the Bush White House did not understand Iraqi culture and that this was the reason they had allowed Hussein Saeed to take over the IFA.[5] Back in the USA he wrote a devastating piece about the Iraqis' time in England: 'Three of the coach's players sit nervously on an unmade bed in a hotel room two of them share. On the television is a BBC report with the headline "More Iraq Violence". They no longer fear physical harm, but they're certain they'll be thrown off the team if names are attached to their comments. "If you say something, you have no career," one player insists, "no anything".' Farrey listed their complaints. They earned $200 a month, less than most teachers in Iraq. They had to buy their own boots. Promised bonuses rarely materialized. They had to wash their own clothes in the hotel room sink. The association had not insured them, so if they were badly injured they would receive nothing.

Farrey said that the players wondered where the money was going. They knew that the IFA received a share of the $10 million the coalition devoted this year to the Iraqi Olympic committee. FIFA gave $700,000 in October 2003. Sponsors had committed more than $600,000. Farrey continued:

> The cost of most of the trips to Europe and the Far East was picked up by the host countries. Then there are more informal cash flows, such as the $30,000 in British pounds that Yamam Nabeel says was handed to an association official on the England trip. Nabeel described it as a blackmail payment, supplied at the last minute by a fellow Iraqi exile to quell a threat to cancel the two scheduled games. 'Did you get the money?' Nabeel recalled asking the official. 'No, what money?' the official replied. Nabeel was incredulous: 'I could see the money in his hand. It was an open envelope, a big stack. It was like talking to a kid who says he didn't eat an ice cream cone and the ice cream is dribbling down his mouth.'

Farrey said that players joked that under Uday there had been one thief, but now there were many.

Farrey reserved his special contempt for Hussein Saeed. He said that players saw him as 'Uday's all-purpose stooge', and that even Bernd Stange doubted Saeed's competence. Stange told him: 'More and more I feel it does not work. Hussein Saeed has taken all of his old mates and put them back into the association. That is a problem.'[6]

Like Farrey, I also hung around the lobby of the hotel. I was struck by the number of heavy, middle-aged Iraqis in leather jackets who were puffing on cigarettes – incongruous for a sports team – and bellowing into mobile phones. Hussein Saeed had gone by then, to attend to his commitments with the Asian Football Confederation. I asked one of the Iraqis, a big man, if he was with the IFA delegation. 'I am Basim al-Rubai', he said. 'I am the president of the technical committee.'[7] While I waited for Stange, we chatted. Had Mr al-Rubai worked for Uday? He mumbled that he had been sacked by Uday. I asked him if he knew Ammo Baba. He smiled. 'Nice man, always nervous.' What about Ammo's academy, I asked. 'We support his school.' And did Ammo defy Uday? 'Uday liked Ammo Baba and gave

him a big salary and cars, but Ammo did not trust Uday.
to say Ammo resisted the government. He was a coach. W
he do? He could not fight Uday.'

Another, smaller man was enveloped in clouds of cigarette smoke.
He was eating, smoking and shouting into his mobile phone. His
name was Abdul Khaliq. He was the IFA treasurer and a Kurd. I asked
him about the association's finances – where their money came from,
how spending was controlled and so on – but he did not speak English
and no one was available to translate.

Players wandered through the lobby. One of them, Hussam Fawzi,
was wearing a track suit with the Iraqi flag of Saddam Hussein emblazoned on it. 'This flag represents me and all of Iraq and that is what
all Iraqis would say', he said. Another, Razzaq Farhan, said he had
been forced to give 40 per cent of his salary to Uday when he played
for a club in the Gulf. He had played for Iraq when Ammo Baba was
the coach and thought he was 'a serious man'. He said: 'He has football in his blood. He has great experience.'

Then Stange arrived, a tall man with wispy white hair in a polo
shirt and casual trousers. I had never met him before, though I felt like
I knew him well after so many long-distance telephone conversations.
In photographs he often looked drawn and unwell, but in the flesh he
was tanned and exuded health. He was carrying his autobiography,
which had recently been published in Germany. He told me that it
was already a stunning commercial success. This was odd, as a friend
who lived in Berlin had told me the previous day that he had never
heard of Stange or his book. As usual, he was not sure whether he
would stay in the job. 'They shot my driver. But people love me. They
try to kiss me. The danger comes from foreign terrorists. It would be
great for them to take the German coach of Iraq hostage. I will go
back to Baghdad after 30 June,[8] when the Coalition Provisional
Authority gives power to the Iraqis. I cannot go back until then. My
life insurance is not valid.'

'I am tired. I have had many offers of jobs. Big money. But I cannot
let the Iraqis down. But if the security situation doesn't improve, I will
have to decide. I cannot coach from outside the country. If I left, I
know the team would forget everything I have taught them.'

ıned with his usual passion and honesty.
enowned for their patience or frankness –
d they usually deliver a few platitudes and
as remarkably patient and candid. I had heard
gripped. He said: 'From my point of view the
irst hotel was awful. It had no facilities, and it
to Bisham. I was so disgusted I said I would go
.ot professional. But now everything is fine.'
en vital that the players felt valued in England: 'I
have players ... ll over Iraq. There are British troops in Iraq. It was important that this was a perfect trip, to show the players and Iraqi people what England is like. My players are not well educated. They did not understand what had gone wrong when we got here. They thought it was because the English do not like them.' He had lofty ambitions; if the team did well, he said, it would inspire the country. 'I want to bring peace, democracy, the good life to this country. My next step is to go from 44 in the world to 34. For that I will need amazing support. We will need international support for training camps like this. There must be a budget for salaries. I have still not been paid this year.' He was dismayed by the battle for power between Hussein Saeed and Ahmed Radhi, until recently the IFA vice-president, which ended with Radhi being arrested with a colleague, Bassim Jamal, the former general secretary, for allegedly trying to kill Saeed by lobbing a grenade at his house. 'Every day I am surprised by what these people do. Radhi gave me great support. So did Hussein.'

I asked him about Basim al-Rubai. He snapped. 'Who? I don't know him. These people change every week.' He decided that he was bored with being diplomatic about the IFA. He scowled at the Iraqi 'officials' in the lobby. He said: 'I told Hussein Saeed, "You should stay as president." But I said, "You must choose people for marketing, financial control and youth development so we can go forward." You know what he did? He chose his mates from the old days of Uday. They cannot manage anything. They came to England for a holiday. They do nothing. I am running around, doing everything. These people are used to working in a dictatorship. There were no financial controls. If a player did well, he would be given a lot of money in cash. There's a horrible fight going on at the association between people coming back to Iraq from abroad and those who have always lived there. The people who have lived under Saddam won't change. They are against everything new.'

After Stange and the team left,[9] I pieced together what had happened on the tour. It was a tragicomedy of misunderstandings, broken promises, impossible dreams and bad behaviour. At first Nabeel was upbeat when we talked: 'The tour achieved its main aim, and no way will I ever give up on Iraqi football. But it's going to be a harder job than I thought with many obstacles along the way. Without being arrogant, I managed to bring the Iraqi national team to England. As an individual that is a considerable achievement, and I have had a few people thank me for it, which was enough in itself. I am proud of what I achieved. The team had first-class training facilities. They stayed in good hotels. There was a lot of press activity. Their morale was raised.' He said that he hoped to travel to Iraq and work in sport, though he could not go until he had a British passport. (Although he had been in the UK for many years he did not have one.)

However, over the next few weeks, as we talked more, another story emerged. He said: 'Bernd told me to be careful of these people. He said I should trust no one. I thought I'd get advice, help, from the Foreign Office, the Football Association. Companies who said they'd back the tour pulled out because of what happened in Fallujah.' (On 31 March four American bodyguards had been killed and their bodies mutilated there.) Now he was telling the truth and not pretending that he was a media mogul. He was angry and disappointed and felt that he had been exploited by everyone. 'Everyone got what they wanted, except me', he said. 'I just wanted the recognition that I had achieved something. I admit it, I was using my father's name. He is a big cheese. I wanted to get to Iraq to help build football there.'

He said the tour group was packed with people invited by Saeed. 'He wanted their votes in the election for the presidency of the association. These guys came on a holiday and to make money. They left people behind who should have been with them, like the doctor and translator, because these people wanted to come. They embarrassed us. I thought Saeed was a good guy, but the IFA is effectively a Mafia. There are always money problems. They should all be sacked. An Iraqi who lives in England said to me, "What do you expect from them? It is the way they have been brought up." One said to me: "Give us money or we won't play the game." Another one called me a liar and a thief. The Kurd, Abdul Khaliq, shouted in Arabic at a press conference, "We are the richest people in the world." The only way they know how to get anything is by threats. All they care about is money in their pockets.'

'They left bills at the hotel totalling £1,500. For premium TV – that is, pornography. For beer. For whisky. They wanted me to pay. I wouldn't.' He said that money had been a constant problem. 'Hussein Saeed told the players that I would give them money. They kept asking me, "Where's our money?" I persuaded someone who was sympathetic to what I was trying to do to give me some money – I think it was about $37,000 in all. Plus we got mobile phones for the players. I gave the money to one of the officials. I think the players got $1,000 each. But I don't know for sure.'

For Stange and the players he had only praise. 'The players are good boys. They are from poor homes but are honest. But they don't get paid. They were not insured in England. I get emotional when I talk about them. I love them. Some of them are good enough to play in Europe. I will stay with them when I go to Iraq. Everything will be done for them. If it was up to me, they would have the best league in the world.'

He explained that he had hoped for support from British and Arab companies. But, apart from the generous Bashar Alkadhi in Macclesfield and a few bits and pieces, he had not persuaded anyone to back him. In the weeks before the team was due to arrive he said he had been frantically trying to cut costs. 'I got a good deal with the hotel, which was why I put the team there. I got half-price flights. The whole thing cost £41,000. Originally we had budgeted for £150,000.'

Bashar Alkadhi, however, was delighted. He said that it had been a wonderful moment when he watched the Iraqi team, with his fourteen-year-old son Rami as mascot, run out on to the pitch at Macclesfield. 'It was such an honour to be involved. To see my country's team play on our pitch. I don't know about the issues that caused problems, like the first hotel in London not being right. For me the tour was very positive, a big success', he said. Bashar and his brother Amar had been majority shareholders in Macclesfield Town FC since late November 2003. The local media estimated they had spent £600,000 on the club, although the brothers, who were quiet, shy and reserved, never discussed money. Journalists in the town said that they were the kind of people who would support charities on condition that no one ever knew.

The Alkadhis came from Baghdad. Their father, a banker, had brought the family to Britain in 1978 because, Bashar told me, he wanted to 'pursue business opportunities'. Bashar insisted that the family was apolitical and that the decision had nothing to with the rise of Saddam, who became president a year later. Bashar was sixteen years old when he arrived in London, three years younger than Amar. They had been keen football fans in Iraq. Bashar supported the Police, and Amar was a fan of the Air Force. 'We loved the big games between Baghdad's top clubs', he said. 'You could get crowds of 50,000 for these matches.'

The brothers were capable students in Britain. Both went to university in London, where Bashar read mechanical engineering and Amar took a degree in civil engineering. But they were keen to become businessman, like their father. Bashar became a key figure in Coca-Cola's global empire and spent a decade in the Gulf as the company's marketing and public relations supremo in the Middle East. Late in 2001 they set up a company called Itsalat, based in Jordan, to distribute mobile phones in the region. Itsalat expanded rapidly and by 2004 had offices peppered around the Middle East and Europe, although Bashar remained in London with his family. In November 2003 he returned to Iraq for the first time since 1978, to launch Itsalat there. He decided that the company should sponsor al-Zawraa, which had just been saved from bankruptcy by Ahmed Radhi, the former Iraqi international. This was generous but also shrewd public relations. Bashar calculated that Itsalat could only benefit by being linked to one of Iraq's top clubs. 'Iraqis are crazy, mad, about football', he said. ' It is unbelievable.' Then the brothers took control at Macclesfield Town, where they had been on the board since the spring. 'We had been looking to invest in a club', said Bashar. 'Macclesfield seemed right. Amar had connections in the region. It was a nice little club and did not have big debts.' He said that it had felt 'right' when Yamam Nabeel asked if the brothers would like to sponsor the Goodwill Tour. 'I know it sounds corny, but it felt the right thing to do', said Bashar. He smiled and said that he preferred not to answer when I asked him how much his company had spent on the tour. He did not have a bad word to say about anyone. He said that Stange was a 'lovely man' who had done 'great things' for Iraqi football. He said that he had worshipped Hussein Saeed as a boy. He said he had met Abdul Khaliq, the IFA's treasurer, during the tour and thought he was 'interesting'. The closest he came to criticizing anyone was to say that perhaps Nabeel had been a little over-optimistic to claim that the Iraqis would play a team of stars from the Premiership. 'I did not think their managers would let them play because these players are worth so much', said Bashar.

Nabeel had more or less covered the bills for the tour, thanks to Alkadhi, the English FA and the Foreign Office. Income from the two matches had been almost zero. (The game against the MPs had been on a public pitch next to the Royal Hospital that is also the site of the Chelsea Flower Show.) 'We made about £1,600 from the game with Trinidad. We made £27 profit at Macclesfield', he said. Officials at the Coalition Provisional Authority in Baghdad agreed with Nabeel: that Hussein Saeed had packed the tour party with low-life cronies to ensure their support in the IFA election in late June. They agreed, too, that the IFA was riven by feuds and corruption and said that some Iraqi 'officials' had behaved appallingly. They thought Stange was a good man who was being treated badly. But they also thought Nabeel had been naive and foolish.

Mark Clark, a thirty-year-old solicitor from Scotland who specialized in sport, had been in Iraq since June 2003, as a CPA adviser to the Ministry of Youth and Sport. He had watched the tour develop, with mounting concern. 'It was the brainchild of Yamam Nabeel, who is a nice guy', said Clark.[10] 'He had a great personal interest in football in Iraq. However, it turned out that he could not organize well, was naive and had zero experience in this kind of event.'

Clark said that they had met months earlier in London. 'Everyone was there – the FA, the Foreign Office, the British Council. Yamam told us his plan. But the dates were all wrong, and the FA said he would struggle to get any decent matches for the Iraqis. He insisted he would manage. We pressed him over the coming weeks to give us costings in writing, to tell us who was backing the tour. We said we wanted written guarantees. He wouldn't put anything down on paper. He called and said it was all OK. The alarm bells were ringing by then. Of course, the IFA took no interest. Hussein Saeed had only agreed to the tour because Yamam said all the costs would be covered. Three months before the tour maybe we should have cancelled it. But the Foreign Office thought we should go ahead because we had come so far. Yamam assured us that the revenue would be there. The team were in Jordan and flying to London next day, and Yamam called me. He said, "We don't have enough money. Some of our sponsors have pulled out." I asked him how much he was short by, and he said £45,000. Then he said that we, the British government, had never offered money. When I told the Foreign Office, they went ballistic. But they agreed to underwrite the tour. All those people had promised him money, but he never got it in writing. That was the problem.'

Clark's problems continued when Stange saw the hotel in central London. He said that Stange was furious and demanded that they move to a decent hotel near Bisham Abbey. Clark said it got worse. 'Bernd and Yamam were constantly on the phone to me complaining about the behaviour of the delegation officials. They said: "No matter what you do, they want more. They won't thank you. They will say, why haven't we got this. They expect everything to be done for them. They think that if you whinge and complain, then other people will be weak and give you what you want." Of course, many of these frustrations were caused by the failure of Yamam's planning in the first place.'

'The Iraqi officials started behaving extremely badly. Bernd Stange complained to me that there had been shouting matches in the hotel and verbal abuse of hotel staff. Abdul Khaliq, the Kurd, was supposed to be the head of the delegation but appeared to do nothing to solve the issues. They refused to pay for things. Bernd was very stressed. One Iraqi had only come for a dental appointment. Bernd said they stayed in the hotel, that they didn't go to training, that they did nothing. They were Hussein Saeed's mates. He was building support for the election. He had done them a favour. It was a jolly in return for a vote at the forthcoming IFA elections.

'I wrote to FIFA to make them aware of the situation and said that such behaviour could not be acceptable. I explained that I believed the situation was a symptom of the lack of administration and management skills in the IFA and that I believed this should be a priority to focus on if the IFA was to develop.'

Other officials in the CPA thought the alleged attack on Saeed's home by Radhi and Jamal was a symptom of what was wrong with not just the IFA but the entire country. A source at the CPA told me: 'A cynic would say that the attack was staged to provide an excuse to have Radhi and Jamal arrested. The truth is perhaps most likely to lie somewhere between the two extremes. I don't trust any of them. They are all the same. They have no leadership skills, they are immoral, they don't care about the association, only themselves.'

At the end of June 2004 Saeed was elected president of the IFA, as expected. A few days later he sacked Bernd Stange and replaced him with Adnan Hamad, who would do as he was told, unlike Stange. Hamad was in his early forties. He had been born into a wealthy family in Samarra, in the area that became known after the fall of Saddam as 'the Sunni triangle'. He had played for some of Iraq's leading clubs, such as al-Zawraa, and had been capped twenty times by his country, including games under Ammo Baba. But he was often injured and had moved into coaching in his early thirties. He studied coaching in Europe and the Gulf before becoming Iraq's national coach in 2000. A few months later he was sacked. He was a Sunni, which meant that he was instinctively sympathetic to Ba'athism, which was the party of his people. This was the fourth time he had coached the national team.

People who liked him, such as Sharar Haydar, said that he was a decent man who only joined the party because it was expected of him. But another Iraqi said: 'He was a good player. He is a good coach. But he will not tolerate criticism of Saddam or Uday. He was never imprisoned or punished. He had lots of dollars. He could leave the country whenever he wanted.'

Stange insisted that he had not been fired. 'It is with deep regret that I dissolve my contract with the Iraqi Football Association', he said. He said that he had enjoyed the work and was proud of his record: 40 games, 96 goals scored, 21 wins, 8 draws and 11 defeats. He said that he no longer felt safe in Iraq, though anyone who had listened to him over the previous year knew that he had been saying this for many months. He said the IFA had told him that they would welcome him back if the security situation improved. But he did not think this was likely. 'I believe a clean break is better, much as it pains me', he said.

Mark Clark, who had just started working with the Iraqi National Olympic Committee, said: 'Bernd was treated badly. I have a lot of respect for him. He was entitled to a good salary as a national team coach: he deserved that. But his passion and devotion went beyond money. It is fair to say the IFA found that they couldn't afford him.' Other sources in Iraq said that the IFA had tried to avoid paying Stange his monthly salary of $10,000. These sources said that the IFA had told Stange that he should ask FIFA to pay half his salary. He did, and FIFA refused. 'Of course then the IFA "misunderstood". They said he had agreed to accept $5,000 from the IFA. Poor Bernd. He had a really rough ride', said a CPA official.

Nick Ask, the Iraqi who lived in Michigan, told me: 'Stange was honest, devoted and talented. When I heard in 2003 that the IFA couldn't renew his contract, citing financial difficulties, I lobbied my contacts within the CPA to chip in some money in order to retain Stange's service. I wrote to Mark Clark:

Dear Mr Clark,

This morning I heard disturbing news that the IFA may not be able to fulfil Mr Stange's contract for the next year due to financial difficulties. Mr Stange has been an inspiration for the rebirth of Iraqi soccer in addition to bringing some badly needed international recognition. I fully understand the bases for such financial difficulties and also do expect the IFA revenue to pick up steam as time goes by. I wonder if the CPA can intervene in such a dispute since it means a lot for the Iraqis if Mr Strange remains as the head coach of the national team.'

Ask said that Iraqi football was the poorer for his departure. I agreed. Stange was a first-class coach, who had transformed Iraq from an ill-disciplined shambles into a decent side that could give anyone a match. And he had done this in awful circumstances. The Iraqis had always been skilful, but Stange had brought European nous and they were the stronger for it. He had kept the team together and fostered a spirit that was usually found only in club sides. He would be missed.

IO

Horror stories

Many people would not talk about Uday until the fall of the regime in April 2003. There were good reasons for this. Some who lived abroad had relatives in Iraq, and feared they would be punished if they attacked Saddam. Others wanted to live quietly. Those who were still in Iraq had no choice but to remain silent: if they had told the truth, they would have been killed. After the fall of Saddam, however, they were prepared to speak to me, though many were nervous, as if they could not believe that the nightmare was over.

Nick Ask was born in 1962 in a poor Shia suburb of Baghdad.[1] In 2004 he was a prosperous executive with an energy company in Michigan, married and with three children, and with a B.Sc. in electronic engineering from the University of Baghdad and an M.Sc. and Ph.D. in electrical engineering from Strathclyde University. It had required sacrifices and hard work. He told me that he had played for the under-16 team of the Air Force club, one of Iraq's top teams. When he was eighteen, he had joined another club, Baladeyat, where he played until he was twenty-one. He said: 'I was paid 6 dinars a month [$20], which was barely enough to pay for my transport costs from my home to the club's training ground. I was also receiving 20 dinars a month [$66] allowance from my parents to cover my personal expenses as a student. When I was eighteen, I turned down an invitation to train with the national under-19 team, because I could not afford the transport. Also, I used to work part-time in the summer to earn money for clothing, books and entertainment. If I had joined the national team, I could not have carried on with my summer job.'

He thought about becoming a professional footballer. He would have had a basic salary, as a policeman, soldier, port worker or train driver, with bonuses for playing. But it would not have been much, and it was insecure because an injury could end a career instantly – Iraq's medical facilities for footballers were notoriously bad unless you were a star, in which case you would be sent abroad, usually to London. 'I gave up football in 1983, two years before I left Iraq', he said. 'I saw great players from the past struggling to make a living in Baghdad. For example, there was a man called Sahib Khazeal, who had played at left back for the national team in the 1960s and '70s. He had been captain of the Air Force. He was now a street vendor. It was terrible, sad.'

'I realized that I would have a better life if I had a profession. The terror in Iraq was getting worse. The brutality was hard to ignore, even if you kept away from politics. Saddam's Iraq was not the place to raise a family. The government used to grant students who finished in the top five in the scientific and engineering disciplines scholarships to pursue their postgraduate studies abroad. It was hard to get permission to travel abroad and I thought that I could go, if I did well enough in university. I worked hard and won a scholarship to Glasgow. As I was preparing to leave, Uday took over football.'[2]

Ask was horrified by what happened after that. He said: 'It was much worse than in Eastern Europe under Communism. The people who ran sport there knew what they were doing and rewarded success. But Uday knew nothing about sport. The people he appointed to run sport knew even less than him. The only incentive for players was to avoid being tortured. It will take a generation or more to repair the damage Uday caused. He believed that you could pick players at random, terrify them and they would beat Brazil. It was like Saddam in the first Gulf War, thinking his army would beat America because Iraqi soldiers were afraid of him.' Ask said that the sanctions imposed on Iraq after the 1990 invasion of Kuwait had crippled the country. Football, like everything else, had been badly affected: there was a shortage of boots, track suits and even balls.

In 1993 Uday lifted his ban on players signing for clubs abroad. Over the next decade there was an exodus of players to Qatar, Bahrain, Lebanon, Algeria, Yemen, Tunisia, Jordan and the United Arab Emirates. It was not altruism: the players had to pay half their salaries to the Iraqi Football Association, which meant the money went to Uday. One of the many players to 'benefit' from this dispensation was Ahmed Radhi, captain of al-Zawraa and Iraq, and arguably a greater player than Ammo Baba, who moved to a club called al-Wakra in Qatar, where he became the league's top scorer. Other top players, such as Radhi Shnishel, Ali Khadim, Ahmed Daham, Laith Hussein and Habib Ja'far, also moved to Qatar, where wages were many times more than the few hundred dollars a month they had earned in Iraq. Most players stayed in the Arab world, where everything was familiar, though a few moved to clubs in Malaysia, South Korea, Bangladesh and India.

Ahmed Radhi was born in 1964. He played seventy-two times for Iraq and scored forty-two goals, an astonishing ratio in international football, even if Iraq did usually play third-rate teams.[3] He had won his first cap when he was nineteen – he was picked by Ammo, who was Iraq's coach – and his last in 1997, when he was thirty-three. In 1994 Uday decided that Radhi should play for his club, al-Rasheed. 'I knew Uday wanted me to join al-Rasheed. I did not want to. Uday's men came for me one night. They took me from my house. They beat me. They said they would accuse me of having a relationship with the girlfriend of one of al-Zawraa's officials. I had to join al-Rasheed. They said if I didn't, I would never play again. I went. Soccer was my life.'[4]

He hated the club, as did most fans. 'It was a total failure in one sense because having all the best players in one club destroyed competition in the Iraqi league. But you could argue it helped the national team because so many players came from al-Rasheed. We knew each other well.' Radhi said that after a defeat, for club or country, players always wondered if they would be punished. He said that he was gaoled three times.

Hashim Nasif Jasim, an Iraqi player who had defected in 2002, was in Portsmouth in 2004, studying for a coaching badge and hoping to be given political asylum. Jasim, who was a friend of Ahmed Kadoim, the referee whom I had met in Birmingham, was thirty-five. He was a Shia from Baghdad and, like Kadoim, had fled Iraq because he had been abused by Uday.[5] He said: 'Uday was a dictator, like his father, but also mad. When he was in charge of sport, the Iraqi FA could do nothing. You could not argue with Uday. The people at the association only wanted to please him. They did not care about football. I was tortured in 1996. I was playing for Uday's club, al-Karkh, in a pre-season friendly against Diyala. We lost. Uday took all the players to prison. For two days we were beaten and tortured.'

Jasim came from a large, working-class family, with six brothers and four sisters. He had always loved football and hated school. He knew that he would never be rich as a player, but at least he would enjoy himself, unlike his father, a taxi driver, who worked to live. Jasim was tall and well built, and became a first-class full-back. He played for the Air Force's youth team. Then he joined a club called Alselekh, before moving to the Police. He went back to the Air Force, then the best team in Iraq. He appeared for the national youth team and twice for the Olympic side. He supplemented his pay from football with casual work outside the game. He was increasingly unhappy. 'Football is a passion for the people of Iraq. For thirty-five years all they had was war. Football was important for them to get rid of the heartbreak. But the problem was that the big clubs were run by Saddam's family. They were gambling all the time. Each one would do anything to make money or get his club to win the league. They bought players and referees. I am a sportsman and did not like it.'

He said that he did not blame people like Ammo Baba ('a great player and coach') for collaborating with Uday. 'Everyone had to keep quiet if they wanted to live. If Uday said something you had to say, "Yes sir",' he said. Unlike many Iraqis, he was optimistic about the future. 'Football will recover. So will the country. I don't think Iraq has been ruined by Saddam.'

Basil Gorgis had been a powerful midfield player for Iraq in the 1980s. Like Ammo Baba, he was an Assyrian, but he had been brought up in the Kurdish north, where many Assyrians lived, and in 1992, aged thirty, sickened by the violence and corruption of Uday's Iraq, he had fled to Canada, where his brothers lived.[6] He had hoped to play in Canada's professional league, but the IFA refused to release his registration. He still played in Canada, but as an amateur, and coached a youth team.

He remained silent until Saddam had gone. Then he explained why he had left: 'Uday was a thug. The atmosphere was horrible. When he first came, he wasn't that involved. But as the 1980s progressed, he got more and more obstructive. I remember we were playing in the Gulf Cup. We were playing Qatar in Doha. The weather was very hot and humid, and we played badly in the first half. At half-time Uday called us and threatened to torture us or send us to the front line against Iran. In the second half we played much better, but it had nothing to do with him. We were just a good team and knew how to adjust our game under different conditions. We won the tournament. But because of instances like that, he thought that his bullying tactics were working.'

He recalled how Uday had interfered with the team's preparations for the World Cup finals in Mexico in 1986. 'We went to Brazil, where we had a horrible training camp. We played local, non-professional teams in mediocre facilities. England had wanted to play us in Wembley and pay us $25,000. They had Morocco in their group, and we had just beaten Morocco, so they were interested in playing us. But Uday didn't want us to play England in case we lost.'

Uday even upset the team before their first game in the tournament that June, against Paraguay, by telling them they would wear a blue and yellow kit instead of the traditional green and white. 'Everyone was astounded', Gorgis said. Iraq lost the match 1–0 and had a goal disallowed in the last minute because the referee said he had blown for full-time before the ball crossed the line. The players wondered if this bad luck had something to do with the kit. They lost their next match against Mexico 1–0. 'The game was in the Aztec Stadium in Mexico City, filled with over 80,000 screaming fans. The crowd charged me. I was the type of player that fed off the energy off the crowd, and wasn't intimidated by it. We played very well, but lost', he said. Their final game was against Belgium. Ahmed Radhi scored – the only goal Iraq have scored in a World Cup finals – but the team lost 2–1. Gorgis said it was not a happy day: 'I got a red card in that match. Because we were considered a poor team, our matches were usually assigned to less experienced and less qualified referees. The referee mistook me for my team-mate Ghanim Uraybi, who was

went over to them and tried to reason with them not to punish us. But they would not listen. They said they had been ordered to punish us by Uday and had to do what he said. They took us to a room. Uday had told them how to punish each player. He had set out what would happen to each of us according to how we had played. I was the seventh into the room. My punishment was to have my head shaved. Uday's behaviour was completely immoral. It was against Islamic law. We had to accept it because we would have suffered more if we had objected. We hoped for the mercy of God. After they had finished with us, the guards took us by bus to the Olympic headquarters. We were put in cells. They were bright red, the walls, the ceiling, the floor, the lights. We spent three days there, with little food. It was summer and very hot. There was no air. We were treated like criminals by Uday. He knew nothing about sport or being human.'[7]

Kadhum was born in 1965 in Sadr City, into a poor Shia family. He had begun his career playing for army teams from 1985 until 1989. Then he joined the Air Force club. In 1993 Uday said that Iraqi players could move abroad, providing they gave him half their salaries. Kadhum calculated that he would still be better off abroad than in Iraq. For the next decade he played in Qatar, Lebanon and Jordan, though he remained a stalwart of the Iraq national team. He retired in the summer of 2003. His time abroad meant that he was rich, at least by Iraqi standards.

He was gaoled again in 2000, when he was playing for the Air Force. He said that the team had been to a pre-season training camp at Duhok, 240 miles north of Baghdad. 'One day we all went to the market in the city. We bought televisions, CD players. Some players bought blankets. It was simple stuff. When we got back to Baghdad, Ahmed al-Fayad, who was security director of the Olympic committee, accused us of buying satellite receivers, which were banned under Saddam. I said it was not true. I said I had bought two chairs for a barber's shop I owned. I had bought them to earn extra money because players weren't paid much in Iraq.'

'We were questioned for two days. Then they told eighteen players that they had to report to the Olympic building at 6 p.m. I was one of the players. When I heard the time, I knew that we would be beaten because the Olympic offices closed at four. I told all the players who had been listed to get ready for a big punishment. They asked me, "How do you know what will happen?" I told them I had experience of these things. I told them to bring hats to wear after they shaved our heads and to wear thick socks in case they beat our feet. Then we could walk afterwards. Next day we went to the committee building. I was right. Uday's bodyguards were there, waiting to beat us. I knew two of them. I had a good relationship with them. Then two young players started crying. It would not be right to name them. I told the bodyguards to leave them, to give me their punishment. But the bodyguards refused. They said Uday would find out and they would be punished.'

'When my turn came to be beaten, I had to sit on a chair with my legs in the air. They started lashing my feet. But they weren't hitting me hard. Their boss, who was from Tikrit, Saddam's town, saw this and got angry. He said, "Why aren't you hitting him hard?" The bodyguards said, "He is Samir Kadhum, he has done many good things for Iraqi football." The boss said this was rubbish. He said, "I will show you how to beat someone." He started hitting me very hard. He was shouting. I said, "Why are you treating me like an animal?" He said, "This is Uday's order, and we must carry it out." One of the bodyguards whispered to me to be quiet. He said that Uday would gaol me for weeks if he heard I was shouting. So I shut up and bore the pain. My feet became swollen, and I could not train for two weeks. Afterwards I got a contract with a club called al-Sahel in the Lebanon.'

Yasir Abdul Latif was another top-class player who suffered horribly. In the early 1990s he was playing for the Salah-al-Deen club, in the north of Iraq, run by Saddam's half-brothers Barzan and Watban. Latif said: 'In 1991 I was playing against a club called al-Diwaniyah. One of my club officials came from Tikrit, Saddam's home town. He was also an officer in the Special Republican Guard. He became very angry with the referee during the game and walked onto the pitch. He shouted at the referee and hit him. The referee knew who had hit him but was afraid to accuse the officer. I was standing near him and he pointed at me and said I had done it. Two days later guards came and said they had orders from Uday to take me to al-Radwaniyah prison. They said they did not know how long I would be held there. I spent fourteen days there. I was beaten with electrical cables, and my hair was shaved, I was humiliated. They did not show me any respect. They were very rough. My family did not know any thing about me or where I had been sent.'

'Seven months later I was sent to al-Radwaniyah once again. I was still playing for Salah-al-Deen and had been late for training. One of the coaching staff yelled at me. He was from Tikrit. He was very rude. I got angry and shouted back. He ordered me to be sent to prison. I was there for a week. They shaved my head again. Then I was gaoled again in 1995. I was playing for my club, al-Zawraa, against the Air Force in the league. The head of the Iraqi Air Force, a general, was watching. He saw me make a gesture and thought I was making fun of him and his club. So he wrote to the Olympic committee and complained about me. Uday sent me to prison again. I was in a small cell, 1 metre by 2 metres. I was beaten there with cables and sticks. I did not eat or sleep properly for a week. It was really unforgettable. In total I was sent to al-Radwaniyah five times. It was pointless. Uday was an ignorant person. This kind of punishment destroys a player psychologically and kills his enthusiasm for playing football. Above all, it destroys your dignity.'

Latif was born in 1971. He played for the under-23 Olympic team in the early 1990s and won his first cap for the full international team in 1996. Like many Iraqis, he often played abroad – for al-Salam in Lebanon, al-Jeel in Yemen and al-Rai in Syria – because wages abroad were higher than in Iraq, even after Uday had taken his cut. He said: 'It was very difficult. All I thought about was making some money for my family to ensure their future. I worked hard to get a good reputation so I could get contracts to play outside Iraq. Thank God I did.'

He said that he came from a large Sunni family. He had two brothers, one of whom was a career soldier, and four sisters. He said: 'My father wanted me to go to college but I wanted to be a professional footballer. I remember he beat me once because I refused to give up football. He said that I must study, go to college, or I would be sent to the army. This was in the 1980s, and the war against Iran was still going on. He said I would die in battle. Like all fathers, he was worried about his son.' In 1989 he was conscripted into the army. 'I was sent to Salah-al-Deen province in the north, where Saddam came from. I was playing in a tournament for military teams and was spotted by a well-known coach called Saas Jabar. He thought I was a good player and told my officers that they should let me join Salah-al-Deen, where he was the coach. Of course they agreed because this was known to be the club of Saddam's family. They said I would have to stay at the club for the three years of my military service.'

He recalled the days when Uday had run al-Rasheed. 'I admit they did well sometimes, but no one liked the club. Uday took all the best players for himself. Once al-Zawraa beat al-Rasheed and Uday was very angry with his players and sent them to prison. Referees were always scared when they had games with al-Rasheed. They were afraid Uday would get upset with them.' However, there were advantages for players when their club had powerful patrons. 'The head of al-Zawraa was Arshed Yassin, Saddam's brother-in-law, and his deputy was Rokan al-Taa'l. Both were Saddam's bodyguards, so they could do a lot for the club. The club had lots of money and equipment. Others clubs had nothing. Sometimes they could not feed their players. There was a negative side. These men were dictatorial and would not allow anyone to argue with them. If they had wanted to punish players, they could have. But, to be honest, they did not punish us physically. Sometimes they stopped a player's salary for a week, but I think they gave the club great support.'

In 1999 Latif married. (His wife's father was a fanatical supporter of al-Zawraa.) The club paid for the ceremony. 'They took care of everything', he said. 'Because I was one of the best players in the club. The players were like brothers. We had a great spirit.' But that was not enough to keep him in Iraq. He wanted to play abroad, where he could earn a thousand dollars a week, instead of a few hundred dollars a month. But to do that he had to pay Uday. 'I was offered contracts abroad. Uday said I could not go because I played for Iraq. I said, "But why? Many players for the national team play outside Iraq." Then his aide, a man from Tikrit, came to me and said Uday wanted more. Usually players gave him 40 per cent of their salary. I offered him half. I also had to bribe people at the football association. I paid them $2,000.'

Latif said that he had cultivated Uday's cronies, such as Basher Rami, Saher Burhan and Assil Tabra. 'They were the direct route to Uday. They were the best people to bribe', he said. 'In 1999, when I was with al-Zawraa, we played in Qatar. I was offered a contract with the al-Shimal club there. They said they would pay me a lump sum of $3,000 for three months and a salary of $3,000 per month. An official from the Iraqi Football Association called Laith al-Rawi said I could not accept. He said that I had to go back to Iraq, and then he would see if he would allow me to play in Qatar. When I got back to Iraq, he said he would not let me go to Qatar. Later I found out why. A friend of his was playing for al-Shimal, and they wanted to exchange him for me. That is how Iraq was. Everyone was corrupt.'

Anyone who tried to outwit Uday suffered. 'One day Uday ordered all the Iraqi football players in Yemen to come back to Iraq. There were thirty-three of us. He suspected that one player had done a secret deal with the Olympic committee and was not paying him. They found out that one player, Juma'a Kudayer, had bought a contract from people from the committee. He was sent to prison. So were three Olympic officials. Uday knew so much about corruption you could never cheat him!

Raad Hammoudi, the goalkeeper who had captained Iraq at the World Cup in 1986, said: 'My dream is that sport in Iraq will be led by people who are here to serve the country, not their own personal interests. We have been liberated. Now we can say what is right and wrong.'[8] A goalkeeper called Majid Abu Kheir, who was only twenty-three when Saddam fled Baghdad, had been picked to play for Iraq in an international competition in Thailand in 1999. He said Uday called the team manager before the matches against Japan and South Korea. Kheir said: 'The manager said that Uday told him we would all be punished if we lost.' He added that the players were so nervous they lost both games, 4–2 to Japan and 3–0 to South Korea. When the team returned to Baghdad, a bus was waiting at the airport to take the twenty-four players, manager, two doctors and a journalist who covered the games to the Olympic building.

'Uday's aide came on the bus and told us we would never see our families again', he said. 'Everyone was shaking and crying.' But instead of going to prison, they were driven to a farm outside Baghdad that belonged to Uday. For twenty-five days they worked as labourers. At night they slept in barn. Bassim Jamal, who was sacked by Hussein Saeed as IFA general secretary in the spring of 2004, had been one of Uday's lieutenants at the IFA since 1992. Unlike Hussein Saeed, he admitted that he had known that players were abused. 'I knew they were being taken to gaol, but I couldn't do anything about it', he said. 'After games Uday's office would call me and say, "This player, this player." I would collect them and they would wait in a room. Then they would be taken away to gaol.'[9]

Habib Ja'far was tiny – 5 feet 4 inches and just over 140 pounds – but was one of the most popular players in the country. He played in midfield, where his 'agility, sheer talent and fighting spirit'[10] made him an outstanding player. He was quiet, polite, modest and devout. One Iraqi said: 'Everyone loves him.'[11] Yet he was also persecuted by Uday. 'Uday sent me to prison five times. Maybe I was hurt more than any player by Uday. I was like a hostage to him. Once I was gaoled for five days because I was sent off in a league match. What would have happened to me if I had been sent off in an international? Maybe Uday would have said it was treason! My team-mates called me Prisoner of Uday.'

Ja'far was born in 1969 and spent his entire career in fear of Uday. He was seventeen when he was gaoled after arguing with a coach at al-Talaba, the club where he was playing. He was in prison for twelve days. He was not tortured, but it was a taste of things to come. In 1989 he was sent to the notorious al-Radwaniyah prison for five days after his team, al-Rasheed, lost a match. Among the team-mates gaoled with him were Ahmed Radhi, Laith Hussein and Karim Alawi. He said: 'They put me in a cell that was so small I could not breathe. It was impossible to sleep.'

He was back in the same gaol that year after Iraq were knocked out of the Gulf Cup. He said: 'They beat me. They kicked me. They would not let me sleep. I was humiliated. Ask people who were in prison for political offences what that place was like! Uday called it a concentration camp, and he was right. I thought about committing suicide to find release from the pain. There was no other salvation. I did not know if I could live until they freed me. There was a smell of death in every corner. In my heart there is still a lot of pain.'

'I cannot forget the humiliation that I faced in prison. Imagine the moment when they have brought you there, and the guards have been told they get to punish someone who is a famous footballer. They liked to torture and humiliate someone like me. It was a lot of pain. After a long day, of being beaten, they would knock on the door of my cell and shout, "What are you doing?" I said, "I am trying to sleep." They shouted, "You are not allowed to sleep." At that moment I really hated life, the world, even myself. Uday was imitating his father. He wanted to be more than him. He punished everyone who was near him. Once Iraq lost a match and he punished a bodyguard, although the guy had nothing to do with football. I do not understand a man like that.'

Ja'far came from a large Shia family – six brothers and three sisters – in Sadr City. His father, who died in 1983, aged forty-four, had been a useful but not outstanding footballer. He had been an NCO in the army and became a driver after he retired from the military. Ja'far was always religious: 'I pray every day. I fast. I read the Koran. I like to help people', he said. He joined al-Talaba in 1980 as an eleven-year-old of great promise. Although he moved clubs frequently as a professional, al-Talaba remained his favourite team. He often played for clubs outside Iraq, such as al-Rayan, al-Wakra and al-Arabi in Qatar, al-Anssar in Lebanon and al-Duhfar in Oman. But Uday always had to be paid. 'The Olympic committee, which controlled all the contracts for players, was Uday's private company. I spent five seasons outside Iraq, and Uday took almost half my money. There is no income tax like that in the world. Once I gave the Olympic committee in Baghdad $16,000. Some of it was supposed to go to my old club, al-Talaba, as compensation for me leaving them, but people from the club told me they never saw the money. No one dared ask where the money went. Uday treated the clubs, the players, the Olympic committee, as his private property. Now that we are free, God willing, we can talk about such things.'

Ja'far said it was not easy to get permission to play abroad. 'It took two months to get agreement from Uday that you could play abroad. In that time the club who wanted you could lose interest. Once I asked Uday's secretary if she could hurry up and get the contract signed, and she said, "Just wait until Mr Uday is in a good mood to sign it or you will regret it." Uday was always away, hunting – he liked to kill animals – or abroad, and his secretaries never knew when he would be back. This hurt players, because clubs abroad knew that Iraqi players were always a problem.'

Of course, he said, corruption was part of the system under Uday, but, to the poor, football represented hope. 'We did not care who was Christian, Sunni or Shia. We were players. The majority of us were Shia, because football is a game for the poor and most Shias are poor. Football was a chance for these poor young men to become prominent.'

Laith Hussein, who had played for Iraq over 100 times and been captain more times than he could remember, said that players were frequently gaoled and tortured. He said he had been gaoled at least ten times, maybe more. 'I thought many times of giving up football', he said. 'But how could I? I was afraid of what Uday would do to me and my family. I would sit and cry when I was by myself. I wanted to play for myself, and for the Iraqi people, not for Uday.'

Anwar Jassam also suffered. He had been a rising star for al-Zawraa, based in Sadr City, and had just been capped by the national team when he hurt his right eye in a car crash in 1970. He was twenty-one. As a young star, the Iraqi authorities were happy to spend money on him. He travelled to London for treatment, but doctors there told him his playing career was over. So he became a coach. Unusually for a footballer, he came from a middle-class family. His father worked for the Transport Ministry and hoped that he would go to university and have a respectable career. 'My father was very encouraging when he realized football was what I wanted', Jassam said.

In 1971 he joined a club called al-Sikahk as an assistant coach, and the following year he became coach there. In 1980 he was asked to help coach the Iraqi team at the Moscow Olympics. Then he took charge of the national youth team. In the 1990s he had spells at clubs in Qatar and Oman.

But Uday was never far away. 'He used to call me and say, "This player is good and you should pick him." Obviously it was an order.' Once Uday accused Jassam of criticizing him. 'The people around Uday were a problem. They told lies all the time. They said that I had called Uday bad names, which was not true. They were trying to impress Uday.' Jassam said: 'All Uday cared about was winning. He used to send players to prison, beat them and shave their heads. I told him this was destroying the players physically and psychologically. I said it would be better to fine them. But he was sure he was right. He thought footballers were soldiers.'

Uday made Jassam's life almost impossible. 'He banned me from working in Iraq or leaving the country for five years because our Olympic team lost a match against Saudi Arabia in 1996. I said at a press conference after the game that we had done well in view of sanctions, but Uday did not like what I said. I was out of work for two years. Friends helped me, and then someone who knew Uday well spoke for me. I was able to go abroad and work in Yemen, Jordan and the United Arab Emirates.' He added: 'Under Uday the Iraqi Football Association did not exist. He made all the decisions about football. And no one could argue with him.'

Mowafak Nuri, a defender for al-Zawraa and the national team, who retired in 2003, said: 'We played every match in fear.'[12] Salam Hashim, another top player, said that, before he was shot and badly wounded in 1996, Uday often summoned players to his home in the early hours. 'He wanted to play football with his friends. None of us dared tackle him.'

In 2000 Muhammed Mohammed, a wrestler from Baghdad, was picked to go to the Sydney Olympics but then told he would not be going. Muhammed, then twenty-three years old and approaching his prime, said that Uday preferred to send his cronies rather than athletes to the Games. 'They took six people from the Ba'ath party – and only four athletes. It didn't matter if you were a good athlete. If you knew somebody in power, that's how you got selected.'[13] Jamal Hassan, the coach of Iraq's wrestling team, said: 'As soon as Uday became head of the Iraqi National Olympic Committee, sport in Iraq was destroyed. It was all about money. If athletes had professional contracts, he would take 50 per cent of their earnings too.'

Uday said that athletes could only travel within the Middle East, but he also made sure that he profited. Hassan said: 'The government would give money to an athlete who had to travel. We'd get the money and then we'd have to go to the Olympic committee and hand it over. The money went straight from the bank into their hands. Then you had to sign a paper to say that you personally were responsible for all the expenses for the trip. That's the way they did it, making us pay from our own pocket. You had to sign a paper saying that you would come first, second or third, If you did not achieve that, then you would be punished, either fined or gaoled.'

He said that Uday had punished him and his team after they came second in the Arab Championships in Syria in 2001. Uday was also furious because one of the wrestlers, Maiham Ali Hadi, had defected to Syria. Back in Baghdad, officials and wrestlers were taken to a military compound and jammed, five each, into dark rooms. Showers were banned. Every forty-eight hours Hassan and the others were interrogated and beaten. 'Two administrators from the wrestling federation were thrown into prison with us, and they hadn't even gone on the trip. Every day they would tell us that we would be let out the next day. Uday was crazy, so random. If he was in a good mood, he'd let you out; if he wasn't, you would stay in. We were in for thirty-five days. There were people in there with us who had been in that prison on his whim for two years', said Hassan. 'The shocks were delivered with an electric stick. They would hit you with it anywhere on your body and that was the worst of all. When they hit you, your body would lurch backwards and hit the wall. Two of the coaches almost didn't survive. One of them had a heart attack, and the other, his blood pressure rocketed. They did get given some treatment, but they so nearly died. Five weeks later they were released, though some wrestlers never returned to competition. 'Some of us stayed because we love our country and we love our sport', Hassan said. 'That's what kept us going.'

Perhaps most sickeningly, Uday even targeted the disabled. Fakher Ali al-Jamali, who had led Iraq's handicapped team, said he had been whipped with electric cables after two members of his team went missing briefly in 1988.[14]

A general, a scholar, Mr Fatfat and a solicitor come to the rescue

Many people in Iraq thought that Ahmed al-Samarrai arrived in Baghdad in April 2003 on the back of an American tank, symbolic of the fact that this 62-year-old former general in Saddam's army was an American puppet. The story was almost true. Al-Samarrai, who had defected to the West in 1983, had travelled with American Special Forces as they swept down from northern Iraq but had not actually been sitting on a tank when they reached Baghdad. To Iraqis this was an irrelevant detail: many condemned him as a creature of the White House.

There is no doubt that he was a favourite of the Americans, who had decided before the invasion that he would be in charge of sport in post-Saddam Iraq because he was so compliant. (Al-Samarrai insisted that Iraqis freely elected him to the job, which no one in Baghdad believed.) Uday's Iraqi National Olympic Committee had vanished with the Saddam regime. The Iraqi Football Association had ceased to exist, like its offices, which had been blown apart. Hundreds of sports clubs and stadiums in the city and the rest of the country had disappeared. They had been run by Ba'ath activists, who had been killed or arrested or had chosen to forget they used to be party activists. Looters stripped these clubs of everything: equipment, furniture, even electrical wiring. Sometimes they actually demolished the building.

Al-Samarrai was appointed president of the Interim Committee to Administer Sport, established by the Americans in May, after the IOC dissolved Iraq's Olympic committee. Al-Samarrai faced a daunting task: to restore the entire system of sport, from small clubs in towns to the giants such as al-Talaba and al-Zawraa. He said that it was a daunting task because sport had become part of the state and party apparatus. 'The system of the regime, its control over life, started in primary school. It was exactly like the Nazis in the 1930s', he said. To be fair to al-Samarrai, he realized the dangers of being seen to be too close to the Americans and after the fall of Saddam made it clear that he was not entirely happy with the way they were behaving. To demonstrate his independence he told me that the Americans had needlessly alienated ordinary Iraqis, who had been delighted when Saddam had fallen but then been antagonized by the insensitivity of the US forces. 'The Americans created the resistance. There was none at the beginning', he said.[1] As a leading member of Iraqi exile groups in the USA and Europe, dedicated to overthrowing Saddam, he said that he had often briefed the American State Department, the Pentagon, the CIA and other agencies on how to best to remove Saddam – and, equally important, on what should replace him. He told me: 'Two weeks before the war I was in Washington. I asked the Americans what they were going to do with the Iraqi army, which they said was 700,000 strong. I said that meant there was another 1.3 million were also dependent – families and so on. I said, "You must keep the army. You must negotiate with the commanders. You must use the Iraqi army to control the cities." I said, "Think what will happen if all those soldiers lose their jobs. They will become suicide bombers." Unfortunately, the Americans did not listen to me. Of course I supported regime change. I told the Americans they must be patient after Saddam had gone, but they thought everything would be fine immediately. They should have listened to the British, who understand Iraq better. It should have been American muscle and British brain.'

Al-Samarrai was born into the Sunni élite of Baghdad society. At school he was clever and a natural athlete. When he was eighteen, he was playing top-class basketball. At university in Baghdad, where he studied physical education and political science, he switched to athletics and ran for Iraq in the 200 metres and 400 metres. He became a career soldier, though he continued as an athlete. He once scored 30 points in a basketball match against an American military team in Damascus, Syria, in 1971. He captained the national basketball team from 1962 until 1973. He retired in the mid-1970s and coached various military teams. Then he was given control over sport in the Iraqi military, an immensely powerful position since many of the best athletes in the country were, at least nominally, in the armed forces.

But he was uneasy. 'My son was eleven, starting secondary school in Baghdad. It was one of the best schools at the time, and it was run by the Americans. Then Saddam came to power in 1979, and he brought in other teachers that were not as good as the American teachers. My son was in a class with Qusay, and he used to play sports with him and Uday. The head of the school was my close friend. She advised me to take my son out because he played very hard and you never knew what would happen if he made a hard foul against Uday or Qusay. The bodyguards could have shot him on the spot. It was a great offence to hit one of Saddam's sons. The penalty was death. So I sent my son to boarding-school in Britain.'

He was horrified when Saddam invaded Iran in 1980. He thought it was a pointless war, which would be long and bloody. 'I used to read all the secret documents, including material from the Americans and the British. I could see what was happening. But Saddam did not care. Saddam only cared about himself.' He decided to defect. Hs son was safe, but he did not know what would happen to his wife. 'I was at a sports conference in Switzerland. That was my work then, administering military sports for the country. On the last day I left the delegation. I didn't tell anybody, even my family. At first my wife was afraid they would execute her family. They took her brothers into custody for a long time. They killed my driver, because he didn't know why I left. My handyman where I lived was tortured for three months. The authorities wanted any information about my associations.'

'My wife was blacklisted from travelling. Her name was on a list at the airport, so she couldn't leave. I tried, through a friend, to smuggle her through the north, but because of the war anyone travelling through there was being detained at the border for six months. When she learned about this, I was able to trust a very powerful friend, who took a big risk by taking her to the airport and making sure her name was not checked. She flew out two months later.'

In Britain he lived quietly. 'I kept a low profile for years, because Saddam was sending people abroad to assassinate people like me. After a couple of years I started a real estate business. Then I started a pub-lishing business for Islamic manuscripts. I made a lot of contacts with VIPs in different countries. I always followed Iraqi sports as best I could, but I didn't think it would be a part of my life.' By 1990 he was confi-dent enough in his personal security to help launch an anti-Saddam group called the Free Iraqi Council. On the eve of the first Gulf War he moved to Saudi Arabia, hoping that Saddam would fall so that he could return home and take his place as one of the country's new leaders. When this did not happen, al-Samarrai returned to London.

In 2001 he was involved in the establishment of another anti-Saddam, pro-American group, the Iraqi National Movement.[2] In February 2003 the Americans sent him to Turkey to await the inva-sion. He knew what his job would be when American troops moved into Iraq: to try and convince senior figures in the Iraqi military and government to work with the Americans.[3] Iraq had had a long, if unsuccessful, Olympic pedigree. It joined the IOC in 1948. It sent athletes to the Games in London in 1948. (It never entered anyone for the Winter Games.) A weightlifter called Aziz Abdul Wahid won its only medal, a bronze, at the 1960 Games in Rome. Iraqi sport fell apart under Uday. Iraq sent forty-three athletes to the 1980 Games in Moscow; only four went to Sydney in 2000.

Sport in Iraq was morally and materially bankrupt after the Saddam regime collapsed. Al-Samarrai set to work, but his resources were pitiful. The Coalition Provisional Authority had been given $18 billion to spend in Iraq but only gave $10 million to sport, with an extra $3 million to repair the national football stadium in Baghdad, which the Americans had wrecked by using it to park their tanks. This was an absurdly small sum and showed how the Americans under-estimated the importance of sport, especially football. The CPA argued that sport could not take place until the necessities of a civilized society – security, electricity, clean water and so on – were established, but, even so, Iraqis and many officials within the CPA felt they could, and should have, spent more.

This was certainly the view of Mounzer Fatfat, a Lebanese-American who advised the CPA on sport. He said: 'We tried to get more. $10 million was not enough. Nowhere near. Paul Bremer was very keen on sport. But his hands were tied. The Americans had their priorities, and sport was not one of them. The Iraqis had suffered thirty-five years of abuse. There was nothing. Saddam had fifty-eight palaces, and sport had nothing. He didn't spend a single dollar on fixing up a single stadium. Sports brings normalcy to any country. We wanted the young people of Iraq to live their lives, to have another way of expressing themselves.'⁴ He pointed out that 60 per cent of the country's population were under twenty-five. These young men – and women – had energy and ambition, which needed to find an outlet. Jobs were vital, but so was sport, in order to channel aggression, instil discipline, foster a sense of national identity and teach tolerance.

Fatfat said that another challenge in the early weeks had been to decide which Iraqis should be excluded from sport because they had worked for Saddam. He said: 'It was not easy. People said, you can't take this man or that man because he was in the Ba'ath Party. But I estimate that only 2 per cent of the Ba'ath Party, maximum 5 per cent, believed in it. People had to join to live. Coaches, people like that, who had been in the party, said to us, "What could we do? We had to join the party."'

They were working alongside Don Eberly, who had advised the White House on what were called 'faith-based and community initiatives' – which meant that he believed society had to be bound by faith to have any strength. He was also passionate about the importance of fathers in the upbringing of children, a reaction to the growth in the USA of single-parent families, and had founded the National Fatherhood Initiative in 1994. He was an amiable, intelligent man – and too decent to cope with Iraqis as they jostled to take over powerful and lucrative positions in Iraqi sport.

One of Eberly's colleagues in the CPA said: 'He had a very difficult task to face, and he did set in place the foundations of the process towards regime change in sport. He also had the vision to realize getting an Iraqi team to the Athens Olympics would potentially be an extremely powerful symbol of the new Iraq. He lacked resources (both experienced manpower and funding) and was really in the country for too short a time to be able to see any strategy come to fruition.'

Before he left in August 2003 Eberly often talked about his vision for sport in Iraq. It was dreamy stuff, which had little relevance to the plotting and squabbling of men such as al-Samarrai and Hussein Saeed. 'Iraq is a nation of young people. We must influence this group. The good news is that ordinary people are stepping up and helping to meet the needs of civil government. We must remove the remnants of the Ba'ath Party and democratize sport. We must build a dynamic sports programme, starting with an infusion of footballs.'[5] But Eberly did not understand the ferocity of the battles that were taking place among Iraqis. Sharar Haydar, the ex-international who had become president of the Free Iraq Olympic Group, arrived in Baghdad soon after the fall of Saddam determined to play a role in creating new, honest sports organizations. It is not easy to be certain about what happened next since everyone involved told a different story – always to their own credit – but it is undeniable that men sought to win positions that would give them status, power and wealth, using whatever methods they thought necessary.

Haydar told me that he only wanted to help his country.[6] 'I wanted nothing for myself', he said. 'But the others, they wanted to get into office, to get a title. Then they would sit there and do nothing. They are all corrupt. It is the Arab culture and I hate it. All of these guys had worked for Uday. They all had brown noses from those days.' He said that Hussein Saeed had begged him to take over the Iraqi Football Association. 'He said, "Sharar, we miss you. I want you to be president of the association." He said that people like Ahmed Radhi were against him. He said he would be my assistant. He called me "sir". I was embarrassed by this. He thought I was strong, powerful.'

'I said I did not want to become president. I told Don Eberly that Hussein Saeed should run the association. I thought Hussein Saeed was a good man, quiet and well educated. I did not know how much he had learned from Uday. He had become a snake. Don Eberly did not want Hussein. He said to me, "Sharar, you know that Saeed worked for Uday." I said, "Yes, but he had to, and he had nothing to do with the torture." I said, "Saeed is a big name in Iraq and has connections abroad." I convinced him to let Saeed stay at the association. Eberly liked me very much and wanted me to do the job. I said no. I said that, if I do anything, I will be president of the national Olympic committee. I said I wanted to be involved in all sports, not only football.'[7]

During the early summer of 2003 Haydar battled with al-Samarrai to control the Interim Committee to Administer Sport. But Haydar lost and returned to London in July. He told me that he had been disgusted when he had met other members of the committee. 'They were the same old faces. The Mafia of Uday. They were all corrupt, liars. I was naive. I could not believe what I saw. Uday was dead, but the tail was alive. So I resigned all my positions and left Iraq. But I will not give up the fight. I will be back, and these people will have to go. Everyone knows they are thieves. No one trusts them.'

Haydar was also unhappy about Raad Hammoudi, the former goalkeeper who had captained Iraq in the 1986 World Cup in Mexico. After the American-led invasion Hammoudi had returned from Jordan, where he had become a successful businessman since leaving Iraq in the late 1980s. Hammoudi had saved his former club, al-Shurta, which had been controlled by one of Saddam's relatives, from bankruptcy and set up various businesses, distributing mobile phones and electrical goods for Western companies. He also established a sports newspaper.

Haydar said that Hammoudi wanted to become a force in Iraqi sport, by taking control of the Olympic committee or, failing that, becoming president of the IFA. 'He was close to Uday. He was given a factory in Baghdad by his friends in the government. He is an opportunist. He is not popular', Haydar said. But an Iraqi businessman, who shuttled between his homes in London and Baghdad, thought this was simplistic nonsense. He told me: 'Hammoudi is a much loved national hero. Sure, there is a lot of speculation about him. The word is that after he retired he set up a sports retail business. Uday said he wanted to become his partner. Hammoudi had no choice. You could not refuse Uday. It was like the Mafia. You did what you were told. After a while Hammoudi got fed up and left for Jordan.'

This source said that there were 'no saints' in Iraq. He said Hammoudi had settled in Jordan, married the daughter of a local television presenter and become a successful businessman. It was rumoured, he told me, that Hammoudi and Uday did business together. But he emphasized that this was only a rumour and, even if it was true, it did not mean Hammoudi was a bad person. 'Hammoudi is like a lot of people. They left Iraq and made money. After Saddam fell they came back and invested. Without him al-Shurta would not exist.'

Hammoudi had been born in 1958. He made his international début when he was eighteen. In his twenties he captained al-Shurta and the national team but then, for reasons he never explained, retired before he reached thirty. Haydar said: 'He voted against me in the elections for the Olympic committee. He would not tell me why. All these people are the same. They want to get a position for themselves so that they can make money.'

Al-Samarrai and Fatfat were joined in the late summer by the unlikely figure of Mark Clark, who became the CPA's main adviser on sport to the Iraqi Ministry of Youth and Sport. When the CPA dissolved itself in June 2004, Clark became an independent adviser to al-Samarrai's Olympic committee.[8] He had gone to school in Scotland. After Edinburgh University he became a solicitor, specializing in intellectual property law and sports law. He helped set up the Scottish Premier League in 1997 and worked for Glasgow Rangers and the Scottish Rugby Union. He had had a spell in India, where he worked in cricket and in the Bollywood film industry. He was one of those rare characters who give off positive energy. He was restless and a natural adventurer. Had he been born 150 years earlier, he would probably have been an explorer.[9]

He was an officer in the Territorial Army, Britain's reserve, and had arrived in Basra in June 2003 for a six-month tour of duty. There was a vacancy within the CPA for someone to investigate how to repair sport in the south, and Clark jumped at it. He said: 'I had a blank piece of paper. I went around meeting people, finding what they needed.' After Eberly returned to the USA, Clark took over and moved to the capital. There were several hundred sports clubs in the city and the rest of the country, small, medium and large, which had always been funded and run by the government. There were forty sports federations, twenty-one of which were entitled to send athletes to the Olympics. All these clubs and federations had been run by the Ba'ath Party. Clark told the Iraqis that they would have to start again, from the bottom upwards. He said that Iraqis would have to elect people to run sport. They gasped and said that would mean hundreds of elections. So be it, said Clark; that is democracy.

Iraqis were always complaining to Clark about people who, they said, should be banned from holding office in the reconstituted sports system because they had belonged to the Ba'ath Party. Clark understood how people felt – he told friends that he understood why people thought it was unfair that those who had prospered under Saddam should do well in the new Iraq – but he said he could not ban everyone who had worked for Saddam. He told me that he had established these rules: 'Anyone who was in the top three tiers of the Ba'ath Party, plus anyone even in lower ranks who had an association with criminal activity, such as fraud, murder or torture, was banned from either voting in, or being a candidate for, any election for any club or federation position. Was it the right policy? I don't know. It was crude, but the CPA was facing exceptionally difficult challenges in trying to effect some visible regime change. What alternative was there? The regime was so embedded in every walk of life and even pervaded sports organizations. How do you make a fresh start after thirty-five years of a regime like this?'

Clark grappled with the problem of how to finance sport. Clubs in Iraq had always been financed by local or national government or by state enterprises. Who would pay for them now? Was the new Iraq always going to be a socialist state? This seemed unlikely since it was controlled by the free marketeers of the White House. If it was a capitalist economy, then who would pay for sport? The major clubs, such as al-Zawraa, would probably survive – they were national institutions that would attract private investment – but what would happen to the provincial clubs in the smaller towns? Clark fretted about this, conscious that it would be a disaster for the country if these clubs went bankrupt.

He said that he hoped to persuade the government to help clubs become self-sufficient by, for example, allowing them to develop their land, which in theory belonged to the government. 'It's not going to be a quick fix', he said. 'There are all sorts of problems and grey areas. In the long term the object is to make clubs independent of government. Any solution that involves private funding depends on the state of the economy in Iraq. But there will probably always have to be state support for some clubs.'

In September new officials were elected to run sport in Iraq in over 500 separate elections. In January 2004 the sports federations sent delegates to Dukan, a resort in the north of the country, to elect a new national Olympic committee – Baghdad was considered unsafe since many Iraqis regarded the new sports set-up as a symbol of American domination. Journalists who went to Dukan were not impressed; they thought the voting had been rigged by the Americans, though there was no evidence to support this. Al-Samarrai was elected president, unopposed; Hussein Saeed, of the IFA, became one of three vice-presidents although, strictly speaking, this should not have been allowed as he was only interim president of the football association.

'This paves the way for Iraq to compete in the Summer Games if the International Olympic Committee accepts the new committee and lifts the suspension it imposed on Iraq in May 2003', wrote one journalist. 'Iraqi officials, many of them smoking and overweight, sat in rows of a hotel auditorium and applauded each delegate as they cast ballots in a glass box.'

Al-Samarrai said 'the historic elections' showed how far Iraq had come since the fall of Saddam. He promised not to forget 'the painful past'. He said: 'We have turned a new leaf, just as the country of Iraq is turning a new page in its history.'

He said: 'I hope Iraq will send athletes to the Olympics in Greece so that everyone knows that we are still on the sporting map. Uday was only interested in football. Now we have less money, but it's shared better. We have six sports in which Iraq will participate in Greece, plus the soccer team. We have two swimmers and some wrestlers. Boxers are in qualification. We have weightlifters, a tae kwon do athlete and two track competitors, including one female, who was not allowed to participate under Saddam. We want to encourage women to compete in sport. Uday's behaviour was so bad that women did not dare practise any sport on a professional level because they were afraid of being mistreated, humiliated, even raped by him.' He said that Iraq had almost no sports facilities. 'In Baghdad we have only the main stadium complex for football, track and field, a gymnasium, a pool and tennis. But it has been damaged, it is not ready for normal events. The football field has been replaced, but we've only just started reconstructing things.'

He claimed that 'all Iraqis' were desperate to see the team walk out at the opening ceremony in Athens beneath the country's 'new flag'. This was odd since there was not really a new flag, just the old red, white and black one, with the three green stars across the white, with the words *Allahu Akbar* in the middle, but written in a different style in view of the rumour that the original script was in Saddam's handwriting. But al-Samarrai seemed unaware of this and of the fact that he was despised as an American stooge.

The IOC had urged the Iraqis to elect a woman to their new Olympic committee, but the one female candidate, Dr Iman Sabeeh, a former runner, stood aside when she tied with a man for the fifth and final place on the NOIC executive board. Al-Samarrai soon found a place for her, however, which showed he had a shrewd eye for public relations. She was an instant hit with the international press.

She was forty-one, attractive, modest, had a Ph.D. in biomechanics, and was a wife and mother. She was head of the Iraqi Women's Sports Federation and was a legend in Iraq, though her running career had been ended by injury when she was only twenty-four. She remembered how Uday punished athletes: 'The bodyguards brought a coffin and put it in front of the athlete. They told them, "You're dead. We're going to bury you alive." Then they closed the coffin and nailed it shut. Twenty-four hours later they would open it and let the person out. They were alive but scared. Some of them thought they were going to die. Maybe some did, psychologically anyway.'[10]

Sabeeh was a fine 400 and 800 metres runner in the 1980s, though her times were unimpressive by the standards of 2004. What mattered most, however, was not how fast she could run but the fact she was doing it at all, because Uday did not believe that women should be athletes. She said she had been training hard for the 1984 Olympics in

Los Angeles. Then Uday took control of sport. She said: 'Once he took over, women athletes never travelled outside Iraq again.' She was voted the most popular female athlete in the country every year from 1980 until 1987, which infuriated Uday, who hated anyone being popular.

In 1985 she needed surgery on an ankle injury. Uday said he would send her abroad for treatment if she joined his new club, al-Rasheed. She refused and was forced to retire in 1987. She said: 'If I had gone to his club, I would have lost my reputation and the love of the people, so I refused. I was forced to retire so young. I wanted to be a world champion, but I cannot bend the left foot the same as the right. I have no spring in it.' She wanted more Iraqi girls to play sport. 'Sport gives you such confidence. Remember, not all of the Islamic culture follows the conservative side you see; some of it is also modern. Iraq is not a fundamentalist country. It is well educated. Girls are not forbidden from sport. It helps them grow.'

Football was treated differently from other sports in 2003. Although it was an Olympic sport – teams at the Games consisted of players aged under twenty-three, with three over-age players allowed – football owed its allegiance to FIFA, not to the IOC. Football was professional and generated huge amounts of money, in a way that most Olympic sports never could. It was the most popular sport in Iraq by far. Although it had been simultaneously pillaged and starved of invest-ment by Uday, it was capable of turning over millions of pounds, even in a developing country such as Iraq. Under Uday tickets for top matches had been virtually free. There was no attempt to organize sponsorship and advertising or to sell television rights. Football existed as a hobby, a propaganda weapon, for the regime. Organized properly, there was money to be made from ticket sales, from advertising, spon-sorship and, most important, from the sale of television rights. The Iraqi diaspora around the world was big and affluent and wanted to watch games involving their favourite clubs and their country. The possibilities were limitless in the new millennium, thanks to the Internet and mobile phones as well as television.

Iraq did not have the social and economic infrastructure to support other big-money global sports, such as tennis, golf and horse-racing.

It could not compete in events that required expensive equipment, such as gymnastics. Most Olympic sports, from archery to weightlifting, would always be small and poor. But football was a cash cow.

Because it was so popular, Clark had to be careful. The heroes of Iraqi football were national celebrities. They squabbled constantly – over who had done what and when under Uday, over who should run the sport now that he was dead, over who was a crook and who was not – but Clark knew it would be dangerous for the CPA to favour one man over another since each had hundreds of thousands of fans. He told the Ministry of Youth and Sport that the Iraqi Football Association should be allowed to carry on, under the control of people who disliked each other – such as Hussein Saeed and Ahmed Radhi – while the other forty sports federations belonging to the Olympic movement elected new committees to replace the Ba'athist ones which had been dissolved. Clark said this was the sensible decision, though he knew that it meant that the men who ran the IFA would continue to bicker and cheat while other sports had to come to terms with the new realities. 'It would have been difficult and controversial to tackle the IFA at the beginning because of the personalities involved. These were big names, with big followings. We had to move slowly', he said.

He had little time for the men who ran the association. He told friends that they were all the same – egotists who wanted to exercise power and to be famous and rich. They thought that the act of being elected was enough; being in office did not involve doing work, only enjoying the prestige and perks. He said: 'People think they are suitable to run a big sports organization like the football association because they used to be a great athlete. It doesn't work like that.' He said there was 'a lack of transparency' at the IFA, which was a polite way of saying that no one knew how money was spent. 'You must have transparency', he told me. 'There is virtually zero transparency in the IFA at the moment. This is a problem if you want to build a good relationship with the media, sponsors and donors. Without transparency there is a real risk that people will suspect, rightly or wrongly, that people are lining their own pockets.'

I asked him about a company called Iraqi Sport in London, which handled sponsorship deals for sport in Iraq. I asked him if he knew about rumours – which people such as Ahmed Radhi and Yamam Nabeel treated as fact – that this company was part of a conspiracy involving himself, al-Samarrai, al-Samarrai's relatives and other people. He laughed and said that he had heard these stories. He said that they showed that Iraqis saw conspiracies everywhere, which was not surprising after Saddam.

He said that Iraqi Sport had approached him in 2003, with a proposal to handle sponsorship for every sport. Clark said they had made such an impressive presentation that he gave them a contract. For the record, and to show that he was not part of a plot to rob Iraq, he explained in detail how it worked. He sent me a long e-mail, detailing what he called 'the legal rights structure that attempts to keep some sensible interim controls on commercialization by the federations'. I read it once, twice and again and still did not understand it fully. There were clauses and sub-clauses and sub-clauses of the sub-clauses; it read like a proper contract and, while I was not a lawyer, it seemed beyond doubt that Clark had behaved entirely properly. He told me that he had been forced to employ Iraqi Sport because there was no one in Iraq with similar expertise. In essence Iraqi Sport went out and found sponsors; they kept 10 per cent of whatever they raised, which seemed fair to me.

Another source in Iraq said that Clark had been right to be cautious about sacking Saeed and his pals at the IFA: 'It would have been relatively easy for Clark to engineer the removal of people at the association. But the alternatives were no better. That was the problem throughout the country. There weren't any good people who hadn't been involved with the previous government. There was no middle-management. There was no such thing as budgeting or accountancy. Everyone was terrified of making a decision. They couldn't grasp the new way of doing things.'

'There's a problem throughout sport in Iraq, throughout the country, of honesty. If you asked me how corrupt the football association was by Western standards, I would say seven, maybe eight, out of ten. Of course, they were lining their own pockets. That was how things were done in Iraq. That was all they knew. We need figureheads like Hussein Saeed but, on the other hand, the football association must have an efficient administration. We have to give the people there incentives to perform. They would still benefit materially, but it would be linked to performance.'

Al-Samarrai was also unhappy about the IFA. But, like Clark, he realized that men like Saeed were national heroes, who could not simply be fired. He knew that the Olympic committee had limited influence over football. However, Iraqis believe that a man must believe in himself if he wants to be taken seriously – in plain English this means that they boast constantly – and al-Samarrai talked to me as if he could make or break the key figures in football. 'There were a lot of politics in the association. A lot of people there told me that they had important relationships with the Asian Football Confederation and with FIFA that could benefit Iraqi football. I am talking about Hussein Saeed, Ahmed Radhi and others. Radhi wanted to be president and to run all football. Each one claimed that FIFA supported them. I asked for proof, a document. Only Saeed produced one.'

Al-Samarrai said that he had been concerned about the way that the association handled money. 'You have to remember that Hussein Saeed worked with Uday for many years. We investigated but found nothing seriously wrong. There are still rumours about accounts abroad and money being missing, but we cannot do more.' Mounzer Fatfat, the Lebanese-American who monitored sport in Iraq for Washington, said: 'People tell me that Saeed is a Ba'athist. I have talked to him and he has said, no. He said that he loves football. He said he had to do what was necessary to survive. He said that, yes he worked for Uday, but he was not his God. He said he did his best but did not want to be killed.'

Dr Basil Abdul Mahdi, the veteran bureaucrat who was an adviser to al-Samarrai, also had strong views on Saeed and the football association. 'Many people do not like the association. All over the Asian world Hussein is respected as a great player, but he uses the association for his own interests. I have told him this to his face, that he is running football for himself. The national team is a travelling circus. The players don't want to stay in Iraq. You see the Kurd [Abdul

Khaliq, the association's treasurer] everywhere except in Iraq. They are a club team now.'

'Hussein gave Ammo Baba a job because he wanted his support for the election in June for the presidency of the association. I told al-Samarrai that it was a problem. Hussein was not popular. Everyone knew he used the period after the invasion until the election to get support by giving people money, giving them trips abroad. Hussein came to my house before the election – he is my student – and said, "Herr Doctor, I have been nominated by FIFA to head the Iraqi Football Association." I said, "Hussein, respect yourself. Go and sit in your house and everything will come to you." I said, "For thirteen years you were a servant of Uday. Now you must be quiet." Then he tried to co-operate with Sharar Haydar. Then they kept postponing the election so that Hussein had more time to get support.

In the days before the Iraqi Olympians – twenty-two footballers, six male athletes, one female sprinter and nineteen officials – left for Greece the media swarmed around the team, eager to hear how they had overcome adversity. American reporters were especially keen to hear how grateful the footballers and athletes were to be rid of Saddam. The Iraqis agreed that life had been hard, often brutal, under Uday, but otherwise did not say the right things. Raad Abbas Rasheed, a 28-year-old baker who was competing at tae kwon do, said: 'My childhood was tough. I had to fight to survive. Some kind of cruelty rose up. That is why I feel satisfied when I fight.' A swimmer, Mohammed Salih Abbas, was even less satisfactory for the American media. He said the pool where he trained in Baghdad had been taken over by Saddam's militia just before the invasion. Afterwards the Americans had taken it as 'their own club Med'. He said: 'The US army is not in Iraq for recreation, to swim and drink Coca-Cola. They don't need my pool. I kept asking if I could use it, and they said, "Come back tomorrow, tomorrow". We are not stupid people. We don't need the Americans to show us how to live.' The only woman in the squad, nineteen-year-old Ala Hikmat, who was competing in the 100 metres, said that the Olympic committee had given her £30 a month to live while she trained and wondered where all the American money was going. She said she was sick of the fighting outside her home. 'I can run, but not faster than a bullet', she said.

The feel-good story that the media wanted came from Houston, Texas, not Baghdad.[11] It centred on a 48-year-old American called Maurice Watkins, nicknamed 'Termite' by the press since he had spent a few months working as a pest control contractor for the CPA in Iraq. Watkins was a former professional boxer who had won fifty-nine out of sixty-seven fights and had once fought for the world light-welterweight title. He had met an official from the CPA towards the end of 2003 and had mentioned his boxing prowess; he was immediately invited to train the group of young men who passed for the Iraqi boxing team. He met them in a gym in Baghdad. 'They had no head-gear, no groin protectors, no mouth guards; half of them were bare-foot. The coaches told them to start fighting and they did. There was blood everywhere. I told them to stop. I said, "Let's learn to do it the right way."'

Over the next eight months Watkins trained the team. He was a dream for the CPA: he was garrulous, approachable, fun and, above all, positive about Iraq. Every training session opened with the team shouting, 'Iraq is back!' None of the team qualified for the Games, but the IOC said he could take a boxer to Athens anyway, which was 'a wild card' in sports-speak. He chose an amiable 24-year-old flyweight called Najah Ali. He was clean-cut, intelligent (he was a graduate in computer science) and spoke excellent English; best of all, he loved America. As he prepared for Athens in Houston, where he had been training, Najah said: 'There's a lot of hope in Iraq now. Being in Greece will be the biggest thing in my life. I am very proud. I will fight for my country, for my people, for our freedom. We want to prove to the world there is normal life in Iraq.'

Meanwhile, in Baghdad, Mark Clark had been having more problems with the IFA. He said: 'When we came to choose the football delegation for Athens, the rules allowed us to take seven officials and eighteen players. Hussein Saeed wanted twenty-two players. That was the normal number for a FIFA tournament, and he was used to operating by FIFA rules. But the Games are different and only permit eighteen accredited places for a football team. That was a big problem because it meant any extra players would not be paid for by the Games' organizers, wouldn't be allowed into secure areas and so on. Hussein also wanted to bring nine officials. I said I would see what I could do, but there was no way. The Games' organizers said seven officials was the limit. Hussein was away and could not be contacted so I explained the situation to Abdul Khaliq, the treasurer, and he decided which two officials to drop from the delegation: he chose the doctor and an assistant coach.' Clark told friends that he was 'disgusted' by the episode. 'All these people care about is having jolly trips abroad. How can you leave the doctor behind?' said one of Clark's friends.

12

Ammo changes his mind and the boys do well in Greece

It was the summer of 2004, and Ammo Baba was glad to be back in Baghdad. The temperatures were soaring, and violence was spreading, but he was in his own home, being visited by friends and admirers. He told me: 'I have guests here in my house in Baghdad all the time. We are eating Iraqi food. I am sorry I could not invite you to eat with me in France. It was not my house. I have so many invitations to go abroad. I have one from Assyrians in Detroit. They want me to bring a team. They insist I come with the boys.' He thought it would be safer if I visited him after the Americans dissolved the Coalition Provisional Authority and handed power to the interim Iraqi government on 30 June. 'Bombs shake my house all the time', he said. 'It is not good. It will be better after the Americans have gone. Safer for you then.'

He did not want to go to Detroit, which was too far, but he was looking forward to taking the under-16 team to Gothenburg for the Gothia Cup. He said that his boys would do well there, playing against teams of the same age, unlike in France, where he felt he had been misinformed by the charity organizing the event. I said that it would be good to see him again and offered to buy his brother Pnouel a ticket. This was not wholly altruistic; I thought the meeting would make for a good episode in my book. But Ammo did not care one way or the other about seeing Pnouel. I asked Pnouel if he would like to meet Ammo, and he shrugged and said that would be fine, but was obviously not bothered.

I told Ammo that the Gothia Cup was a major event. Two hundred and seventy-five teams had taken part in the first competition in 1975, but in 2004 the organizers expected 1,500 teams, in age groups ranging from eleven years old up to eighteen, from sixty-one countries around the world. Ammo clucked approvingly, pleased that this was a serious tournament. I said that there would be over 4,000 matches, that a quarter of the teams were female (he had been told by Shia extremists to forget his plan to run teams for girls at his school in Baghdad) and that 40,000 people would watch the opening ceremony. I said it would be like the World Cup. It seemed to me that a man like him, who had been such a great player and coach, deserved more than a tournament for boys in the French country-side. The French organizers in Brittany had worked hard and had put on a first-class show, but it was hardly the big time, which Ammo deserved.

A group of Iraqis who lived in Sweden had raised the money for Ammo's trip. One, Layth Alattar, an engineer with a mobile phone company who had lived in Gothenburg for fifteen years, told me: 'There are eight of us working on this. We have raised the money for the fares and other expenses. We want to show Swedes there is more to Iraq than war. Iraq has sent teams to Gothenburg before and twice won cups in the 1980s. We want to wind the clock back to that golden age.' I asked him where teams stayed, and he said in schools or with families. 'Ah,' I said, 'so Ammo would not be in an hotel.' 'No,' said Alattar, 'we don't have the budget for that.' I real-ized that, just as in Brittany, money was tight. Ammo envisaged chauffeur-driven limousines and decent hotels; instead, he would be staying at the home of an Iraqi exile. I thought about mentioning this to Ammo and decided that it would only upset him.

With a few weeks to go there were problems. Alattar said that they did not have Swedish visas yet for Ammo and his team. He said that he had sent someone to Amman, Jordan, to negotiate with the Swedish embassy there. But it was too late: the Swedes would not issue visas to Ammo and his team. Alattar was distressed and said that he had trusted colleagues to do the necessary work and they had let him, Ammo and the boys down. Later he wrote to me: 'One of the main reasons for the rejection of the visas is that most of the young players have a "travel document" issued by the CPA and not a real passport. The Swedish authority does not recognize the CPA travel document. As a matter of fact, they do not recognize the CPA itself! The man in the Swedish embassy said that they would "never" accept travel documents issued by the CPA.'

I was baffled. Surely Alattar and his friends had asked about visas long ago? I e-mailed the Swedish embassy in Amman. A diplomat there replied: 'During the contacts we had with the Iraqis (in Sweden and in Iraq) we informed them extensively which documents are needed to apply for a Schengen visa.[1] In accordance with Swedish laws and regulations we also offered guidance to the envoys/representatives of the team on how to fill them out. I understand fully the problems involved in communicating in a language alien to both us and the Iraqi applicants – English – therefore the procedure has also been explained by our Arabic-speaking colleagues. I also appreciate the difficult circumstances presently at hand in Iraq. The Gothia Cup is a tournament that has been taking place for a number of years, and Swedish embassies around the world understand the importance of broad participation.'

Once again Iraqis saw themselves as victims of a conspiracy, just as Ammo had done in Brittany. I wondered again if Saddam had damaged the national psyche. Iraqis assumed that they were going to be cheated, because that was what always happened. They had grown up in a society where you survived through cunning, by cultivating the right people, not by behaving decently. Even exiles had been infected by this virus. After all, Yamam Nabeel, who was an intelligent young man, was convinced that Mark Clark had struck a dubious deal with a group of businessmen in London, which I knew was nonsense. Yamam was sure that Clark must be crooked because that was how everyone in Iraq behaved. Nick Ask, who was so articulate about football in Iraq, told me: 'Iraq has been so corrupted that dishonesty is part of the culture. It will take many years to recover. Saddam destroyed honesty and integrity. He stripped Iraqis of their dignity. The only way to rebuild is through a clear, just and adequate law and judicial system.'

Ammo was more concerned about what was happening in Iraq than about the Gothia Cup. It was clear that he had been mistaken about the situation improving after the CPA was dissolved. During

July 2004, the month after the Americans handed power to the Iraqis, there were an average of sixty attacks a day, from bombs and mortars to shootings. On 28 July 129 people died.[2] That day a suicide bomber killed seventy-one people in Baquba, north of Baghdad, when a minibus packed with explosives blew up near a market and a queue of men waiting to enlist at a police station. There were attacks in Ramadi, Fallujah and Balad-Ruz in the west, Kirkuk in the north, Suweira in the south and in Baghdad. In Suweira, a mainly Shia town, Iraq's armed forces fought Wahabbites, extremist Sunnis who had originally come from Saudi Arabia and who had regularly attacked the Shia majority and police. One man said: 'The Wahabbites say we are Jews – collaborators with America. That is why they are killing us.'

Journalists speculated that the violence was temporary, that it was aimed at disrupting a conference to elect the interim parliament that would sit until elections in January 2005. But they were wrong. The bombings, kidnappings and the videotaped beheadings of hostages went on, and on. People in Baghdad tried to live normally. They went to funfairs, took their children to playgrounds and promenaded along the banks of the Tigris in the evening. The more prosperous ones went to the Baghdad Equestrian Club, a race-track, which infuriated Muslim fundamentalists, who abhorred gambling. One young man, after he had been swimming at a fashionable club in the city, said: 'It's a release to be here. I forget all about security.' But then he added: 'At home I think about the rogues and thieves, how they could burst in at any moment and rob me.'

There were growing fears that Iraq would become a new Iran, ruled by intolerant clerics. For example, Moqtada al-Sadr, a Shia cleric from Najaf, whose followers were habitually violent, issued an edict in July permitting the murder of people who sold alcohol. Anyone who worked for the new Iraq was a target for the militant Shias and Sunnis. If these thugs had a coherent plan – and many did not – it was a desire to destroy everything so that another country would emerge, built on whatever religious principles they espoused. But many kidnappings were carried out by criminals, who sold hostages to religious groups.

Zawadi Shaati, the chairman of the district area council set up by the coalition in Sadr City, was a typical victim. He was seized, tortured and shot in the head because he had co-operated with the Americans. His body was left hanging from a lamppost, a sign around his neck proclaiming that he had been killed by the 'Mahdi Army', showing that Shia followers of Moqtada al-Sadr were responsible. But 'collaborators' like him were also being killed by Sunni extremists who were loyal to Saddam and by foreign terrorists who had imported their mad *jihad* to Iraq.

A woman who was an interpreter with US forces was killed and her head placed on top of a box containing her ashes. An Iraqi told journalists that women like her were seen as 'the whores of the occupation'. He said: 'Some Iraqis are so backward they expect their women to be serving them and hate the idea of them working with foreigners.' The media also found a new hate figure to rival Osama bin Laden: Abu Musab al-Zarqawi, a 38-year-old Jordanian who the Americans said had masterminded scores of bombings, shootings and kidnappings and who, they said, personally beheaded hostages. He was a Sunni, preached violence against Shias and was devoid of humanity. The Americans offered a reward of $10 million dollars for his capture, the same as for bin Laden.[3]

Understandably Adnan Hamad and his team were glad to escape all this when they travelled to China for the Asian Cup, the continent's equivalent of the European Championship. Hamad took the Olympic squad, all but three of whom were under twenty-three, because he thought this was the best way to prepare for Greece. But other countries sent their full teams. As a lifelong Ba'athist, Hamad thought the invasion had been a crime. 'What have the Americans done for Iraq? They have destroyed everything', he said when he arrived in Beijing, *en route* for Chengdu, where they were based for the first round. Officials with the team, anxious not to offend the Americans, without whom the IFA would have been broke, intervened and said that actually things were improving in Iraq. One said that he was 'off to get mobile phones for the players so they can call their families'.

Hamad said that the violence in Iraq had forced the suspension of the league. Often players could not train because of the fighting. 'We have no proper pitches. Teams won't come to Baghdad, and we don't have the funds to send our teams abroad. But the Iraqi people need us to win to lift their spirits', he said. The Iraqi players were delighted to arrive in Chengdu, 1500 miles south of Beijing. It is a bustling city of almost 9 million people, the centre of Sichuan, China's most populous province. It is renowned for its cuisine and its night life, though the players knew that Hamad, a fearsome disciplinarian, would send home any player who broke his many rules.

They had been drawn in a tough group, with Saudi Arabia, ranked 26th in the world, Uzbekistan, at 51, and Turkmenistan, ranked 90. Iraq were ranked at 40, but that was their senior squad and Hamad had brought mostly youngsters. The Saudis were a first-class team, and the Uzbeks were under-rated; the only match that seemed relatively easy was against Turkmenistan. The first match, against the Uzbeks, was a bad-tempered disaster. Iraq lost 1–0 and had a man sent off (as did the Uzbeks). Afterwards Hamad growled that his boys had missed easy chances. The next game, against Turkmenistan, who had drawn 2–2 against Saudi Arabia, ended with Iraq winning 3–2, though Hamad admitted later that they had been 'lucky'. To reach the quarter-finals Iraq had to beat Saudi Arabia, which no one thought likely. But Iraq won 2–1.

There was uproar in Baghdad. The city had shut down for the game, which was broadcast live on radio and television. At the final whistle the city shook with gunfire, as Iraqis celebrated this famous victory. Al-Jazeera, the Arabic satellite station based in Qatar, which prided itself on its commitment to serious news, interrupted its news bulletin to show the final minutes of the match. In Baghdad people surrounded Western reporters, eager to explain why they were so excited. They said that football was a relief after so much violence, that Iraq's players could play without fear now that Uday had gone, and that every Iraqi – Sunni, Shia, Kurd or Christian – could unite behind the football team.

A few days later Iraq were heading home after losing 3–0 to China in Beijing. (The Chinese lost to Japan in the final.) Once again an Iraqi player, the goalkeeper this time, was sent off. Hamad apologized to the Chinese but, overall, said he was delighted with his team. 'We have energy and potential', he said. 'Our aim is to do well in Greece and to qualify for the World Cup.'

On the morning of Sunday 8 August 2004 the Iraqi Olympic team – twenty-two footballers, six male athletes, one female sprinter and nineteen officials – drove under armed escort from Baghdad to the airport. Their bags were searched, in case someone had planted explosives, and they boarded a Royal Australian Air Force C-130 Hercules for the short flight to Amman, from where they would fly to Athens by more conventional means. The drive to Amman would have been tiring and dangerous. The Olympians would have been a target for extremists, who did not approve of Iraq's participation in the Games, and for criminals, who knew the ransom value of this party.

They arrived in Athens the next day. Before they could leave the sparkling new terminal, built for the Games, they had to be accredited. This was the first crisis. The athletes and their coaches, the officials, including al-Samarrai and Mark Clark, were dealt with quickly. But the football squad was different. Hussein Saeed had brought twenty-two players, instead of eighteen. Other teams had also brought an extra player or perhaps two, who could be moved into the squad if someone was injured. But no one else brought twenty-two players. Saeed thought that, as a valued colleague of Sepp Blatter, FIFA's president, he could do as he wanted; FIFA rules allowed for twenty-two players at a tournament, and he thought that it was the Greeks' problem if they did not understand that. One of the Olympic volunteers assigned to look after the Iraqi delegation told me: 'It was a right old muddle at the airport. The Greeks did not know what was going on. They thought there'd be eighteen Iraqi players. But there were twenty-two. And the names didn't match the lists that the Iraqis had sent the Greeks in advance. In the end the Greeks gave up and said that the Iraqis would have to sort it when they got to their hotel. I think that only one official, the physiotherapist, and half a dozen of the players were accredited. The Iraqis' attitude was, we are here so let's get on the bus and get to the hotel. They did not understand, or want to understand, what was required of them.'

This volunteer, who asked to remain anonymous, was one of thousands at the Games, all wearing the same yellow T-shirt and shorts. Many were young, from Greece and around the world, but there were older people too. The volunteers had many jobs, from selling tickets to escorting athletes. They were always charming and helpful and ensured that the Games ran smoothly. It was kind of the Greeks to let the squad leave the terminal without accreditation. They had spent almost £1 billion on security for the Games, much of it donated by other governments, which was fifteen times the security budget for Atlanta in 1996. The precautions against terrorism were astonishing – including missiles to shoot down unauthorized aircraft, special forces trained to combat every conceivable threat and 70,000 police and troops. Accreditation was central to this. It took the form of plastic badges, covered with fraud-proof logos and symbols, which hung from the neck. These were issued to athletes, officials, the media, police, soldiers and volunteers. There were many grades. The best badges, for officials from the IOC, corporate sponsors, politicians, star broadcasters and so on, allowed the bearer to roam anywhere; the worst gave access to only the outer limits of the Olympics. You could tell by glancing at the badge whether someone was important. Without a badge you were nobody; the paying spectators did not have them, but they were only there because athletes perform better in front of a crowd and because television needs atmosphere.

The Iraqis strode out of the terminal building into the suffocating heat. There were flags everywhere, proclaiming that this was the home of the 2004 Olympics. The opening ceremony was scheduled for Friday night, but the airport and the city were already buzzing with anticipation. The Greeks had been planning this since 1997, and after so much effort – and controversy about costs, delays in construction and the best way to combat terrorism – they seemed bewildered that the big day was so close.

The Iraqis were surrounded by journalists, as they would be for the next three weeks. Al-Samarrai said that he hoped that sport would unite his country. 'It overcomes the differences between ethnic and religious groups. Through sport we hope to bring safety and security to the people. Our hope is to live in peace', he said.

The delegation divided. Hussein Saeed led his squad – Adnan Hamad, Abdul Khaliq, the football association's treasurer who so enjoyed his trips abroad, a physiotherapist, two coaches and an all-purpose fixer, and twenty-two players, average age twenty-two years and eight months, over half of whom came from the Shia slums of Sadr City – to a bus. They faced a three-and-a-half-hour journey to a hotel near Patras, on the north coast of the Peloponnese, where they were playing their first match against Portugal on Thursday 12 August, the day before the opening ceremony in Athens.

The rest of the delegation were driven to Athens. The athletes, coaches and Mark Clark, who was acting as press officer for the Iraqis, went to the Olympic Village, in the north of the city, where most of the 10,500 competitors at the Games would be staying. Al-Samarrai went to his five-star hotel, where rooms cost more than $600 a night. His friend and adviser Basil Abdul Mahdi did not rank as highly as al-Samarrai and had to make do with a four-star hotel where rooms cost $400 a night. Despite pleas from their government, the Games' organizers and travel agents, hotels in Athens increased prices massively for the Olympics. This meant many potential visitors did not come. The best hotels were still full, with Olympic officials, media, sponsors and assorted guests, but the city was far from fully booked. The football squad were staying at the Porto Rio Hotel, at Rio, 5 miles east of Patras. It was a four-star hotel, where double rooms cost about $270 a night. It had a private beach and had the usual trappings: swimming-pools, restaurants, gym, sauna, jacuzzi and superb gardens. It had a good view of the awesome new suspension bridge that linked Rio and the Peloponnese with Andirio and the mainland and which was about to make dozens of ferries in the port of Rio redundant. I checked into a more modest establishment in a resort near by. It was called the Florida Blue Bay and was owned by an English family.

The Porto Rio Hotel was ringed by police. It was the base for the men's and women's football teams who were playing in Patras over the next ten days. Rival teams never stayed at the same hotels in professional football, but this was the Olympics, where taking part was as important as winning, and teams were encouraged to mix. The Olympics and football were no longer happy partners. In the days when sport was divided into amateurs, who played for love, and professionals, who did it for the money, football had been an integral part of the Games. During the 1970s and 1980s, as money poured into sport, transforming it into a global industry, this distinction became a nonsense, known as 'shamateurism'. For example, everyone knew that top athletes were paid fortunes to appear at meetings, though they were nominally amateur. That was history now. All top-class performers at the Games were openly professional. It was not only in the glamour sports, such as athletics and tennis, that the big names earned their living by competing; so too did top competitors in the so-called minor sports, such as table tennis, sailing and rowing, who were sponsored by companies and governments and did not have regular jobs.

Most major football nations did not bother with the Olympics. Clubs did not want to lose their best young players, and national and regional football associations did not want players to take the Olympics seriously because that would threaten their own tournaments, such as the European Championship. FIFA had no official view but privately made it known that the Olympics were a football non-event. As a result there was a second-rate feel to the football. Portugal had a surprisingly strong team of players from major European clubs, including Cristiano Ronaldo, of Manchester United, who earned more in a week than the highest-paid Iraqi made in a year. The Argentines were useful. The Italians looked solid. But the rest – Australia, Tunisia, Serbia–Montenegro, Costa Rica, Ghana, Mali, South Korea, Japan, Morocco, Paraguay, Greece and Mexico – would have struggled in the English Second Division.[4]

It took time to get inside the Porto Rio Hotel. Police searched me on the outer perimeter and again at the hotel's entrance. But again there was a contrast with, say, the World Cup. There it would have been impossible to get into the hotel used by, say, the England team unless you were an accredited journalist attending a press conference. At a World Cup journalists could not wander around teams' hotels looking for people to interview. Young men and women from the various teams flip-flopped around the lobby of the Porto Rio. On the pitch footballers always look like adults, but close up they seem much younger. Most of these players looked like super-fit teenagers.

Most football teams, national and club, are transitory, with players coming and going constantly. But Stange had kept the Iraqi national squad, which was almost identical to this Olympic team, together permanently since the invasion. The Iraqis were more like friends from the same village than a group of professional footballers. Many were responsible for supporting their families. Without their son, who played in midfield, Hassan Atia's parents and eleven brothers and sisters would have been destitute. Hassan also had a wife to look after, the sister of a team-mate. Another player, Yassir Raad, helped his father, a driver in a government ministry, support his four siblings. It was clear to me that this team would be playing for themselves, to impress scouts from clubs outside Iraq. No one could blame them for that: for players who were attached to clubs in Iraq this was their big chance, to find a club that would pay them decent salaries. They would play for each other, too, because they were friends. Finally, they would be pleased if they could cheer up people back home, but that would not drive them, though I imagined that they would tell the media they were motivated by patriotism rather than self-interest.

I had heard much about Hussein Saeed, most of it bad. I told myself it was essential to approach him with an open mind. It would be absurd, I wrote in my notebook, to demonize him. He is an ex-footballer who did what was necessary to survive in a brutal dictatorship. Yes, he worked for a psychopath, Uday, and yes he prospered, but there was no evidence that he was a criminal. As one of Uday's lieutenants he must have known what was happening – the smuggling, extortion, rapes, murders and torture – and had done nothing about it. But, I reasoned, what could he have done? If he had protested, then he would have been killed. Most people would have behaved like him. He could have fled, but he had a life, a family and a home in Iraq.

I sat in the hotel lobby as journalists who had travelled from Athens to report the game against Portugal queued to interview him. They came from France, Italy, Germany, the USA, the Gulf and the Far East. He was keen to talk to the Americans, because their government paid the bills in Iraq. I assumed he would be idiotically pro-American, but he was not; he said that he did not think the Americans had done enough to provide security for ordinary Iraqis. However, he said that the invasion had been a good thing, which was not what his coach, Adnan Hamad, and most of the players thought. He had put on a considerable amount of weight since his playing days but still had the presence of a star. He reminded me of Ammo Baba; he had the same charisma.

I listened as he gave interview after interview. Some of the journalists were clutching Tom Farrey's story on the ESPN website about Saeed's malevolent influence, which Farrey had researched during the disastrous 'Goodwill Tour' of England in May.[5] But the story was too detailed for them, and assumed too much knowledge of Iraq; all they wanted were some punchy quotes from Saeed about Saddam (and Uday, if they knew who he was), about the struggle to rebuild football, about how proud and excited the Iraqis were to be at the Games. They were sports writers, not investigative journalists. The game between Iraq and Portugal on Thursday night was a side-show. They planned to weave quotes from Saeed into their match reports and get back to Athens as quickly as possible. So they scribbled his platitudes and were grateful. Most of what he said was uncontroversial, though occasionally he made claims that were plain wrong, such as saying that top players in Iraq earned $50,000 year. I thought this was harmless pride: he did not want to admit that Iraq's best players were paupers.

Then it was my turn. I started gently because I did not want to alarm him with questions that showed I had been studying Iraqi football closely. So I began with his career. Like most Iraqis who held important jobs, he was not what you would call modest. He told me he had played in three Olympic Games – in 1980, 1984 and 1988 – and at the World Cup in Mexico in 1986. He said that he had once been voted Asia's best player. He said he had scored so many goals in his career that he had lost count. We talked about Ammo Baba: 'We give his school equipment. We bought all the kit for the team that went to France. We gave the children pocket money. When Ammo was national coach, the players did not like him because all he cared about was fitness and they are Arabs. They like to relax, like Brazilians. If Ammo was a young man, he could be a coach for us. He is too old, so I have given him a job as an adviser on technical matters, how to develop football in schools.'

Other journalists were lining up to collect their quotes, so I asked Saeed if we could talk again another time. He smiled and nodded. He displayed the characteristics of Iraqis who had prospered under Saddam: evasiveness, arrogance and cod concern for 'the people'. But most of the exiles who had returned since the invasion were like this.

The Olympic volunteers who were assigned to the team soon became disillusioned. They had thought the Iraqis would be grate-ful to the Greeks but told me privately that they were surly and arrogant. 'The players and officials wouldn't carry their bags into the hotel. They thought someone else should do it', said one. The day after they arrived, the Iraqis negotiated their accreditation with the Greeks. The organizers were generous – they accredited twenty players, all of whom would be paid for by the Games. This left two players with no badges, which meant they could not travel on the official buses, sit on the touchline during matches or feel involved.

Olympic volunteers took a particular dislike to the football asso-ciation's treasurer, Abdul Khaliq. One volunteer told me: 'Khaliq sits around eating and smoking. He is always on the phone.' Nor did they care for Saeed: 'He is a pig. He is not interested in the team. He is arrogant and doesn't give a shit about anyone except himself. He has a single room, of course. So do Adnan and Khaliq. Everyone else has to share', said one volunteer. Another said: 'Iraqis who live in Greece keep coming to the hotel with pots of food. They think they can bring it into the hotel restaurant and eat with the team. We told them that they couldn't. Saeed and the others weren't very gracious about this. Maybe it's a cultural thing.'

That Thursday evening I drove into Patras for the match. Patras, with a population of around 250,000, is Greece's second port, after Piraeus. It is home to dozens of ferries, which sail to Italy and the Ionian Islands. It is a typical port, a place to stop for a coffee before heading off somewhere more interesting. However, because the Olympics are obsessed with sharing events around a host country, the Greeks had awarded Patras the honour of staging five men's and three women's football matches. They were the sort of games — a women's game between Germany and China, for example, and a men's game between Serbia–Montenegro and Tunisia — that would normally be played at small stadiums used by semi-professional teams. But this was the Olympics, and millions of pounds had been spent on top-class facilities that far outstripped local demand.

The new, 20,000-capacity Pampeloponnsiako Stadium on the outskirts of the city was stunning. Its grandstand was a work of art. It had soaring, super-bright floodlights. It was overlooked by the beautiful Mount Panachaikon. There were hundreds of police and Olympic volunteers to guide, advise and control. Roads were closed. Crash barriers were in place. Inside the ground a tannoy system blared out pop songs. All that was missing was a crowd. It was peculiar, like a lavish party with no guests.

In the dressing-room the Iraqis sat and waited for the new kit that Hamad had promised them. The two strips they had brought with them from Baghdad were, one Olympic volunteer said, 'a mess'. He said: 'They were worse than the kits that pub teams wear. There were no names, numbers were peeling off. It was shocking.' Thankfully, two sets of kit arrived just before kick-off. The Iraqis changed into all-white and trotted out. The official attendance for the match against Portugal was 5,689, but it looked to me as though they organizers had included everyone who was in the ground: police, volunteers and press. The crowd consisted mainly of young Iraqi men, many of whom were soon drunk.

There are many thousands of Iraqis in Europe, North America and Australia. There are thousands, too, in Greece — mostly illegal immigrants. They work on building sites, in restaurants, doing anything they can find that does not require documentation.[6] Most are

Kurds and Assyrians who have fled persecution in Iraq, but there are some Arabs because they can earn more working illegally in Greece than working openly in Iraq.

The Portuguese were expected to win the game easily. They went into an early lead, when an Iraqi scored an own goal, but then they lost interest and the Iraqis, in an Olympics football finals for the first time in sixteen years, discovered a new, previously undreamed of, gear. They equalized and then scored again. Early in the second half Portugal's Luis Boa Morte, who played for Fulham in the Premiership, was sent off. As he trudged off the pitch the Iraqi fans hurled abuse, coins and bottles at him. A middle-aged Iraqi woman scowled at these yobs. She said she had come from Australia with her husband to cheer on the team. 'Those people are not Christians', she told me. 'They are Kurds and Arabs.' The fans were not an attractive bunch. They had painted faces and waved Iraqi flags. Many were tattooed. Some were dressed as if they were suicide bombers, which was odd since they were clearly not devout Muslims from the amount of alcohol they were consuming. They were not violent, but they were disturbingly, hysterically patriotic.

The police stared at them and fingered their truncheons. Greece is not renowned for its racial tolerance, and it seemed to me that the police were looking for an excuse to thump the Iraqis. The Olympic volunteers, meanwhile, looked terrified. They had been told that the Olympics were about world peace and now found themselves surrounded by yelling, drunk, shirtless Arabs with hard faces.

Iraq scored a third goal, and then a fourth in injury time. It was hard to believe, but these unknown players from the slums of Baghdad had beaten a team whose value on the transfer market ran into tens of millions of pounds. This was what the media had been waiting for in Greece: a feel-good story. The news went around the world, that the brave Iraqis, who had suffered terribly under Saddam, had beaten the mighty Portuguese. At the post-match press conference Hussein Saeed, flanked by his friend Sepp Blatter, beamed. Blatter waved aside questions about whether it was right for him to embrace a man who had been one of Uday's lieutenants and said that Iraq should be proud of its team.

Hamad was delighted too. But he was not going to let anyone think he approved of the occupation of Iraq: 'There are bandits and violence in Iraq. There is no law. No one is happy. Everyone is afraid. We are afraid to go into the street, afraid for our children. America has destroyed my country', he said. But he added, to show that he was not really interested in politics: 'Football is important for the people of Iraq. It helps them forget their problems.'

I called Stange, who was at his home in Jena, Germany. He had watched the game on an Arabic satellite channel and was thrilled. 'I am very proud. It is the best ever game for Iraq. I worked with them every day for more than year. The team played like a computer tonight. They are like a club side. I made them spend so much time together.' He added, without conviction, that it was not his victory: 'My ties are cut with Iraq forever. I cannot go back. German intelligence says I am a target for terrorists. There is terrible, dirty fighting going on in the Iraqi Football Association. They all accuse each other of working with Uday. It is no good.' Then he told me, without seeing the irony, that he would be coming to Patras for the final game in the group, against Morocco. He said that he was looking forward to seeing his good friends Saeed and Hamad.

Yamam Nabeel had also been glued to his television in London. He was so excited for the team that he sounded as though he was going to cry. But he was angrier than ever with Saeed and his cronies. 'It looks like they are making as much money as they can from Iraqi football. But I believe they will be kicked out soon. People are still chasing me for payment for the Goodwill Tour.'

Iraq left the Porto Rio Hotel next day for Athens since they were playing Costa Rica in Piraeus on Sunday 15 August. Iraq was now *the* good news story of the Games. Journalists battled for interviews with al-Samarrai, Saeed, Hamad and the players. Mark Clark's phone bleeped constantly as reporters begged him to fix a time with the squad.

The opening ceremony in Athens on Friday 13 August was the kind of lavish spectacle that the world has come to expect from the Olympics, a superbly choreographed extravaganza of art, dancing, music and fireworks – a far cry from the last time the Games were in Athens, in 1896, when the opening ceremony consisted of athletes from the thirteen competing nations strolling past King George of Greece and saluting. It had taken years to plan the ceremony. The organizers said that everything was significant; nothing had been done simply to entertain. For example, the Greeks said that a model of a human torso that hovered in the air at one point 'represented the first free citizen of Europe, the citizen of the first democratic regime ever born'.

But the crowd did not know or care; they thought it was all splendid and cheered the 11,000 or so athletes from 202 countries who paraded around the stadium. And the biggest cheer came when the Iraqis appeared. The locals in Patras, however, were not so keen. Fiona Fisher, whose family owned the Florida Blue Bay Hotel, where I was staying, told me that her friends who had been Olympic volunteers in Patras had resigned. 'They were really frightened of the Iraqis', she told me. 'They were horrible people. Nasty and dirty.' That Sunday Iraq beat Costa Rica 2–0 in Piraeus, watched by a crowd of just over 12,000. It meant they were through to the quarter-finals. They did not even have to get a point in their final match, in Patras against Morocco.

Most of the press coverage was still favourable. Journalists from the major American newspapers – the *New York Times*, *Washington Post*, *Los Angeles Times* and so on – were wary about drawing comfort from the team's unexpected progress; they said that it did not mean that Iraqis welcomed the Americans. Reporters from smaller, less cerebral American publications were not so cautious and talked as if the Iraqi's performance vindicated the invasion. One journalist babbled that 'NBC should wake up to the biggest story of the Athens Olympics and put Iraq's soccer team on its main network.' The reporter, from a newspaper in Florida, said that Iraq's heroics were 'a wonderful mystery'.[7] He added: 'No other team at this Olympics has drawn so much on the emotions of its fans.' Some journalists, however, were disturbed by these fans, who were angry and unable to control themselves. A veteran from the *International Herald Tribune* wrote: 'Many were drinking from plastic beer bottles

. . . many were smoking, despite the futile and polite efforts of Olympic volunteers. None were sitting. Many looked pretty tough. Many wore a glazed Heineken stare.' He said that, compared to hard-core hooligans in England, they were harmless, but he added that it was 'easy to feel the power of the mob standing amongst them'.[8]

Next day the squad returned to the Porto Rio Hotel. They were besieged by reporters. Saeed was in full flow in the lobby, though it was hard to catch everything he said as his treasurer, Abdul Khaliq, was always yelling into a mobile phone, which he had been given by the Games' organizers – though, to his obvious irritation, it did not allow calls outside Greece. Saeed said: 'I collected this team. I gave from my personal money for equipment and hotels. We had nothing. All the other countries have money and are rich. We have nothing. There are many people in Iraq dependent on salaries to my players. If there isn't any money, they can make problems for our country.'[9] It was obvious from listening to him that he regarded himself as the new Uday, minus the violence; he ran football in Iraq and the association was his, to shape and exploit as he saw fit.

There was a darker side. Al-Samarrai had told a reporter from an Israeli newspaper that the Iraqis would compete against anyone. He said: 'I want to send a clear message to the Israeli people. It does not matter if you are Israeli, Palestinian or Iraqi. Each one of us has the basic right to live. We have no problem meeting the Israelis. This is sport, not politics.' Al-Samarrai must have known that this was rubbish. Many Iraqis had hated Jews since the establishment of Israel in 1948; they regarded Israel and Judaism as the same, equally loath-some, thing. An Iraqi athlete in Greece who competed against an Israeli knew that he or she would not survive long back home.

Israel was not playing in the football tournament, but Israeli jour-nalists were eager to test al-Samarrai's pledge, and one drove from Athens to Patras to watch the team train. The session was open to the press. One source told me what happened: 'There were some television crews and reporters. We heard there was an Israeli reporter. Adnan said he would have to go. The guy begged to be allowed to stay. He said he would not take any notes, he would just watch. But Adnan would not have it. The guy left and said he would complain. We never heard any more, so I guess he didn't. I thought Adnan only did it because he was afraid people in Iraq would find out. He said no. I got the impression that he it was his decision. He didn't want an Israeli in the ground.'

Iraq had had a pro-Nazi and anti-Semitic government in the early 1940s.[10] After Israel's victory in the Six-Day War in June 1967 Jewish property was expropriated, Jews' accounts were frozen, they were dismissed from public posts, their businesses were shut and their telephones were disconnected. Jews were placed under house arrest or restricted to the cities. In 1969 fourteen men – eleven of them Jews – were hanged publicly in Baghdad after being accused of spying for Israel. Radio Baghdad announced: 'We hanged spies, but the Jews crucified Christ.'

Although Iraq was secular by the standards of the region, Saddam encouraged religious hatreds, as Hitler and Stalin had done, to distract his people from everyday problems. In 1948 there were 150,000 Jews in Iraq; in 2004 there were just 17.

In response to international pressure Saddam allowed Jews to emigrate in the early 1970s, though he maintained what Jewish commentators described as 'anti-Semitic rhetoric'. In 2000 the government described Jews as 'descendants of monkeys and pigs, and worshippers of the infidel tyrant'. Many Iraqis – like others in the Arab world – believed that the attacks on the Twin Towers in New York on 11 September 2001 were a plot by the Israelis to discredit Muslims. In mosques throughout Iraq clerics interchanged the words for Jew (Yahudi), Zionist (Sayuni) and Israel (Israeli.) Many Iraqis thought the US-led invasion of their country had been organized by Jews to destroy Islam.

On the eve of the final match, against Morocco, I plopped myself down beside Saeed in the hotel lobby. I congratulated him on the team's performance and said that he must be proud. He smiled, pleased by the flattery. I thought it was time to ask about his relationship with Uday. 'Please, the past is finished. I was in the federation. I did it for my country. I could have gone abroad but wanted to help my people', he said. Had he known about the torture? He shrugged and fiddled with his mobile phone. 'Some of the stories

are true. We have so many stories. Uday made many mistakes', he
said.

He started to get up, so I changed direction. I asked him about al-
Rasheed, the club Uday founded in 1984, when Saeed was at his
peak as a player. I knew that this was safer ground. 'I refused to join
him', he said. 'After that Uday made many problems for me.' 'And
what about when you ran the IFA for him? 'He fired me many times.
But he never sent me to gaol because I am too popular. Please no
more on the past. It is not nice. People know. Politics is not for me.
I do not support any party.'

I asked him about Ahmed Radhi, whom he had accused of trying
to kill him. He shook his head and would not answer. I thought he
asked me who Radhi was, but he spoke so quietly I could not be
sure. He said that the future was promising. Adnan Hamad was an
excellent coach – and cheaper than Bernd Stange. 'I am paying
Hamad $60,000 a year, which is good for Iraq', he said. There was
a new league, divided into a northern section, two in the centre and
one in the south. He said he had exciting plans to develop football,
using advanced marketing techniques. He told me that he would sell
television rights for a lot of money.

Was he concerned that so many players were going abroad, I
asked. I said that seven of the eighteen players in the Olympic
squad were based abroad. 'I will stop players leaving', he said. 'I have
to sign the certificates and I make the rules. I will not let players go
to countries where the standard is lower than ours. They can go to
England and Europe, but not to Syria and Egypt. I have told people
my vision and they liked it and elected me president.'

I thought this was odd. Since the early 1990s Iraqi players had
gone to clubs in the Middle East because they could not make a
decent living at home. Few had gone to Europe, because standards
were so much higher there and because they were happier in the
Arab countries. I asked if this meant that he would, somehow, stop
players signing for clubs outside Iraq. How could he do this? Surely
it would be illegal? Did he intend to take a percentage of any transfer fees? But he did not reply. He got up and walked away. I had asked
the wrong questions.

Meanwhile, Stange had arrived from Germany to meet his friends Saeed and Hamad, though some newspapers reported that he was at home in Jena, brooding that they had stolen his glory.[11] He said that he had been fortunate that he had been able to treat the players as if they were a club side. He said: 'I hope they will stay together as a team, but I fear it will disintegrate. The players will go abroad. If Adnan gets the right offer, he will go too. I would understand if he did, because one of the reasons I went to Iraq was that the financial package was right.' He had no time for romantics who said that the players only cared about their country: 'They are egotistical, like players around the world. They want lucrative contracts abroad, and who can blame them? Of course they are playing for their country, but many are also spoilt now. The players have tasted luxury with me, and it has gone to some of their heads. They complain if can't eat *à la carte* or have to stay in a guest house.'[12]

Iraq lost 2–1 to Morocco, watched by just 4,000 people. It was another bizarre occasion. Once again there were hundreds of volunteers and police and the paraphernalia of a major event: the refreshments stands, the crash barriers and so on. But the stadium was almost empty. The game was a wretched, scrappy affair, the standard of a relegation battle in the old English Fourth Division, though it must be said that Hamad had rested half of his first team. It struck me that only Iraqis and Moroccans would have watched the match, though the more excitable members of the press corps were writing about the Iraqis as if they were being cheered on by billions of people around the world. But Hamad and his team did not care about this because they were meeting Australia in the quarter-finals in Iraklion, Crete.

There was a new problem. In the USA the campaign to re-elect George W. Bush had produced a television advertisement, entitled 'Victory', which said that the Olympic teams from Afghanistan and Iraq proved that the USA was winning its war on terror. A spokesman for the Bush campaign said: 'Two countries that no longer operate under dictatorships are now competing in the Olympics.' The advertisement opened with a shot of Bush looking rugged in a rural setting and then cut to footage of athletes. A voice said:

'Freedom is spreading through the world like a sunrise. At this Olympics there will be two more free nations and two less terrorist regimes.'

The Iraqis were furious. 'Iraq as a team does not want Mr Bush to use us for his presidential campaign. He can find another way to advertise himself', said one player, Salih Sadir, who was twenty-one and used to play for Najaf, which had been almost destroyed in fighting between the Americans and Iraqis loyal to the cleric Moqtada al-Sadr.[13] 'I want the violence to go away from the city. We want the Americans to go away.' Another player, Ahmed Manajid, aged twenty-two, from Fallujah, said: 'How will he [Bush] meet his God, having slaughtered so many men and women? He has committed so many crimes.' He said that he had lost friends who had fought the Americans and said that he would be fighting too, if he had not been a footballer. 'I want to defend my home. If a stranger invades America and the people resists, does that make them a terrorist? Fallujah people are some of the best in Iraq.'

These comments did not go down well in Athens. Privately Mark Clark thought that the advertisement by the Bush camp was incredibly crass, but he could not say so publicly; instead he said that the Iraqi players were young and naive. But Adnan Hamad was not young or naive. He said: 'You cannot speak about a team that represents freedom. We do not have freedom in Iraq. We are occupied. This is a miserable time. Freedom is just a word for the media. My problems are not with the American people. They are with what America has done in Iraq. The American army has killed so many people. Many people hate America now.'[14]

The row was soon forgotten, not so much because of Clark's tactics but because this was the Olympics, and the media and public wanted straightforward sports news or, failing that, good news. On Saturday 21 August, watched by 10,023 people, Iraq beat Australia 1–0 in Iraklion, Crete and qualified for the semi-final. The team's captain, Wahab Abu al Hail, said: 'Life is tough at home. We want to show the world there's more to Iraq than Saddam, that Iraq is for peace and we are friends of all countries. For me personally, I have these feelings inside me all the time at these Olympics.' There were wild celebrations in Iraq. 'In Baghdad a stream of red tracer bullets cut through the night sky amid a hail of celebratory gunfire. Fans who had watched the game in cafés and hotels spilled out and drove through the streets with national flags fluttering from their cars and screaming "God is great"', said one report.

The Iraqis were physically and emotionally exhausted. In Greece's second city, Thessaloniki, on Tuesday 24 August, before a crowd of 6,213, they were outclassed by Paraguay and lost 3–1. By now the FA and Olympic officials based in Athens had decided that there were too many questions about politics. They decreed that Adnan Hamad would only talk about football. But he could not resist taking another swipe at the Americans for 'destroying my country'.

A few days later Iraq lost 1–0 to Italy in the same stadium, in the match to decide the bronze medal. Only 5,203 people turned up. It was not a happy occasion. An Italian journalist, Enzo Baldoni, had just been kidnapped and murdered in Iraq by militants, ostensibly to protest against the presence of Italian troops in Iraq, though extremist thugs were also killing foreigners from countries not involved in the invasion. An Olympic volunteer said: 'The Italians were very upset. They wanted a minute's silence before the game and for everyone to wear black armbands. Don't get me wrong: the Iraqis were upset too. None of them said it was a good thing that the Italian had been killed. They were all shocked. But they said, "Look, you must remember that sixty Iraqis die every day." There was no minute's silence, and the Iraqis didn't wear armbands, but the Italians did.'

In his five-star hotel in Athens, behind the lines of troops and police and barriers to prevent suicide bombers, Ahmed al-Samarrai was delighted. He said that the Games had been a triumph for the new Iraq. He was a big, fit man, glowing with health and confidence. He was tanned, smartly dressed and looked like the chairman of a multinational. He told me that he was glad that he had not been intimidated by terrorists to leave Iraq, like other exiles who had returned home and then fled again. 'There were two ministers in the new Iraqi government who gave up and went back to London. I said to them, "No, you have been away from Iraq for twenty years in opposition." I could not do this. I had to stay. Soldiers had sacrificed their lives to bring us freedom.' He said that he was a target – he had escaped an assassination attempt a few days before he came to Athens – but would fight on. Mark Clark was also pleased. Iraq had not won any medals, but the football team had performed heroically and had won many friends for its energy and skill. Some of their criticisms of the Americans were, Clark told friends, unfortunate but warranted.

On Tuesday 31 August, Hamad and his team returned to Baghdad.[15] At a welcoming ceremony they were showered with sweets while a singer crooned: 'Oh, coach Adnan, the things you did in Athens!' But nothing had really changed. The players who did not play for clubs abroad knew they would be lucky if they were paid $200 a month by their clubs or the IFA. A league was supposed to start, but no one believed it would and, if it did, Iraqis knew it would soon shut down. Athens had been great, the players agreed. They weren't fools. They knew it was low-grade stuff. What mattered now was joining a club abroad, because that was the only way they could earn a living.

13

The game goes on

On the first Sunday of August 2004, as Iraq's athletes and footballers were preparing to leave for Greece and the Olympics, four churches in Baghdad and two in the northern city of Mosul were bombed. Eleven people died in Baghdad and one in Mosul. Scores more were injured. Worst hit was the Chaldean church in Baghdad, when a car exploded outside as the congregation was leaving. One worshipper said: 'We knew it was a matter of time before they got to us. They are trying to divide Iraq but they will never succeed. When will they learn that only peace and love can restore our country? I pray for their forgiveness.'

Clergymen tried to calm Iraq's estimated population of 750,000 Christians[1] by blaming 'foreign insurgents', Sunni extremists who hated everyone, Jews and Shias as well as Christians. But many Christians did not believe this. They said that there had been a growth in anti-Christian feeling since the invasion. One woman said: 'We never talked about religion at work, but now I hear it all the time from the Muslims in my office. They say we should be part of the insurgency, they say we should all fight together against the Americans, that we should be involved.'

Many Christians looked back with affection to the days of Saddam, when they said that they had been free to practise their faith. Now, they said, Islamic radicals ordered them to shut down their shops selling alcohol and women's beauty salons. Christian women who had been proud of their femininity and fashion sense complained they were stared at, as if they were whores, if they wore make-up. Other Christians said that Iraqis accused them of being pro-American. 'Muslims say that we are collaborating with what they call "the crusader" invaders of the coalition', said a spokesman from the Assyrian

Democratic Movement, which had a seat on the interim government's council.

Ammo Baba told me he could not meet me again. He said it would
be too dangerous, for me as well as for him. He did not even want to
talk on the phone because he had heard that insurgents could tap
phones. He said that he could suffer if 'they' knew he was talking to
a British reporter. This was a blow. I had wanted to see him at his
home, to watch him with friends, to study a national hero. I had
wanted to visit his school for the deprived Shia children of Sadr City,
to go with him to the stadiums in Baghdad, Najaf, Arbil and Basra
that he had graced as a player and then as a coach. I had known for
several months that this was probably not possible, but nonetheless I
had hoped that Iraq would settle down or, to quote the American
spokespeople, 'normalize'. But the country was not 'normalizing': it
was getting so bad that one of the legends of Iraqi sport, Ammo Baba,
was too scared to meet a writer to discuss matches from the 1950s that
existed only in the memories of those who had played or watched.

I did not blame Ammo. When we had met in the spring in Brittany,
he believed that he was so popular that no one would ever harm him,
or anyone who was with him. That was not the case now. Past glories
meant nothing; everyone was a target. His assailants could be Saddam
loyalists, Sunni fanatics from Iraq, al-Qaeda madmen from Yemen,
Saudi Arabia or Jordan or Shia radicals from Sadr City, all of whom
loathed the West. He sounded disappointed, confused and frightened.
How could it be, he obviously wondered, that Iraq's greatest player,
who had never been involved in politics, who had never discriminated
against anyone because of their religion, could end up cowering in his
house, unable to entertain a Western reporter who wanted to write
about him?

But then it occurred to me that there might be other reasons for his
change of heart. Had someone from the Iraqi Football Association
advised him not to speak to me because I was asking awkward questions? Ammo complained that the association had not supported his
football academy or given him a job. But Hussein Saeed had told me
in Greece that the association supported the academy and was employing Ammo as a consultant. Had someone told Ammo that he should be

paid for talking to me? Or perhaps he thought he should write his auto-biography. Was he annoyed that I had talked to people like Sharar Haydar, who thought he was a fraud? I asked Mark Clark how I could find out. He laughed and said: 'Good luck. It is almost impossible to discover the truth in Iraq, about football or anything else.'

I wondered if, like many Iraqis, I was becoming a conspiracy theo-rist. Then an Iraqi journalist in Baghdad, who had been helping me with research, e-mailed me: 'Ammo is not only worried about his security if he meets you. He feels you want to go too deeply into his life. He said, "Simon wants to use me to make himself very famous because I am so loved around the world." He is also angry with the new government. He said they were very stupid and had marginalized people like him. He said he had only a pension from the Ministry of Sport of $200 a month. He talked about Hussein Saeed. I think he is fighting Saeed. He is angry because Saeed took his job.' This was baffling. Ammo told me that Saeed was a respectful former 'student'. But now he was attacking Saeed for stealing his job. Saeed had spoken warmly of Ammo when we met in Greece and had told me that Ammo was a valued adviser to the association, who was paid well for his opinions on how to rebuild the game. Football in Iraq, it seemed, was a microcosm of the country itself, made up of lies, half-truths, feuds and shifting alliances.

I was disappointed that Ammo would not talk to me again but still hoped it would be possible to interview people in Iraq about football. Yet even this was looking difficult. A friend of a friend, who had been a senior NCO in the SAS, ran teams of bodyguards in Iraq. He said he would be happy to 'provide protection' for me, though I pointed out that I could not afford to pay. (A good bodyguard cost $1,000 a day.) I asked him what would happen if I wandered around Baghdad with an unarmed driver. He frowned. He said I *might* be OK in the Green Zone, the fortified area of Central Baghdad where the US mil-itary had its headquarters and where most Westerners, journalists, aid workers and 'contractors' (meaning anyone with a contract to work in Iraq) stayed, but said that I would be in severe danger outside that zone if I did not have 'protection'. I said that I needed to drift around Baghdad and Iraq, chatting to footballers and fans about the game and doubted this would be possible if I was accompanied by men in wrap-around sunglasses carrying automatic weapons. He said he saw my point.

Men who have served with the SAS rarely exaggerate. But they view the world as soldiers, so I asked a Westerner who was a consultant to the Iraqi government for advice. He said: 'Security concerns for foreigners are very high at the moment – as the recent spate of very blatant kidnappings in Baghdad, from houses which supposedly had armed guards etc., shows. It would be extremely difficult for you to achieve your task in Baghdad at this time, and I personally would advise against travel to Baghdad until things calm down again. You should be accommodated within the international Green Zone, and have proper security measures in place (secure accommodation, transport and driver and personal bodyguard detail). Bear in mind that security is expensive, but you very much get what you pay for. You would also need to plan in detail what movement you wanted to make around the city, and ideally have as many meetings as possible in one location since your security personnel will have to recce in advance anywhere new you want to go.'

This was absurd. If I did as I was advised, I would be running a military campaign costing thousands of pounds a day. I was writing a book about football, not testing the efficiency of bodyguards who used to be in the SAS. The news from Iraq kept getting worse. It was considered suicidal to drive from Jordan to Baghdad. The only way to Baghdad was with Air Jordan, which charged almost £700 for the return flight from Amman. But that did not solve the problem: the road from the airport to the city was a death trap. Taxi drivers were reportedly charging more than £2,500 for the short trip.[2] It was a surreal world where you needed to spend thousands of dollars to have a hope of staying alive. In any case, there were no guarantees. Another friend, who was also a bodyguard in Iraq, told me that there were risks, even if you had the best 'protection'. He said: 'They are hitting us with rocket-propelled grenades, roadside bombs, you name it. If you are hit then you are gone', he said, with what sounded like relish.

One friend, a veteran television correspondent who had reported dozens of conflicts, e-mailed me: 'I have not left the hotel in over a week aside from a quickie visit to the interim government in the fortress-like Green Zone. I was in Beirut twenty years ago, and this is much worse. Last time I was here I could walk around with my security guys in the shadows. Now the place has gone to Hell, no matter what Messrs Bush and Blair tell you. It's a mess.' I was shocked by this. It was the job of bodyguards to see risk everywhere, but this correspondent was famously brave. I had never heard him worry about his own safety. Another journalist said: 'Travel outside Baghdad is off-limits at the moment. I only make strictly necessary and limited journeys. I've been making one trip a day – to the US military protected Green Zone and various ministries. On each trip I've been distinctly nervous. There is a risk of being caught in a suicide bomb attack at these locations, or of being followed by insurgents who may be keeping surveillance. I'm not sure how much an armed escort would help in these situations.'

Another journalist talked about Iraq's fascination with violence, epitomized by the sales of videos of hostages being beheaded by hooded terrorists. (To be fair, websites showing these videos were popular throughout the world.) He said that these killers wanted to drive away foreigners – and it did not matter whether they came from the USA, France, India or Japan, or whether they were telephone engineers or truck drivers – so that reconstruction was impossible. The terrorists were saying that anyone, even if they meant well, such as doctors or aid workers, would be in danger because they were associated with the invasion. Other commentators said this analysis dignified people who were monsters; they dismissed them as simply evil. Whatever their motivation, these 'insurgents' had turned life in Baghdad into 'a fight for survival'.[3] To interview someone journalists ran from their hotels in the Green Zone into cars with blackened windows. But they did not stay long – fifteen minutes at most – because 'insurgents' or criminals, who sold hostages to the religious extremists, would hear about them.

However, an Iraqi journalist called Omar, who worked for an American television station in Baghdad, did agree to organize interviews with past and present footballers on my behalf.[4] Over the following three months Omar and his colleagues spoke to these players, asking questions that I had sent them. Omar understood what these players had been through. He had been gaoled and tortured in 1995, when he was working for Iraqi television and produced a news report in which he mistakenly showed an American flag. 'I was in a huge cell, packed with people. I was beaten. Thank God I did not go mad. I was freed after a month. I was sacked from my job', he told me. He said that it was hard to arrange interviews at players' homes, which was where I wanted them to take place, so that we had a feel for their lives. 'We have to meet the players when they are training. Then we make appointments. We always see them in the day and are always back by the time it is dark. It is not safe, even for Iraqis. They talk to us frankly. They would not say the same things to an Iraqi writer because no one knows who will be in power tomorrow and they must not say anything that could offend someone', he said. He said that most of the players had come from poor Shia homes. Some were illiterate. A few, who had retired, were no better off than they had been as children.

One who had prospered was Ahmed Radhi, who had been the vice-president of the post-invasion IFA until Hussein Saeed, the president, sacked him in the spring of 2004 for allegedly trying to kill him in a grenade attack. Radhi bounced back and became president of al-Zawraa. Radhi said that Saeed had really fired him because he was determined to end corruption within the IFA. He said: 'After the fall of Saddam it was important to organize properly. But some members of the association began to exploit their positions for their personal gain, which was what had happened in the past. I was also strongly opposed to the appointment of al-Samarrai as president of the Iraqi National Olympic Committee. He is a merchant who came into sport in Iraq with the object of making money. I opposed the kind of things that were going on at the association and the Olympic committee. I decided to resign because I did not want the public to associate me with these activities. To try and silence me they accused me of trying to kill Saeed. But I will not be quiet. Sooner or later I will get proof of wrongdoing within the IFA, and then I will return to run the association.'

In 2004 Arkan Mahmood, the Kurdish player, had returned to Baghdad from Syria, where he had been playing for a club called al–Wathba, for a two-week holiday. He said: 'There was fighting in my neighbourhood between the Americans and the Shia militias. I was standing by my door when the Americans started shooting randomly. I was hit in the right knee.' It was not a life-threatening wound, but it was a disaster for a professional athlete. He was thirty years old, edging towards being a veteran, and had hoped to make some serious money in Syria. There he could earn $3,000 a month, with a lump sum of $20,000 at the end of a season. This compared to $400 a month in Iraq and a bonus of $3,000. He said: 'The bullet broke a bone in my knee. I went to Amman and had three operations. The doctor says I should be able to start training soon. All I want is to play again.'

He was angry with the Americans, but he also thought that he had been let down by the Iraqi Football Association. 'When I was injured, they said the Americans had told them that I would be taken to Germany for treatment at an American hospital. Then they denied that they had said this. They offered me $350 instead. I have refused to take it because it is not enough. The operations have cost me $6,000 so far. The association don't care about me.' Like many Iraqis, Arkan was not happy that Uday's lieutenants still ran football. 'They re-elected themselves. But at least they are not as greedy as Uday. He took half your salary if you were abroad. They only took a small amount, $350, from me so that I could play in Syria.' He was not sure that Iraq's top clubs would survive. 'Take my old club, the Air Force. They have lost the support of the government. They are waiting for help from rich investors, like in the Gulf, where clubs are run by the Sheikhs.'

Yasir Abdul Latif, who had been gaoled five times by Uday, was playing for a club called al-Sulaymaniyah in the north of Iraq in 2004. He said: 'I am waiting for a contract to travel to Yemen to play for the Faisal Aziz club there. Jaber Hamid, the coach at al-Sulaymaniyah, told me that his club would like to sign me. I said I would only come on a monthly contract. Bigger clubs in Iraq wanted me, but they would not accept my conditions.' He said that football in Iraq – like everything else in the country – was falling apart. He was intelligent and candid, but his accusations and complaints were familiar. It was like listening to a younger, brighter and less egotistical version of

Ammo Baba. He said that his beloved al-Zawraa was now 'unexceptional'. He was upset that Ahmed Radhi, the club's new president, had not wanted him there. He said: 'Al-Zawraa's golden era was from the 1970s until 1999. Ahmed Radhi was a great player, but no one likes him. He is bad at training players and doesn't know how to analyse opponents during matches. He is dictatorial. He doesn't listen to any one. He got rid of players with experience, like me. He brought in young, immature players. I was surprised when they told me that Ahmed Radhi did not want me in the club. I asked why and they said it was his decision. I tried to talk to him but he refused.'

He said the league was a shambles. 'We are all afraid of bombs and fighting. We see that even innocent people are targeted by insurgents and terrorists. Few spectators come to matches because terrorists might attack a big crowd with mortars or rockets. One of the reasons I chose al-Sulaymaniyah is that it is much safer in the north. When we played in Sadr City a few weeks ago, most of the other games in Baghdad were cancelled. The al-Zawraa club came under attack by mortars a few weeks ago, and a few days later the security officers found a car bomb near al-Zawraa. Things are getting worse. The Iraqi Football Association has divided the league into four sections: one in the north, two in the middle and one in the south. They say it is for security reasons. Maybe it is the first sign that the country will break up.'

He was not impressed by the team's performance at the Olympics. 'It was like Iraqi football had awoken from a long death. The players were not afraid any more. And they wanted to do well, so they would get contracts outside Iraq. But that is over now. There is little football being played in Iraq. The best players have gone. We did not qualify for the World Cup in 2006. I blame the coaches more than the players. The coaches were brought up under Uday. They are dictators. You cannot argue with them.' He looked at the people running the game and was angry. 'Corruption is everywhere. The government gave the football association a lot of money to pay for supporters to go to a game in Jordan [in the spring of 2004]. The team lost, and the association abandoned the fans. They had to sleep in the street. No one knows where the money went.'

'Things will never change unless the people running the associa-tion and the clubs are removed. Nothing has changed since Uday. Most of the people at the association do not deserve their positions. They are the same gang who were around Uday. They are still working for their own interests. You have to bribe them if you want a good contract from a club. It is destroying football in my country. Myself and others players wrote to the Ministry of Sport and Youth, complaining about the dishonesty and the corruption, but it was useless and nothing has changed. You can't get anywhere unless you flatter and bribe them.'

Issam Thamer al-Diwan's return to Iraq after the invasion had ended with him being fired by the Americans because he complained that Saddam loyalists were being given important jobs in sport. Back at his home near San Diego he said: 'A decade later I am reminded daily of the abuse I suffered. Two of the vertebrae in my neck are per-manently damaged from my body staying in one position so long – which is why I am hunched. The doctors say I need an artificial knee but at my age – I am not even fifty – I am too young to qualify. My ankles are bloated and scarred from shackles, so I try not to stand for more than fifteen minutes at a time. I take pills for my pain and see psychiatrists.'

Nick Ask had reluctantly supported the invasion. 'I saw it as the only way to rid Iraq of Saddam. Iraqis failed to remove the regime not through lack of effort but simply because the regime was so ruthless.' But he was dismayed to see that the people who had run football under Saddam had survived. 'People like Hussein Saeed and Ahmed Radhi ran the IFA during the Uday era. They carried out his orders.' Nor could he understand why the IFA had set up such a large league – thirty-six teams in four groups – when, he said, the country only had the resources to support fourteen decent sides, at most. He assumed that someone was making money from the new league.

He said football could only develop if the country became 'peace-ful and civilized'. He said: 'I am pessimistic about this. The liberation plan of Iraq was based on wishful thinking. It underestimated the power of Saddam's die-hards, the segment of Iraqis that are loyal to him. There are also the Sunni fundamentalists of al-Qaeda. Many of

Iraq's neighbours such as Syria, Iran and Kuwait feel that the real motive of liberating Iraq is to democratize the entire region, and therefore they sense they are next on the USA regime change policy.' He said that football clubs in Iraq had to be run like businesses. They had to attract sponsors and build a fan base that was willing to pay reasonable amounts for tickets and club memorabilia because they could no longer rely on support from the state. 'Corruption will be one of the biggest obstacles in this. The IFA and clubs must conduct themselves in a transparent manner so that people can see where the money is going.'

Anwar Jassam, who had become a coach when he was only twenty-two, after being injured in a car crash, had prospered. He had married in 1975 and had three sons and two daughters. His eldest son had just graduated in sports science. He had three brothers. One had also been an Iraqi international and was now a coach in the UAE. Another brother was a coach in Jordan. The third brother, Waleed, was a wealthy businessman. Jassam was content with his own life – 'We have a large house and I am very happy' – but he worried about his country. He said the invasion was 'a tragedy'. He said: 'The Americans have destroyed Iraq. They have entered every house in Iraq. They are stealing our lives, our future.' He was not sanguine about football. 'We are worse off now because the government no longer supports the football association and clubs. We are totally dependent on rich people to keep going.'

Shakir Mahmood, who had played for three unhappy years for al-Rasheed, was married with four young children. He loved his family but thought he had failed to make anything of his life, mainly because his country was so irredeemably corrupt. 'I finished playing in 1995 and had no means to support my family. We are living in two rooms, which I rent. I have not worked for six months and have many debts.' But, he added, the fans still remembered him, which was a comfort. Like many Iraqis, he was outraged that people who had served Saddam and Uday had now been given lucrative jobs by the Americans. He was annoyed too that exiles who had lived comfortably abroad during the Saddam years while Iraq suffered had returned to take powerful jobs.

He said that people like him, who had stayed in Iraq, had been pushed aside by Iraqis who had gone abroad and become wealthy. He was also annoyed that the Iraqis who had prospered under Uday were still doing well. 'There are people like me, who have qualifications, and we cannot get work', he said. His frustration was understandable but simplistic. The people about whom he was talking – such as Hussein Saeed – were not criminals. They had done what was necessary to survive under Saddam and Uday. They were quick-witted pragmatists. Mahmood had not behaved better than them; he just had not played the system as well. He may have considered himself a better person, but it did not follow that material failure, being poor, was a consequence of virtue. He said that he had studied hard to become a coach and complained that the IFA had sent other people, who knew nothing about football but who had the right connections, on coaching courses in Europe, rather than him. And yet he would not accuse anyone of being corrupt or incompetent because outspokenness, candour, challenging those in power, were not part of the Iraqi psyche. Saddam had programmed people like Mahmood to believe that might was right and that it was impossible to resist. So, as he talked about the unfairness of the new Iraq, he also paid tribute to the men who ran football, such as Hussein Saeed, who had ruined his life. In the space of a few sentences he said that the IFA had selected people to attend coaching courses in the UK 'for personal reasons' – which meant that the decision was corrupt – and then told me that the new regime at the IFA was splendid. It was mind-twisting stuff.

Habib Ja'far, the popular midfield player, retired at the end of the 2003–4 season, aged thirty-nine. He had married in 1988 and had three sons and three daughters, whom he adored. He was coaching youngsters at al-Talaba. He lived in a small house in Sadr City. ' I did not make much money from playing, and this is all I can afford', he said. 'Uday took much of what I earned. Now I am only earning $150 a month.' He hoped that football would recover but was not sure that it would: 'The security situation is very bad. Players think that there will be a bomb at every match. We must have safety. There is a large base for the game. Young men want to play football more than ever today.'

By 2004 Saad Qeis, the player who had fled Iraq in 2001, was living in Norway on benefits with his twelve-year-old son Mohammad, who suffered from a protein deficiency disease. Like his friend Sharar Haydar, he was dismayed to see that 'the same old faces' were running football.

Samir Kadhum, who had been gaoled five times by Uday, had been elected chairman of the Air Force club after he retired from playing in the summer of 2003. He was married, with two children, and was realistic but optimistic. He said that looters had destroyed the club's stadium and offices and had taken everything – kit, boots, balls, goalposts, nets, lights, even wiring. But he said the club had a huge fan base and was potentially profitable. 'I have asked the government, the Olympic committee and the football association for help. They have not replied. I am talking to the government about developing land that the club owns. We used to get money from the government, but that has stopped now. The security situation is so bad that we play few games. No one comes to games, so we have no income from ticket sales. Before the invasion we had big crowds.'

Kadhum said that the club had a wealthy patron, who was paying for everything, but added that he did not know how long the man would be willing to do this. He said it was essential to have a regular and substantial income. He said that he had also spent his own money keeping the club afloat. For all these problems, he said, life was better after Saddam. 'I thank God every day that Uday has gone. We are on the road to freedom and democracy. We want an end to terrorism because it is against humanity and our religion.'

Sharar Haydar, big, strong and articulate, told me in London that he feared that the violence would continue. 'No one trusts the politicians. We are better off with the occupation than with Saddam. But it will take time to recover. The Iraqi people are not ready for democracy yet. The Americans have been arrogant. The Arab mentality is such that, if you are nice to them, they will do many nice things for you. But if you point a gun at them, there is no way they will support you. The average Iraqi is against the occupation. It is not only the insurgents. Everyone, in the north and south, is unhappy. We are happy to be rid of Saddam, but so many promises have been broken.'[5]

But the news from Iraq was more depressing every day. A madness, an evil, the spirit of Uday perhaps, had descended on the country. Ordinary men – and perhaps women – had become monsters. Dozens of foreigners were kidnapped. Many were murdered horribly. Britain was convulsed by the killing of Kenneth Bigley, a 62-year-old engineer, a decent and harmless man who had gone to Iraq to make extra money for his life with his new wife. He was beheaded on video by, it was suspected, Abu Musab al-Zarqawi, the Jordanian Sunni, a psychopath who wanted to destroy the modern world. Then a British aid worker, Margaret Hassan, who was married to an Iraqi, spoke fluent Arabic and had devoted her life to helping Iraqis, was murdered by hooded men. Commentators looked for a logic but instead found only the chaos of Sunni and Shia groups who shared one thing: a willingness to kill without compunction. It was possible to erect theories: that Bigley was killed by Sunni extremists to put pressure on the British government to break away from the Americans; that Hassan was murdered by a Sunni group who thought al-Qaeda was becoming too calculating, that it had lost its missionary zeal to convert the world to pure Islam. But it was hard to believe that there was any logic to this. More likely it was just evil.

Since they did not know what else to do, the Americans battered Iraqi towns such as Fallujah, as if blowing up buildings and killing a few hundred young men from Iraq, Yemen and Saudi Arabia would solve Iraq's problems. They talked of winning the battle for 'hearts and minds' and invited journalists to accompany the troops on missions in 'hot spots'. Some writers thought this was the new Vietnam. But they were wrong. This was the Middle East, not the Far East. Iraq's problems were more like those of post-Tito Yugoslavia than Vietnam in the 1960s. The basic question, which the Americans did not want to ask because they did not know the answer, was this: is there a good reason for Iraq to exist? The British had created Iraq, but the borders had no logic. The country consisted of religious and ethnic groups – Shias, Sunnis, Kurds and a diminishing number of Christians – who had nothing in common with each other. Iraq had been held together by harsh rule until Saddam took power and then by sheer brutality. It was easy to imagine the country disintegrating into its constituent parts. But, just as with the former Yugoslavia, there were complications because so many areas, especially in Baghdad and central Iraq, were mixed. What would happen to Sunnis in a predominantly Shia area and vice versa?

It was difficult for football to continue, let alone thrive, in these conditions. Middle-class, as well as wealthy, Iraqis were terrified that they would be kidnapped. Everyone was afraid of being caught up in a street battle. In mid-October Iraq lost 2–1 to Uzbekistan in Amman, Jordan, where they played their home matches, and were knocked out of the World Cup for 2006. Greece was a fading memory. Most of Iraq's best players had found clubs abroad. Bernd Stange had gone, a victim of Saeed's scheming and Iraq's desire to have one of their own leading the country's football team. Iraq was ranked at 39 in the world, while Uzbekistan was only 54, but this was misleading, a reflection of past glories rather than present realities. Stange had grafted discipline and method onto the traditional flair of the Iraqis, but Hamad was an amateur to him. Stange had refused to toady to Saeed and his cronies. But Hamad owed everything to Saeed.

In October 2004 the IFA announced that the domestic league would start again, for the first time since May 2004.[6] It said there would be four regional leagues, each of nine teams. The top three from each would move into the next round and eventually to a grand final in May 2005. However, the association put the four major clubs from Baghdad – al-Zawraa, al-Shurta, al-Talaba and al-Quwa-al-Jawiya – into separate groups since they were the strongest teams in the country.

Hussein Saeed said that security was a problem, but not an insurmountable one: 'It is essential to resuscitate football for everyone: players, referees and coaches. Re-launching the league is central to that. Football is an important part of Iraqi society, and the fans are very happy to see the return of the league. As far as the Iraqi people are concerned, it is another sign that conditions are improving. The managers of our national teams also thought it was very important to get a domestic league up and running again, so that they could once again pick locally based players.' He said that the association was helping teams prepare for the new season: 'We are helping teams get the basic necessities, such as jerseys, balls and so forth. Then there are TV rights, which also add a little something to the coffers. We are currently in talks with several companies over marketing opportunities. All that is coming together.'

Obviously, he said, teams could not travel far, so the association had come up with the regional format. 'Our biggest concern at the moment is to get the stadiums in shape. Reconstruction of the national stadium in Baghdad is already under way and should be finished in about a month. Once it's ready, we'll inaugurate it by staging a match between two of the city's most popular teams. I'm sure people will come to watch.' He said that he was sure that all would be well: 'A lot of players have gone abroad to play in other Arab leagues, and they'll probably stay there. But I'm not worried. We will have plenty of good teams here at home.' It was fantasy. After a handful of matches, watched by almost no one, the IFA abandoned the league.

The opening game had showed that professional football could not function in a country where there was no law and order. Al-Shurta had met a team called Naft-ul-Junoob, from Basra, in a small stadium in one of the most dangerous areas of Baghdad. Al-Shurta won 5–1, but only 100 people watched. IFA officials said that it was a triumph and the players said it was great to be back, but everyone knew that the league did not have much of a future if people were too afraid to attend matches.

Latif Yahia, who had worked as Uday's double, had married an Irish woman in 2000. He had lived in Dublin for seven years but had moved to Manchester with his wife and children in 2003. He told me that he had many business interests, including an estate agency, but would not go into detail. He said that a Dutch company had made a film of his life, that he had written a second book, about his life in exile, that he was busier than ever. But people who knew him well told me that, understandably, he had been damaged by his experiences in Iraq and Europe and was erratic. He may have been unpredictable – he vanished at the end of 2004 and did not respond to my messages – but he was articulate and well informed.[7] He told me that the continuing debate about Uday – about whether the IOC and FIFA should have done more to stop the abuse of athletes and footballers, and whether it would have been better if Uday had been captured alive – was naive: 'Uday was a sadist. Just that. He was not interested in sport. He was head of criminal operations. He was not human. He was more than evil. Nothing could be done about him.'

He said that he had opposed the invasion. 'I was against the war. I do not want innocent people in my country killed. I don't want people from the outside coming to put a democratic government in Iraq. There's no way for Iraq to be democratic.' He raged about the way he had been treated by Western governments. He said that he was still holding an Iraqi passport because no one – the Irish, the British or the Americans – would grant him citizenship after he had refused to help Western intelligence. That, he said, would have been unpatriotic; like many Iraqis, he despised the regime of Saddam Hussein, but that did not mean he wanted the West forcibly to remove him. He said: 'I refused to work for the Americans and British so they made my life a misery. The CIA, MI6, all wanted me to work for them. I would not be their puppet. They are all bullshit. I have no faith in the West.'

Furat Ahmed Kadoim, the Iraqi referee, had spent his last months in England in a council house in Birmingham, with three other asylum seekers. His application for political asylum had been refused, he told me, because, the British government said that Iraq was no longer dangerous. He was worried. He knew he would find work in Iraq; as a qualified engineer, that would not be a problem. He was looking forward to seeing his wife and two sons for the first time in two years. He said: 'The security situation is not good. But worse is the fact that the same people are in charge of football, the same people who worked for Uday, who told me I could not be a FIFA referee any longer. Hussein Saeed worked for Uday for fifteen years. He knows all about torture.' He said that many of his friends thought Iraq had been a better place under Saddam. 'Everyone thinks the Americans came because of our oil. They do not care about Iraq.'

In late November he flew to Amman. Then he took a bus to Baghdad because he could not afford the airfare. He called me a few days before Christmas. 'The journey from Amman was horrible. There were thieves everywhere', he said. 'I was shocked, really shocked when I saw Baghdad. Everything is different. There are American troops everywhere. There are car bombs, suicide bombs.' He said that people had changed. 'No one has any patience. Everyone wants to fight all the time. I cannot leave my house. There is no security. They say that football will start again soon. But I don't think so.' We spoke again on Christmas Day. He was trying to be positive and said that he hoped to find a job in the New Year. But the omens were not good.

On Tuesday 22 December a 24-year-old man belonging to a Sunni group calling itself Ansar al-Sunna strolled into the mess tent at the American base at the airport outside Mosul, Iraq's third largest city, close to the border with Syria, and blew himself up. He killed fourteen American troops, four American civilians and four Iraqis. Seventy-two people, including fifty-one Americans, were injured, many of them seriously. It was the worst attack on the Americans since the invasion of March 2003.

At first the Americans claimed that the mess tent had been hit by a mortar or rocket, but within hours they admitted that there had been an extraordinary and unforgivable breach of security. They said that the bomber had either worked at the base or had been allowed in, possibly disguised as a policeman, by an accomplice. This showed that they had no idea who was, and who was not, a threat. Frustrated and angry, the Americans swept into Mosul with heavy armour and raided the homes of people who they said were 'suspect'. But it was obvious that they did not know who was behind the attack on their base and that this was a knee-jerk show of strength that would only further antagonize local people.

On Christmas Day the irrepressible Hassanin Mubarak, of iraq-sport.com, e-mailed me from Iraq. He said that he was having a terrific time in Najaf, the Shia holy city 100 miles south of Baghdad. He said that the local club, which hoped to challenge the major teams of Baghdad, had allowed him to train with them, which had obviously thrilled him.

I was impressed. He had gone to Iraq in search of football, apparently oblivious of the dangers facing him, an Iraqi living in Britain. He saw the big problems – the fear, the murders, the kidnappings, the absence of water, electricity, sanitation, jobs and so on – only in terms of how they affected football. At first I thought this was childish or unrealistic, but it occurred to me that perhaps it was his way of fighting the terrorists, the fanatics, the killers; maybe Hassanin was saying, 'look, football will survive, it will prosper, it will be here long after you have been forgotten'. He talked as if Iraq was close to peace.

Hassanin told me that the club in Najaf had always been badly treated by the football association in Baghdad because it was based in a Shia stronghold. But now the club was poised to hit the big time. He told me: 'Al-Najaf Sports Club was formed in 1960, and reached the top flight twenty-one years later; they have stayed there ever since. In the early days their home stadium was made up of only two rooms and a football pitch, but now the refurbished stadium boasts a capacity of nearly 10,000 – a good thing considering the club is known to have some of the most vocal supporters in the land.'

He described a typical training session at the club: 'On a cold winter's day the players turn up for training at 2.30 p.m., after a hard day's work. They come from all over the city and the neighbouring cities of Kufa, Karbala, Nassriya and Diwaniya. The players lace up their boots, jog around the pitch and do stretches to warm up, while chatting about a Spanish game shown on satellite the night before. Satellite was banned under Saddam's rule; being caught in possession of one would have led to a hefty fine and a six-month prison sentence. The players spend ten minutes warming up, before being given instructions by the coach for the day's work-out. At the end they play out a 90-minute practice match. As the players walk off the pitch, they wait to hear if their league match will take place during the week.'

'It's a similar story for other clubs; the new league has been stop-start from the beginning, owing to the country's instability. "Sometimes we'll turn up for training and just play for fun", one player told me. "With no league and no games, what can we do? Sometimes even our coach doesn't turn up for training." Even with daily electricity black-outs, fuel shortages and no hot water during a cold winter, life at the club goes on, as the players turn up for training, dreaming of making their mark on the game they love.'

On Christmas Eve 2004 a French journalist called Georges

Malbrunot, who had just been freed after being held hostage in Iraq since August, said that the West should realize that parts of Iraq were now 'Planet Bin Laden'. Malbrunot, forty-one, wrote in *Le Figaro*, the newspaper for which he worked, that his kidnappers had been motivated by 'the internationalist jihadist agenda' rather than any Iraqi one. But it was also true there were many reasons for kidnapping Westerners; gangs could be radical Shias as well as radical Sunnis, Ba'ath loyalists or merely criminals who wanted to make money. Whatever their motivation, Malbrunot said that Iraq was definitely not safe: 'The country is crawling with armed men on the look-out for Westerners.'

Then Adnan Hamad resigned, a few weeks after Iraq had been eliminated from the Gulf Cup. He had been voted Asian Coach of the Year, but this counted for nothing now. He said that he had failed the players and the country and had to go. He said that he hoped to find work in the Middle East. His successor was Akram Salman Ahmed, reportedly aged sixty (Iraqis were often vague about their birthdays). It was his fourth stint in charge of the national team. Like Hussein Saeed and Hamad, he was a Sunni, though it must be said that religion did not matter to people involved in football, only to those outside it.

Salman was not in the same class as Stange, or even Hamad, and the fact that the Iraqis had hired him showed how far they had fallen since the Asian Cup in China and the Olympics in Greece the previous summer. He had been a journeyman player in the 1960s with a second-rate club called Esla al-Mae (literally translated as Water Liquefaction). He was player–coach there in his late twenties. After he retired as a player, he coached in Karbala. In 1980, aged thirty-five, he moved to Saudi Arabia to coach a club called al-Jabalain. He was back in Iraq by 1982, first with al-Talaba and then with the national team. He coached Uday's club, al-Rasheed, from 1985 to 1988, which suggested that he possessed a certain moral flexibility. From 1989 until late in 2004 he worked in the Gulf, Saudi Arabia and Lebanon.

As news of Salman's appointment spread around the world, there was outrage and dismay among the Iraqi exiles who followed football in their homeland. 'Who is this man?' asked Internet chat rooms on Iraqi football. 'Is this the best we can do?' they said. Salman insisted that he would only pick players for the national team who were based in Iraq, rather than 'mercenaries' who had fled the country and whose clubs might not release them. This was foolish. The fact that players had left did not mean that they were unpatriotic. They had to earn a living and could not do that in Iraq. Salman relented after his new team, consisting of players based in Iraq, who were not good enough or were too old to find work abroad, were thrashed in a practice match against a Baghdad club. Later he said that, having reflected on it, he would indeed pick players who lived outside Iraq. Salman was no Stange. He had never worked outside the Middle East. He knew nothing of the training methods of the top European teams. Critics of the IFA said that he had been appointed because he was cheap and pliable. They doubted that he would be able to reverse the rapid decline of the national team.

The league in Iraq, which had stuttered along in October and November 2004 before the IFA abandoned it, saying that the security situation was so bad that football was impossible, started again in January 2005. Matches were often cancelled, especially in the central zone of Baghdad and the 'Sunni triangle', where the violence was most intense. If games did take place here, 'crowds' consisted of club officials and relatives of players. It was better in the Kurdish north and Shia south. But even there crowds were still small compared with those that had watched games before the invasion. Nonetheless it was remarkable that any matches were being played and a testament to the Iraqis' passion for football, and their desire for a normal life.

I studied the four group tables. Al-Quwa al-Jawiya, al-Shurta and al-Zawraa, the traditional giants of Iraqi football, were leading their groups. However, the fourth mighty Iraqi club, al-Talaba, were third in their group, behind teams called Electricity and al-Karkh. It occurred to me that perhaps none of this was true, that maybe someone in the football association, or an Iraqi football fan in exile, had manufactured these tables and posted them on the Internet, to give the impression that the country was returning to normal. But Ahmed Radhi, the president of al-Zawraa, said that, yes, the tables were genuine. He told me that it was taking longer than expected to complete the group matches but insisted that the second, and final, round would definitely have started by May. A friend who was working in Baghdad told me: 'Crowds are small. It is hard to get to matches. But games happen.'

By late April the clubs in the four groups had almost completed their matches. There had been the familiar problems. Teams had not turned up for matches because it was too dangerous to travel or because they had no money and no players. Some matches had taken place behind locked doors because of security problems. Occasionally teams had walked off in protest against what they thought was corrupt refereeing. One club, Diwaniya, simply vanished. Predictably al-Shurta and al-Zawraa, Iraq's representatives in the Asian Champions League, the regional tournament for top clubs, struggled. Their best players had fled abroad and they had to play 'home' matches outside Iraq. Iraq, ranked 40th in the world by FIFA the previous August, was ranked 53rd by the spring. The team had played a friendly Australia in Sydney and lost 2–1. The new coach, Akram Salman, made the same points as Adnan Hamad and Bernd Stange. 'There is no security in Iraq. It is difficult for teams to train. Pitches are in a bad state.'

The league had been suspended as the country prepared to vote in late January for a national assembly which would appoint an interim government and construct a new constitution. The 'insurgents' – the ragbag of Sunni extremists, Ba'ath Party fanatics and thugs who saw money in chaos – promised to destroy the poll. But they failed. Almost 8½ million people voted, 58 per cent of those eligible. Most of the country's estimated 5 million Sunni Arabs, around 20 per cent of the total population, did not vote, because they were scared or because they objected to the process, but nonetheless it was the first positive news in many months for those who had backed the invasion. President Bush was particularly excited. He proclaimed it as a triumph for democracy ('The world is hearing the voice of freedom from the centre of the Middle East', he said), and so it was, but with some qualifications. Bush's foreign policy doctrine, roughly, was that the world would be a better and safer place (and the USA would profit more) if every country was a free market democracy. He thought that it was America's duty to export this economic and political system. But many people, including senior American politicians, thought this was simplistic and dangerous. They pointed out that there were vast social, cultural and economic differences between countries such as Iraq and Syria and those of Western Europe and North America. This was not the same as saying that Arabs were not equipped for democracy, only that caution, tact and humility were required.

Certainly, there were murmurings in the spring of 2005 from people who had always insisted Iraq would soon 'normalize'. One British official told *The Observer*: 'There is a realization now that we underestimated the level of criminality in Iraq and how that feeds into its instability and violence. There is an understanding now that this is a decades-long problem and we will be here for a long time.' One of my contacts in Iraq agreed: 'It is going to take a long time to change the mindset of people. We are talking generations.'

In Washington the National Intelligence Council, a CIA think-tank, said that Iraq had become 'a training and recruitment ground' for Islamic militants. It said that Iraq was creating 'professionalized' terrorists for whom 'violence is an end in itself' as they sought to destroy, literally, what they saw as a heretical world. Even Colin Powell, who had resigned in November 2004 as Bush's Secretary of State, revealed his fears. He said that he that warned the President in August 2002 that overthrowing Saddam would be easy; the real problem was what to do with Iraq after that. Powell said that he told Bush that Iraq would 'crack like a goblet'.

I thought of Bernd Stange, who had dreamed of taking Iraq to the World Cup Finals in Germany in 2006. I thought of Ammo Baba, sitting at home in Baghdad wondering if 'they' would come for him because he had talked to a British writer. It was all mad, and sad.

One day Iraq will 'normalize.' One day the bombings and kidnappings will stop. The country may fracture, but there will be peace. And football will be played. It will happen because it always does. But it will take time.

Notes

Chapter 1

1. Information on Stange comes from the website iraqsport.com and from newspaper reports.
2. Brian Bennett and Michael Weisskopf, 'Uday's and Qusay's Gulag Archipelago', *Time* (27 May 2003). This is a gripping report on the two brothers.
3. Indict's website was still available in November 2004, although the organization no longer existed.
4. Farrey, e-mail to the author, 2004.
5. Owens won the 100 metres in 10.3 seconds (equalling the world record), the long jump, with a jump of 26′5¼″ (an Olympic record) and the 200 metres in 20.7 seconds (an Olympic record), as well as running the first leg in the 400 metres relay, which the USA team won in 39.8 seconds (an Olympic and world record).
6. One of the best books on Iraq and the war is John Simpson's *The Wars against Saddam: Taking the Hard Road to Baghdad* (Macmillan, 2003), a revealing account of the events leading to the invasion of Iraq on 19 March 2003 by American and British forces.

Chapter 2

1. There were no Jews in the Iraqi team. At the Olympics in Greece in the summer of 2004 the Iraqi coach, Adnan Hamad, refused to let an Israeli journalist watch his team train.
2. Interview with FIFA.com, October 2003.
3. From iraqsport.com.
4. *Iraq Today* (10 November 2003).

5. Interview with al-Ahram, 25–31 December 2003.
6. Comments on teams come from FIFA.com.

Chapter 3

1. David Baran, 'Iraq: The Party in Power', *Le Monde Diplomatique* (December 2000), a brilliant analysis of the way the Ba'ath Party controlled Iraq.
2. A source at the CPA later said: 'Al-Taey's appointment was controversial but then any appointment would have been, and Eberly did seek advice from various eminent sports personalities and the Interim Committee to Administer Sport. It was only later that al-Taey's real nature emerged, and it was a fairly long and twisted route to his eventual dismissal from the Ministry.'
3. Haydar to the author, October–December 2004.
4. *Time* (19 April 2003).
5. John Simpson, *The Wars against Saddam*.

Chapter 4

1. Interview with Michael Horeni, *Frankfurter Allgemeine Zeitung* (January 2003).
2. Nick Ask was his assumed name. He asked me to withhold his Iraqi name.

Chapter 5

1. Pelé, born in 1940 as Edson Arantes do Nascimento, is probably the greatest player in football history. He played for Brazil in four World Cups, winning in 1958, 1962 and 1970. He retired in 1977. Like the boxer Muhammad Ali, he is a legend who transcends sport.
2. The passages on the history of Iraq and the Assyrians are based on many sources, including the Library of Congress's analysis of Iraq, GlobalSecurity.org, Jonathan Eric Lewis's essay in *Middle East Forum* (summer 2003) and Glen Chancy in LewRockwell.com
3. Interviews with the author, April–December 2004.

Chapter 6

1. Mira Kassis, writing in Air Serv International's *Flight Plan* (15 June 2004), the airline's online magazine.

Chapter 7

1. The £20 maximum wage in football was scrapped in 1961. Two years later players were given freedom to move from clubs once their contracts had expired. By the mid-1960s top players were earning £100 a week.
2. David Baran, *Le Monde Diplomatique* (December 2002).
3. Brian Bennett and Michael Weisskopf, 'Uday's and Qusay's Gulag Archipelago', *Time* (27 May 2003).
4. In his book *The Devil's Double* (Arrow, 2003) Latif Yahia says that Uday often ordered men's heads to be shaved. Arabs regarded this as the ultimate humiliation.
5. Furat Ahmed Kadoim, interview with the author, September–October 2004.
6. Basil Abdul Mahdi, interview with the author, Athens, August 2004.

Chapter 8

1. Latif Yahia, interview with the author (2004), interviews with journalists (1992–2004) and writing for amazon.co.uk.
2. Quotations from Sharar Haydar in this chapter are from interviews with the author in April–December 2004, supplemented by interviews he gave from 1998 to 2004 to ESPN and the BBC, and to the *Sunday Times* and other newspapers.
3. Saad Qeis was writing for the website of a London group of Iraqi exiles. He also spoke to the *Sunday Times* on 19 May, 2001
4. Interviews with Issam Thamer al-Diwan and Raed Ahmed on ESPN, December 2002. Sharar Haydar from interview with ESPN and from interviews with the author, April–December 2004.
5. Interviews with the author, October–November 2004.

Chapter 9

1. For an account of Nabeel Yasin's work see 'Poetry to the People', *The Guardian* (25 August 2004).
2. Eriksson is the current manager of the England team, Nancy Dell'Olio is his girlfriend. Eriksson's affairs – and Dell'Olio's protests about them – often featured in the tabloid press. She set up Truce International with his backing to 'mobilize the power of football as a force for peace', but it did little for Yamam Nabeel or anyone else.
3. Jack Warner, a FIFA vice-president from the West Indies, liked to help football in the developing world.
4. Chris Boffey, *Daily Telegraph* (21 May 2004). It should be noted that Truce International was not a charity and never claimed to be one.
5. Tom Farrey, e-mail to the author, November 2004.
6. ESPN, 6 August 2004.
7. In November 2004 he told Reuters that he was vice-president of the IFA.
8. In fact, the Americans formally handed power to the Iraqis on 29 June because they feared a wave of suicide bombings on 30 June.
9. They did not go to Florence to play Italy as planned because the Italians cancelled the match.
10. Mark Clark, interview in Athens with the author, August 2004. Clark was an adviser to the Iraqi National Olympic Committee.

Chapter 10

1. Nick Ask, interviews with and e-mails to the author, 2004.
2. Nick Ask's English was good, but I have tidied it where necessary, as I have done throughout this book when quoting Iraqis. I have tried to retain the tone as well as the literal sense of their comments.
3. The records of Iraqi football are so chaotic that some football historians think that Radhi played 124 times and scored 86 goals for his country.
4. Interviews with Radhi in various newspapers, May 2003, plus interviews in Baghdad with the author's contacts, October 2004. Radhi was reluctant to go into detail about his life because he was writing his autobiography.

5. Jasim, interview with the author, October 2004.

6. A website called Shakomako.net.

7. After this incident Sharar Haydar told Uday that he would not play for Iraq again.

8. Associated Press (12 May 2003).

9. Alan Abrahamson, interviews in Baghdad, 15 August 2003.

10. Iraqsoccer.net's comment on Ja'far in October 2003, when he announced that he would retire, at the age of thirty-seven, at the end of the season.

11. A comment from Ja'far's neighbour in Sadr City, October 2004.

12. All further interviews in this chapter, unless otherwise stated, were conducted in Baghdad in September, October and November 2004 by Iraqi journalists on behalf of the author. To ensure their safety I have not named them here.

13. *Christian Science Monitor* (20 November 2003).

14. *Denver Post* and other American newspapers, 28 April 2004.

Chapter 11

1. Quotations from al-Samarrai in this chapter are from an interview with the author in Athens in August 2004 or from interviews with newspapers and magazines between April 2003 and July 2004, including a lengthy question-and-answer session with *Sports Illustrated* in April 2004.

2. The Iraqi National Movement claimed to represent Shias and Sunnis. It argued that Saddam could be overthrown by a small American force because much of the Iraqi army would defect to them. It thought Iraq should be a federal state, to allow the different religious groups independence.

3. *Iraq Business Journal* (spring 2004).

4. Mounzer Fatfat, interview with Associated Press, May 2004, and with the author in Patras, Greece, 2004.

5. Address to US Chamber of Commerce, May 2003.

6. Interviews with the author, April–December 2004.

7. Despite this, Sharar Haydar was listed, briefly, as the IFA general secretary in 2003. Saeed was president. Ahmed Radhi was vice-president.

8. Information on Clark taken from an interview with the author in August 2004 in Athens.

9. In December 2004 Clark was awarded an MBE, one of fifty civilians honoured for their work in Iraq. There was confusion about his role, however. The BBC reported that he had coached the Iraqi football team. He said: 'It's very nice on a personal level to be recognized. This, like anything else, has been very much a team effort. One of the real satisfactions I get out of this bizarre job I have landed myself with in Iraq is that it's full of people with energy and passion and vision.'

10. Interviews with *USA Today* and *Sports Illustrated*, April–May 2004.

11. This story was covered by major news agencies and many newspapers during 2004. I have taken quotations from a cross-section of them.

Chapter 12

1. The name 'Schengen' is taken from a small town in Luxembourg. In June 1985 seven European Union countries signed a treaty to end internal border checkpoints and controls. More countries have joined the treaty since then. In November 2004 there were fifteen Schengen countries: Austria, Belgium, Denmark, Finland, France, Germany, Iceland, Italy, Greece, Luxembourg, Netherlands, Norway, Portugal, Spain and Sweden. All these countries, except Norway and Iceland, are members of the European Union.

2. The information on violence in July is based on reports in the *Daily Telegraph*.

3. For more on Islamic fundamentalism and bin Laden, see Jason Burke, *Al-Qaeda: The True Story of Radical Islam* (Penguin, 2004).

4. This had been rebranded in 2004–5 as League One, but to most football fans it remained the Third Division.

5. This was published on 6 August. Much of it was about the Iraqi team's 'Goodwill Tour' of England in May.

6. George Packer, 'The Playing Field', *The New Yorker* (30 August 2004).

7. Charles Elmore, *Palm Beach Post* (17 August 2004).

8. Peter Berlin, *International Herald Tribune* (17 August 2004).

9. *San Francisco Chronicle* (19 August 2004).

10. From Michael Bard, 'The Jews of Iraq', Jewish Virtual Library website, and Orly Halprin, 'To Be a Jew in Baghdad', *Jerusalem Post* (October 2004).

11. *The Observer* reported on 22 August that Stange had stayed in Germany.

12. Stange, interview with the author in Jena and Patras, supplemented by interview with FIFA.com.
13. *Sports Illustrated* (19 August 2004).
14. Ibid.
15. Tom Perry, Reuters (31 August 2004).

Chapter 13

1. I have used the term 'Christian' here since this was how the violence was reported by the British media. One newspaper wrote that 'of the 750,000 Christians in Iraq, the majority are Chaldean Roman Catholic, the rest are Syrian Catholic, Syrian Orthodox and Assyrian'. However, many experts argue that all Christians in Iraq are Assyrian.
2. In November 2004 the BBC reported that taxis charged £2,750 for the journey.
3. Richard Beeston, *The Spectator* (25 September 2004).
4. This is not his real name, which he asked me to withhold.
5. Haydar, interviews with the author, April–December 2004, supplemented by interviews with ESPN.
6. The semi-finals and the final of the Iraqi Cup had been played in Arbil, in the Kurdish north, in August 2003. According to iraqsport.com, this was the final stage of the competition, which had been postponed in March. The four teams taking part were al-Shurta (the Police), al-Nafat (Oil Ministry), al-Minaa (Port, from Basra) and al-Talaba (the Students). Al-Talaba won the competition, taking the modest prize of $3,000. The runners-up were al-Shurta, who won $2,000.
7. Latif Yahia, interview with the author, November 2004.

Index

Abbas, Mohammed Salih (swimmer), 172
Abdul-Majid, Mohammed, 24
Abdul-Sattar, Faris, 23
academy *see* football academy
Adnan, Safa, 23
Afghanistan, 27, 195–6
Ahmed, Akram Salman, 217–18, 219
Ahmed, Ala, 93
Ahmed, Hadi, 93
Ahmed, Nashwan, 23
Ahmed, Raed (weightlifter), 10, 11, 12, 115–16
Air Force football club *see* al-Quwa al-Jawiya (Air Force) football club
Air Serv International, 79
AKB Media, 120
Akram, Faleh, 52
Akram, Nashat, 23
Alattar, Layth (Swedish sponsor), 176
Alawi, Karim, 151
Algeria, 113, 140
Ali Hadi, Maiham, 155
Ali Jaber, Ahmed, 67
Ali, Najah (boxer), 173
Alkadhi, Amar, 133–4
Alkadhi, Bashar, 122, 132–4
All-Star XI football team, 68
Amana football club, 50
America (USA): anti-American responses by Olympic athletes, 172–3; attitude to football in Iraq, 36, 43–4, 68; breach of security in Iraq, 215; choice of al-Samarrai as sports boss, 157; CIA, 158, 214, 219–20; football and ethnic minorities in, 3; FIFA ranking, 3, 28; football in, 3, 28; Iraqi suspicion of motives for invasion, 27–8, 214; information on torture of athletes in Iraq, 11; Iraqis' attitude to Americans, 31, 34, 38, 42–3, 69, 158, 172–3, 179, 186, 196, 208, 210; National Intelligence Council, 220; and Saeed, 127; and al-Samarrai, 160

Ammo Baba (Emmanuel Baba Dawud), 36, 53–4, 220; Air Force appointment, 91; appearance, 56, 63–4, 73; and Ba'ath Party, 91; in Baghdad clubs, 88, 92, 93; on Bremer, 69; on Buannic, 79; on change in Iraq, 85; character, 70, 74; children, 92; suspicion over conspiracy, 80, 82; contact with author, 68–9; deaths of family members, 85–6; early life, 55–6; earnings in Iraq, 82, 83–4, 86, 99, 104; in Egypt, 56, 77, 88; family, 62, 63; Farhan on, 129; as footballer, 55, 56, 62, 63, 88–9, 90, 91, 92; as full-time coach, 92–3, 97; Haydar on, 65–6; imprisonment of father and brother, 85; as interviewee, 74–8; on invasion, 75; Jasim on, 142; Josephine (Ammo Baba's wife), 64, 69, 84–5, 92; King Faisal II on, 89; life in Baghdad, 85, 175; love of London, 62, 63; Mubarak on, 55; Pnouel on, 62; quality as coach, 97–8; refusal of interview, 200–1; refusal to leave Iraq, 88–9, 92, 102; religion, 85; retirement from football, 92; al-Rubai on, 128–9; and Saddam, 63, 65, 75, 94, 98, 100, 101, 103–4; under Saddam's regime, 86, 95; and Saeed, 172, 187, 201; Stange on, 64–5; and Uday, 63, 64, 84, 100–2, 103, 104, 128–9; sacked by Uday, 101; on Zaidang, 83; *see also* boys' football team
Amnesty International: complaint to IOC, 33
Ansar al-Sunna (Sunni group), 215
anti-Semitism in Iraq, 58, 73, 193
Arab Cup, 97
al-Arabiya television station, 39
Arbil, 20, 38, 52, 53; finals of Iraqi Cup in, 227

229

Arif, Colonel Abd as Salaam, 89, 90–1
army, Iraqi: football club, 49, 96; growth, 96; al-Samarrai's advice to US government, 158
Asian Cup, 20, 24, 27; Iraq success in, 97; as preparation for Olympics, 179
Asian Football Confederation, 21, 126, 171
'Ask, Nick': on American invasion, 207; background, 139; on corruption in Iraq, 177; on footballers' conditions in Iraq, 93–4, 96, 97; on importance of football for Iraqis, 52; letter to Clark, 137; on Stange, 137, 138
Assyrian Democratic Movement, 199–200
Assyrian Sports Club, 90
Assyrians: in Baghdad, 59; in football teams in Iraq, 59; in Iraq, 56–7, 58–9, 227; in the Middle East, 59; Muslims' attitude to, 58; RAF Employees' (Assyrian) football club, 88; treatment by British, 59; unpopularity in Iraq, 59
Athens Olympics see Olympic Games; Olympic team, Iraqi
Atia, Hassan, 185
attendance at football matches: Athens Olympics, 188, 191, 195, 196, 197; Baghdad, 133, 213, 218, 219
Australia: defeat by Iraq, 196; Iraqi team in, 26; Stange as coach, 8, 44

Ba'ath Party, 48, 69, 91–2, 112; after invasion, 157; Arif and, 90, 91; Communism and, 48, 91; compulsion to join, 161; and control of sport in Iraq, 165; ideology, 94; intelligence network, 94; membership and sport after Saddam, 161
Baba, Ammo see Ammo Baba
Badraddin, Rafid, 20
'Bagdad FC', 73, 78, 80, 81–2, 83
Baghdad: attacks on churches, 199; attempt at normal life, 178; attendance at football matches, 133, 213, 218, 219; British Embassy, 89; dangers, 38, 166, 200, 201–3, 214–15, 218; dangers to football clubs, 206; gunfire after football successes, 19, 180, 197; as centre of football, 48, 50, 51, 94–5; first football club, 59; first football league, 49–50; 'football academy', 36, 72, 80, 84, 103, 128; football teams, 49; Green Zone, 70, 201, 203; police disbanded, 34; Sheraton Hotel, 9; Stange on danger/threats, 15, 16, 26, 43, 65, 66; unwillingness of foreign footballers to visit,

180; see also al-Karkh; al-Quwa al-Jawiya; Sadr City; al-Shaab stadium; al-Shurta; al-Talaba; al-Zawraa
Baghdad Equestrian Club, 178
Baghdad High School for Boys, 106
Bahrain: Iraqi players in, 140; matches against Iraq, 20
Baker, Rustum, 12
al-Bakr, General Ahmed Hasan, 94
Baladeyat (Municipalities) football club, 50
Baldoni, Enzo, 197
Barcelona football club, 90
basketball: importance in Iraq, 44; al-Samarrai's career, 158
Basra: Clark in, 164; football teams, 51–2, 93, 213; players from, 93
Beckham, David, 4
Belize football team, 28
Berlusconi, Silvio, 68
Berluscowitz, Alexandre, 79, 80, 81
Bhutan football team, 28
Bigley, Kenneth, 211
Bisham Abbey sports centre, 119
Blair, Tony, 68, 126
Blatter, Sepp, 21, 181, 189
Boa Morte, Luis, 189
Bookseller of Kabul, The (Seierstad), 44–5
Boskowitz, Alexandre, 79, 80, 81
boxing team, Iraq, 108, 173
boys' football team, Ammo Baba's: in Brittany, 70–1, 72, 73–4, 78, 80; 'football academy', 36, 72, 80, 84, 103, 128; and Gothia Cup, 175; return to Iraq after French visit, 175; visa for Sweden refused, 176–7; see also Enfants du Monde charity
Bremer, Paul: Ammo Baba on, 69; involvement in Iraqi football, 36, 67; and money for sport in Iraq, 160–1; Stange on, 23
Bristol Rovers, 24, 68, 121–2, 123, 124
Britain: backgrounds of professional footballers, 4; British clubs' approaches to Ammo Baba, 88, 89; British understanding of Iraqis, 158; and football outside Britain, 2; foreign players, 4, 46; history of football, 89–90; intelligence, MI6, 214; Iraq under British control, 56–8, 59–61; lack of support for 'Goodwill Tour', 119, 131; refusal to grant asylum to Iraqis, 214; support for Iraqi football, 37; see also England; Foreign Office
British Council: and 'Goodwill Tour', 135
British Parliament: Iraq game against MPs, 124–5

Brittany: football tournament for boys, 70–1, 72, 73–4, 78, 80
Buannic, Yves, 78, 79
Burhan, Saher, 150
Bush, George W., 195–6, 219

Caborn, Richard, 126
Canada: Iraqi emigration to, 62, 85, 142
CARE International, 121
Charlton, Sir Bobby, 51, 222
Charlton, Air Commodore Lionel, 57
cheating and match fixing, 96–7, 101, 109, 117, 118
Chengdu, 180
Children of the World see Enfants du Monde charity
China: Iraq's qualification for Asian Cup, 20, 68, 180; treatment of athletes, 13
Christians: in Iraq, 45, 58, 199–200, 227; see also Assyrians
Churchill, Winston: and Iraq, 57
CIA, 158, 214, 220
Clark, Mark: at Athens Olympics, 183, 190, 198; awarded MBE, 226; and Ba'ath Party members, 160, 165; background, 164; on Bush campaign advertisement, 196; as CPA's adviser on sport in Iraq, 164–5; and finance of sport after Saddam, 165–6; on 'Goodwill Tour', 134–5; and IFA, 173–4; and Iraqi Sport sponsorship, 170; and Olympic sports in Iraq, 169, 173–4; and popularity of football in Iraq, 169; on Stange, 137; on truth in Iraq, 201; see also Coalition Provisional Authority (CPA)
Clarke, Tony, MP, 124
class systems: and football, 4–5
Clough, Brian, 222
Clwyd, Ann, 9–10
coaches see football coaches
Coalition Provisional Authority (CPA), 22; dissolved, 177–8; on football in Iraq, 32; on 'Goodwill Tour' of England, 134, 136; money for sport in Iraq, 160; request from 'Nick Ask' over Stange's salary, 137; Sweden's lack of recognition, 177; see also Clark, Mark
Communist countries: coaches in Iraq from, 5; sport in, 13
Communist Party, Iraq, 90; Ba'ath Party and, 48, 91; links with eastern bloc countries, 90, 91
Cook, William: football coaching in Iraq, 5

corruption: after fall of Saddam, 162, 163; Ibrahim brothers, 53; in Iraqi sport, 32, 52, 93, 112, 145, 170–1; football, 93, 128, 150, 204, 206, 207, 208; Iraqis and, 67, 162, 170, 177; Uday, 9, 10, 12
Costa Rica: defeat by Iraq, 191
CPA see Coalition Provisional Authority (CPA)
criminality in Iraq, 178, 203, 217, 220; Uday, 33, 214
cronyism in Iraq, 26; Saeed's cronies, 130, 131–2, 134, 135–6; Uday's cronies, 49, 108, 150, 154–5
Cruyff, Johan, 35
Ctvrtlik, Bob, 13

Daham, Ahmed, 141
Dawud, Emmanuel Baba see Ammo Baba
Dawud, Josephine (Ammo Baba's wife), 64, 69, 84–5, 92
Dawud, Pnouel ('Tarzan'; Ammo Baba's brother), 61–2, 63, 84, 85, 93, 175
defection: anonymity of athletes, 10; punishment of families, 115, 116–17, 155, 159
Dell'Olio, Nancy, 120, 124
democracy: and Iraq, 219
developing countries: aspirations to join European clubs, 4; football in, 3
Dhibban, RAF base, 60
disabled athletes: punishment by Uday, 156
al-Diwan, Issam Thamer, 12, 31, 33, 114; fired by Americans, 207
Duhok, 53, 146
Dukan, 166

earnings of athletes: Uday and, 153
earnings of Iraqi footballers, 59–60, 130–1, 139–40, 223; after 1976 Olympic qualifier, 93; after Olympics, 67–8; Air Force team, 145; broken promises over, 67–8; compared to Syrians' earnings, 205; dependence on gifts, 112; players working abroad, 23, 140, 148, 150, 205; post-invasion under Saeed, 127; proportion demanded by Uday from footballers working abroad, 23, 112–13, 116, 129, 140–1, 146, 152–3, 155; Saeed on, 186; as supplement to wages of daily job, 59, 63
East Germany: football in, 8, 97
Eberly, Don, 31; and Haydar, 162–3; on Iraqi football, 37; National Fatherhood Initiative, 161; return to USA, 164; vision for sport in Iraq, 162

Egypt: Ammo Baba in, 56, 77, 88; ties with Iraq, 90

election (2005), xiv, 219

Enfants du Monde (Children of the World) charity, 74, 75, 78–80; Ammo Baba on, 79, 80–2; Iraqi employees, 87; press coverage, 124–5; tickets scandal, 80–1

England: 2002 FIFA ranking, 3; Iraqi footballers in, 24; Premiership, money earned, 46; wish to play Iraq, 143; *see also* Britain; 'Goodwill Tour' of England

Eriksson, Sven Goran, 120, 124

Eshaya, Youra, 24, 68, 121–2

ESPN (*formerly* Entertainment and Sports Programming Network) television, 10

Eusebio, 82

Everesto (Brazilian coach), 144

executions and killings: 178, 179, 203, 211; after dissolution of CPA, 179; of athletes and sports leaders, 52, 114; and collaboration with Americans, 179; head of Iraq Football Association, 52; of Jews, 193; ordered by Uday, 49, 100, 102, 106, 108; in Saddam's Iraq, 52, 94, 106, 107; threatened death penalty for hitting Saddam's sons, 159; threats to footballers, 97, 100, 115; of Uday's teachers, 99; willingness to kill, 211

Faisal I, king of Iraq, 57

Faisal II, king of Iraq, 89

Fallujah, 131, 178, 196, 211

fans, Iraqi: after fall of Saddam, 34; attendance at matches after invasion, 213, 218, 219; behaviour, 43; at Athens Olympics, 189, 191–2, 197; Iraqi cup final (2003), 38; in Jordan, 206; in Mexico, 143; opposition to Saddam and Uday, 52, 111; Uday's thugs as, 36; and al-Zawraa, 141

Farhan, Razzaq, 23, 129

Farrey, Tom, 10–11, 127–8, 186

Fatfat, Mounzer, 67, 160–1, 171

Fawzi, Hussam, 20, 125, 129

al-Fayad, Ahmed, 146

Fedayeen, 37, 107

Fédération Internationale de Football Association (FIFA): attempt to prevent rivalries, 13; award to Stange, 26; on football in Palestine, 27–8; and 'Goodwill Tour', 136; investigation of torture in Iraq, 12, 109, 114; Iraq affiliated to, 60; money to IFA, 128; rankings, 3, 17, 27, 28, 124,

125, 180, 212; and Stange's salary, 137; support for Saeed, 171

Ferguson, Sir Alex, 8

Fever Pitch (Hornby), 2–3, 46

FIFA *see* Fédération Internationale de Football Association (FIFA)

Finland: match against Iraq, 97

Fisher, Fiona, 191

flag of Iraq, 66–7, 167

football: amorality, 1–2; as big business, 46, 168; books, 2–3, 46; internationalism, 63; search for new talent, 4, 46; success in developing countries, 3

football academy (Ammo Baba's), 36, 72, 80, 84, 103, 128; and Gothia Cup, 175–6; refusal of visas for Sweden, 176; Saeed on, 187

Football Association (English): on Revie's move to UAE, 5; support for 'Goodwill Tour', 131, 134, 135

football coaches: employment abroad, 5; foreigners as, 5; in Iraq, 5, 8, 19, 66, 154; managers and, 5; vs managers, national teams, 5; successful, 8; under Uday, 206; *see also* Ammo Baba; Stange, Bernd

football in Iraq: after invasion, 157; Ammo Baba in, 55; beginnings, 59; British and, 59; business potential, 168; cash shortages, 93; cost of kit, 78; decline, 43; FIFA ranking, 3, 17, 124, 125, 180, 212; finance by Saddam, 96; first international game, 60; first recorded match, 59; funding for 'Goodwill Tour', 122, 128, 132–4, 190; importance for Iraqis, 32, 34, 38, 52, 53, 153, 168; Iraqi Cup Final, August 2003, 38; journalists on, 32; match fixing and cheating, 96–7, 101, 109, 117, 118; organization, 48–9; Nabeel's plans for, 120–1; as outlet for frustration, 90; over-age players, 97, 109; post-invasion, training in Najaf, 216; post-war conditions, 19; as propaganda weapon, 168; proposed TV documentary, 17–18; reaction to win in Asian Cup, 180; religion and, 16, 20, 153, 180, 217; reputation, 111; satellite television transmissions, 216; as Shia sport, 37, 80, 84, 93–4, 153, 204; decline in attendance after invasion, 213, 218, 219; under Saddam, 52; websites, 48–9, 50–1; *see also* boys' football team; al-Shaab stadium

football kit: for Athens Olympics, 188; payment for, 78

football literature, 2–3
footballers: earnings, 4; interests, 8; as multimillionaires, 4; professional, backgrounds, 4; retired, employment, 92
footballers in Iraq: accused of theft, 146–7; acquiring permission to travel abroad, 153; chosen by Uday, 141, 146–7, 154–5; in Europe, 24; families, treatment of, 10–11, 102, 108, 110, 115–16, 117, 151, 159; fear as incentive, 140, 149, 154; as labourers, 151; lack of security, 140, 209, 215; living conditions, 93; playing abroad, 23, 102, 140–1, 148, 150, 152, 205, 218; Saeed on, 194; poverty, 204; punishments for failure, 11, 12, 20, 35–6, 150–1, 152; punishments by Uday, 20, 35–6, 101–2, 107–8, 109, 111, 113–14, 118, 142, 145, 150–1; threatened with execution, 97, 100, 115; threatened by Uday, 35, 99–100, 102, 111–12, 115, 143, 144, 151; travel restrictions, 155, 176–7; see also earnings of Iraqi footballers
Foreign Office (British government): and 'Goodwill Tour', 119, 131, 134, 135
Forrest, Charles, 33
Free Iraq Olympic Group, 162–20
Free Iraqi Council, 160
free market: and Iraq, 219–20

Galbraith, Peter (former US ambassador to Croatia), 13–14
gambling: Muslim fundamentalists and, 178; Uday, 108, 117
Germany, 4–5, 18, 24, 97; see also Stange, Bernd
Gibson, Dr Ian, MP, 125
'Goodwill Tour' of England, 68, 131–2; accommodation problems, 119, 135; lack of British government support, 119, 131; loss against Trinidad and Tobago, 125; match against Members of Parliament, 124–5; match against non-league clubs, 126; money raised, 134; planned fund-raising dinner, 126; plans for, 121–2; programme for final match, 126; Saeed's cronies on, 130, 131–2, 134, 135–6; sponsorship, 132, 134, 135; Stange and, 119, 125, 129–30, 135–6; unwillingness of players to talk, 127; see also Nabeel, Yamam
Gorgis, Basil, 142–4
Gothia Cup, 175
Greece, Olympic Games see Olympic Games, Athens
Guam football team, 28

Gulf Cup, 51, 93, 152; Iraq success in, 97; Uday's bullying, 143
Gulf states: football in, 51
gunfire: after successes, 19, 180, 197

Habbinaniya, RAF base, 60–1, 63
Hadi, Ali Maiham, 155
al-Hail, Abdul, Wahab Abu, 23, 196–7
Hamad, Adnan, 136, 219; on American invasion, 179–80, 190, 196, 197; and Asian Cup, 179, 180; at Athens Olympics, 183, 187, 190; as Iraqi Olympic coach, 17, 66; and Israeli reporter, 192–3; resignation, 217; and Saeed, 104, 212; as Stange's replacement, 136, 212
Hamid, Jaber, 205
Hammoudi, Raad, 150, 163; background, 164; Haydar and, 163, 164; refusal to join Uday's team, 98
Hanoon, Jalil, 93
Hasan-al-Bakr, General Ahmed, 94
Hashim, Salam, 154
Hassan, Falah, 25, 97
Hassan, Jamal (wrestling coach), 155
Hassan, Margaret, 211
Hassan, Muhsin, 12
Haydar, Sharar, 11–12, 31–2, 108; on Ammo Baba, 65, 113; background, 111; decision to retire from football, 109–10; and Eberly, 162–3; exposure of Uday's treatment of footballers, 109, 110; on future of football in Iraq, 210; on Hamad, 136; and Hammoudi, 163, 164; imprisonment and torture, 109, 110, 111, 112; on IOC, 33; move to London, 110; return to Iraq after fall of Saddam, 162; return to London, s163; and Saeed, 162, 172; and al-Samarrai, 163
Henry, Thierry, 72
Hikmat, Ala (sprinter), 172–3
Hill, Frank (manager of Notts. County), 88
Hill, Jimmy: and Saudi football, 51
Holding the Zero (Seymour), 60–1
Hornby, Nick, 2–3, 46
human rights: Human Rights Watch, xv; and IOC, 14
humiliation: of footballers by Uday, 113, 118, 145, 148, 152; shaving of head as ultimate humiliation, 12
Hundred and One Days, A: A Baghdad Journal (Seierstad), 45
Hussein, Laith, 141; imprisonment, 153; punishment after losing match, 151
Hussein, Mustafa (Qusay's son), 37

Hussein, Qusay (Saddam's second son), 37, 38, 94, 98; at school, 159; as Saddam's successor, 103

Hussein, Saddam: and Ammo Baba, 63, 65, 75, 98, 101, 103–4; approval of, 31, 214; assassination of defectors, 159; atrocities, 6, 48; capture, 39–40; character, 106; contacts with media, 39; early life, 94; family and children, 94, 100; marriages, 94, 100; fear of, 30; financial support for Iraqi football, 96; intelligence and spying, 94, 105; invasion of Iran, 96, 159; and Iraqi football, 52; and Jews in Iraq, 193; popular policies, 106; portraits, 6; rise to power, 91; search for, 38–9; and Stange, 42; support for football, 34, 52

Hussein, Saith, 35–6

Hussein, Sajida ('Sadja'; Saddam's first wife), 34, 94

Hussein, Samira (Saddam's second wife), 100

Hussein, Uday (Saddam's eldest son), xiii, xv, 14, 38, 50, 94; academic success, 99; Ammo Baba threatened by, 100–1; attempt on life, 102–3; attempts to outwit, 150; and black market, 113; bullying tactics, 143; character, 106; choice of footballers and athletes, 141, 146–7, 154–5; conversion to Shia, 103; corruption, 9, 10, 12; criminal activities, 33, 214; cronies, 49, 108, 150, 154–5; death, 37; and defection of athletes, 115, 155; demands earnings of footballers working abroad, 23, 112–13, 129, 140–1, 146, 152–3, 155; disappearance of critics of, 106; disinherited by Saddam, 103; domination of sport in Iraq, 113; early life, 98–9; elected to Parliament, 103; fear as incentive to win, 140, 149, 154; footballers' accounts of treatment by, 105–18, 139–56; and INOC, 14, 33, 49, 98, 152; jealousy, 168; killings, 49, 100, 102, 106, 108; knowledge of sport, 107; legacy, 163, 206–7; love of hunting, 153; 'parties', 107; permission for footballers to work abroad, 23, 113, 129, 140–1; as president of IFA, 49; private prison, 107; unpredictability, 102, 106, 153, 155; punishment of footballers for lost matches, 20, 35–6, 101–2, 107–8, 109, 111, 113–14, 118, 142, 145, 150–1; Qeis on, 113; and al-Rasheed football club, 21; at school, 159; shooting of Watban Ibrahim, 117; and Stange, 42; theft of money from athletes, 116; threats to footballers, 35, 99–100, 102,

111–12, 115, 143, 144, 151; torture of athletes, 5–6, 7, 9–12, 98–9, 113, 125, 142; torture of friends, 103; victims on, 105–18, 139–56; wealth, 102, 107; wish to outdo father, 152; and women in sport, 166–8; Yahia on, 105–6, 213–14; see also Iraqi National Olympic Committee (INOC)

Ibrahim, Barzan (Saddam's half-brother), 53

Ibrahim, Watban (Saddam's half-brother), 53, 117

IFA see Iraqi Football Association (IFA)

imprisonment of footballers, 11–12, 114, 115, 142, 144, 145, 151

Indict, 9, 14; complaint against INOC, 33; identity of sources, 10; on IOC, 33

INOC see Iraqi National Olympic Committee (INOC)

International Olympic Committee (IOC): attempt to prevent rivalries, 13; banning of countries, 13, 14; complaints from Indict, 9–10, 33; decision to dissolve Iraq's Olympic committee, 33; dissolution of INOC, 157; Ethics Commission, 10; Iraq as member, 160; and Uday, 33

Internet research, 47–8

invasion of Iraq, xiii–xiv; Iraqi anger over, 31

IOC see International Olympic Committee (IOC)

Iran: defeat by Iraq (2003), 17; celebrations in Baghdad, 19; FIFA ranking, 3, 17, 212; invasion by Iraq, 96, 159; revolution, 96

Iraq, 211–12; after dissolution of CPA, 177–8; anti-Saddam groups, 160; artificial borders, 30, 211; bombing by British, 57; creation by British, 211; discrimination in, 10; election (2005), xiv, 219; experts on, 30–1; fear in, 45, 69, 206, 212, 213; flag, 66–7, 167; history, 30, 56–7, 89, 90–1; independence (1932), 58; Interim Committee to Administer Sport, 157, 163; Ministry of Youth and Sport, 67, 134, 169, 207; organization under Saddam, 48, 69; rebellion (1920), 57; religious freedom under Saddam, 199; resentment over return of exiles, 208–9; ruling élite, 48, 53, 57, 83; sanctions, effects, 80, 140; as training ground for Islamic militants, 220; under British control, 56–8, 59–61; uprising against Saddam (1991), 114; see also football in Iraq

Iraqi Football Association (IFA): administration and management problems, 136; Ahmed in, 217–18; Ammo Baba and, 86; Clark and, 169, 173–4; coalition money to, 128; contract with Stange, 7, 41, 136, 137; corruption, 93, 128, 150, 204, 206, 207, 208; disappearance after Uday's death, 157; financial concerns, 169, 171; and 'football academy', 84; formation (1948), 60; and 'Goodwill Tour', 135; Arkan Mahmood on, 205; Shakir Mahmood on, 209; Nabeel and, 120; offices destroyed, 157; refusal to release players, 142; Saddam's regime, 52–3; Saeed and, 22, 194; Saeed elected president, 136; al-Samarrai and, 171; Stange and, 20–1, 41, 130, 137, 190; Uday and, 41, 98, 141, 154; see also Baghdad

Iraqi Football League, 48, 49–50; revival after invasion, xiv, 206, 207, 212, 213, 216, 218–19; regional format after revival, 213

Iraqi national football team: in China for Asian Cup, 179–80; international successes, 97; and Iraqi flag, 66–7; as permanent group, 185; qualification for Asian Cup, 20; qualification for Olympic Games, 66; training, 18, 20, 26; see also 'Goodwill Tour' of England; Olympic team, Iraqi (2004)

Iraqi National Movement, 160

Iraqi National Olympic Committee (INOC), 1, 9, 14; coalition money to, 128; as cover for criminal activities, 33; destruction of offices, 17; disappearance after Uday's death, 157; extraction of money from athletes, 155; offices, 17, 107; al-Samarrai as president of post-invasion committee, 166; torture, evidence found, 32–3; Uday and, 14, 33, 49, 98, 152; woman member of post-invasion committee, 167

Iraqi people: Americans and, 32, 36, 68; attitude to Americans, 31, 34, 38, 42, 158, 172–3, 179, 186, 196, 208, 210; attitude to Westerners, 42–3, 217; celebration of football successes, 19, 180, 196–7; character, xiv, 45, 187; and corruption, 67, 162, 170, 177; cynicism, 34; in Greece, 187, 188–9; fascination with violence, 203; importance of football, 32, 34, 38, 52, 53; influence of Saddam's regime, 31; reaction to invasion, 30; survival under Saddam's regime, 31, 65, 67, 84, 177, 185, 209; suspicion of conspiracies, 66, 80, 82, 170, 177; unwillingness to challenge those in power, 209

Iraqi Sport (London), 169–70
Iraqi Women's Sports Federation, 167
iraqsport.com, 50–1, 215
'iron maiden', 32–3
Islam: and terrorism, 211; Uday and Islamic law, 146; see also Muslims; Shias; Sunnis
Israel: creation of, and Arabs, 58; and Iraq at Olympics, 192–3; junior football team, 73, 74
Italy: defeat of Iraq, 197; football organization, 90; footballers' backgrounds, 4–5; proposed game against Iraq, 68; role of coaches, 5
Itsalat, 133

Jabar, Saas, 149
Jaber, Ali Ahmed, 67
Jaed, Jabah, 49
Ja'far, Habib, 109, 141, 151–3, 209
al-Jaish (Army) football club, 49, 96
Jajou, Hama, 100
Jako (equipment company), 44
al-Jama'a football club, 50
Jamal, Bassim, 130, 136, 151
al-Jamali, Fakher Ali, 156
Japan: FIFA ranking, 3
Jasim, Hashim Nasif, 141–2
Jassam, Anwar, 153; after invasion, 208; family, 208; on invasion, 208; as national coach, 154; punishment after losing match, 154; works abroad, 154
Al-Jazeera, 180
al-Jbir, Mohammed, 87
Jena, FC Carl Zeiss Jena, 8
Jews in Iraq, 58, 193; anti-Semitism, 58, 73, 193
Jordan: Hammoudi in, 163–4; Iraqi players in, 140, 154
journalists in Iraq, 45, 70; interviews with Ammo Baba, 74–8; as targets, 70
junior tournament, Brittany: Iraqi players in, 70–1, 72, 73–4, 78, 80

Kadhum, Samir, 145–6, 210
Kadoim, Furat Ahmed (Kurdish referee), 38, 103–4, 116–17; as British asylum seeker, 214; disappearance of sister Wasila, 117; return to Baghdad, 214–15
Kamil, Hussein (Saddam's son-in-law), 96
Karim, Rahim, 93
al-Karkh football club, 36, 98, 112, 142, 218; unpopularity of, 112
Kazakhstan, 12, 109, 114
Khadim, Ahmed, 20, 23

Khadim, Ali, 51, 141
Khalif, Muthar, 35
Khaliq, Abdul (IFA treasurer), 129, 132, 172,
    174; Alkadhi on, 134; at Athens Olympics,
    183, 187, 192; Clark on, 135
Khazeal, Sahib, 140
Kheir, Majid Abu, 150
kidnapping, 178; fear of, 212; of Iraqis, 69;
    motives of kidnappers, 217; of Westerners,
    66, 70, 197, 202, 211, 217; of women by
    Uday, 99
Kirkuk, 178
Kudayer, Juma'a, 150
Kurdish football clubs, 53
Kurdistan: Kurds under British rule, 59; safety,
    20; see also Arbil; Duhok
Kuwait: invasion of, 114–15; theft of sports
    equipment by Iraq, 114–15

Latif, Yasir Abdul, 147–9, 205; wish to play
    abroad, 149–50
Lebanon: Assyrians in, 59; football in, 51; Iraqi
    players in, 140, 146, 147, 148, 152, 217;
    match against Iraq, 89
looters: of Iraqi sports facilities, 157

Macclesfield Town FC, 122, 125–6, 132–4
Mahdi, Dr Basil Abdul, 104, 171–2, 174, 183
Mahdi, Saleh, 114
Mahmood, Arkan, 144–5, 204–5
Mahmood, Shakir, 144, 208–9
Mahmoud, Barakat, 36–7
Mahmoud, Younis, 23
Malbrunot, Georges (French journalist),
    216–17
Manajid, Ahmed, 196
Mashal, Manhal, 23
match fixing and cheating, 96–7, 101, 109,
    117, 118
Medan al-Tarbiya football club, 59
media: British, and football outside Britain, 2;
    see also television
MI6, 214
Middle East: Americans' motive behind
    liberation of Iraq, 207–8; footballers from,
    4; Iraqi footballers signing for clubs abroad,
    140–1; organization of football in, 51; see
    also individual countries
Military Academy football club, 92, 93
al-Minaa football team, Basra, 51–2, 93
Mirza, Sabah, 52, 53, 96
Mohammed, Ali Ahmed, 19
Mohammed, Harda, 34

Mohammed, Muhammed (wrestler), 154–5
monarchy in Iraq, 57, 61
Mondial Pupilles de Plomelin, Le, 72
Morocco: defeat of Iraq at Athens Olympics,
    195
Mosul: American attack after suicide bombing,
    37–8, 59, 215
Mubarak, Hassanin, 50–1, 53, 55, 215–16
Mubarak, Suzanne, 100
Munir, Qusay, 127
Murphy, Jim, MP, 125
Muslims: attitude to Assyrians, 58; and
    gambling, 178; hatred of Zionism, 58; rise
    of fundamentalists in Iraq, 178; see also
    Shias; Sunnis
Mustafa, Jamal (Saddam's son-in-law), 49

Nabeel, Yamam: Alkadhi on, 134; background,
    120; Clark on, 135; CPA on, 134; finance
    for 'Goodwill Tour' of England, 128, 190;
    on Iraqi footballers, 132; motives behind
    and preliminary discussions on tour, 120,
    123, 135; on Olympic success, 190;
    organization of tour, 119–20; press releases,
    120–1, 126; rumours about Iraqi Sport,
    170; on Stange, 132; suspicion of
    conspiracy, 177; verdict after tour, 131
Naft-ul-Junoob (Basra football club), 213
Najaf, 52, 196, 215–16
al-Naqil (Transport) football club, 50
Nasser, Gamul Abdul, 90
Naswari, Ghaith, 50
Nazis: and sport, 13
Nuri, Mowafak, 154

Obaid, Haidar, 23
Olympic Games: Atlanta, 116; Los Angeles,
    167–8; football in, 168, 184; Iraq and, 160,
    166, 168–9; Jassam as coach (Moscow),
    154; opening ceremony (Athens), 190–1;
    security (Athens), 182; sponsorship of
    athletes, 184; Uday's choice of athletes
    (Sydney), 154–5; volunteers (Athens), 182;
    see also Free Iraq Olympic Group;
    International Olympic Committee; Iraqi
    National Olympic Committee; Olympic
    team, Iraqi (2004)
Olympic team, Iraqi (2004), 68, 172, 181;
    accommodation, 183; accreditation, 181,
    182, 187; at opening ceremony, 191;
    attendance at matches, 188, 191, 195, 196,
    197; defeats, 195, 197; Eberly on, 161;
    exploitation by Bush campaign, 195–6;

games won, 189, 191, 196; Iraqi fans, 189, 191–2; Latif on, 206; press coverage, 190, 191, 195; qualification, 97; volunteers on, 187, 189, 191; welcomed back to Iraq, 198

Oman: Iraqi players in, 152, 154; Stange as coach, 8–9

Omar (Iraqi journalist), 203–4

Oraebi, Waleeb, 87

Owens, Jesse, 13

Palestine: football in, 27–8; games against Iraq, 17, 64–5

Pan-Arab Games: Iraq success in, 97

Paraguay: defeat of Iraq, 197

Patras, Greece: stadium, 188

Penmarc'h, Brittany, 72, 73

Plomelin, 72

Pnouel (Ammo Baba's brother) see Dawud, Pnouel

Police football club see al-Shurta

Porto Rio Hotel, Greece, 183–4

Portugal: match against Iraq, 189; Olympic football team, 184

Powell, Colin, 220

Premiership: importance in English football, 2; as multimillion business, 46; proposed team to play Iraqis, 68, 122–3, 126, 134

Presidential Palace prison, 114, 115

'Prisoner of Uday', 151

punishments for lost matches, 11, 12, 20, 35–6, 150–1, 152; by Uday, 20, 35–6, 101–2, 107–8, 109, 111, 113–14, 118, 142, 145, 150–1; see also torture

Puskas, Ferenc: as Saudi football coach, 51

al-Qaeda, 31, 207, 211

Qasim, Amer, 23

Qasim, Brigadier Abd al Karim, 89, 90–1

Qatar: football in, 35, 51; Iraqi players in, 25, 140, 141, 152, 154; Palestine games in, 27; Stange in, 64–5

Qeis, Saad, 113–15, 210

Quimper, 72

al-Quwa al-Jawiya (Air Force) football club, 49, 50, 96–7, 113, 142, 205; after invasion, 210; fans, 210; patron, 210; payment of players, 145; in post-invasion league, 212, 218

Raad, Yassir, 185

racism, 13, 14; in football, 63

Radhi, Ahmed, 23–5, 141; on football in Iraq, 35; move to Qatar, 141; on new football

league, 218–19; power battle, 130; as president of al-Zawraa, 204, 206; protection of fellow footballers, 145–6; punishment after losing match, 151; rumours about Iraqi Sport, 170; rumours of collaboration with Uday, 35; and Saeed, 162, 169, 194; alleged attack on Saeed, 82, 133, 136; al-Samarrai on, 171; and Uday, 207; as World Cup scorer, 143

al-Radwaniyah prison, 107, 151–2; torture of athletes in, 109, 110, 113, 116, 118, 145, 148, 151–2

RAF see Royal Air Force, British (RAF)

Rahim, Abbas, 23

Rami, Basher, 150

Ramsey, Sir Alf, 82, 95, 222

Rasheed, Raad Abas (tae kwon do competitor), 172

al-Rasheed sports club, 21, 53, 98, 111, 141; Haydar in, 111; players forced to join, 141, 144; pressure on Sabeeh to join, 168; Saeed on, 194; unpopularity, 111, 149

al-Rawi, Hilal, 115

al-Rawi, Laith, 150

Real Madrid football club, 90

referees: bribery and intimidation, 53, 112; fear of Uday, 149; match fixing, 96–7, 101, 117, 118; punishments, 147–8; treatment by Uday, 117; see also Kadoim, Furat Ahmed

religion: and football, 16, 20, 153, 180, 217; in Iraq, 30, 183, 211; and kidnappers, 178, 203

Reuters, 1, 7

Revie, Don, 5, 82, 95

Riedl, Alfred, 28

Ronaldo, Cristiano (Portuguese footballer), 184

Rooney, Wayne, 4

Royal Air Force, British (RAF): and Ammo Baba, 55, 56; Habbaniya base, 60–1; in Iraq, 57; move to outskirts of Fallujah, 60; RAF Employees' (Assyrian) football club, 88; treatment of Iraqis, 57

Royal Iraqi Guards football club, 88

al-Rubai, Basim, 128, 130

Rwanda football team, 28

Sabawi, Omar (Saddam's nephew), 53

Sabeeh, Dr Iman, 167–8

Saddam City see Sadr City

Saddam Hussein see Hussein, Saddam

'Saddam's Revolutionary Fighters' (Fedayeen), 37, 107

Sadiq, Shiwan Ahmad, 24
Sadir, Salih, 196
Sadr City, 34, 144, 183, 206; boy footballers, 80; coalition appointee, 179; *see also* al-Zawraa
Sadr, Imam Mohammed, 144
al-Sadr, Moqtada (cleric), 178, 179
Saeed, Hussein, 1, 20, 21–2, 86, 97, 185; Alkadhi on, 134; and Ammo Baba, 172, 201; at Athens Olympics, 181, 183, 185–6, 187, 189, 190, 192, 193–4; attack by Radhi, 82; breach of Olympic rules, 181; character, 162; cronies, 26; and Eberly, 162; desire to control Iraqi football, 172, 192; elected president of IFA, 136; Farrey's investigation, 127–8; in football, 21, 186–7; and 'Goodwill Tour', 119, 130, 131–2, 134, 135–6; and Haydar, 162, 172; on IFA, 22; and Iraqi Olympic football team, 173–4; on 2004 league, 212; Nabeel on, 120, 131–2; as national hero, 171; popularity, 172; possible complicity with Uday, 21, 193–4, 207, 209; on post-war state of football, 22; and Radhi, 130, 162, 169; refusal to join Uday's team, 98; and Stange, 21–2, 212; and Uday, 21–2, 171, 172–3; as vice-president of new national Olympic committee, 166;
Salah-al-Deen football club, 53, 147; and Ibrahim brothers, 53
salaries *see* earnings
al-Samarrai, Ahmed, 157–8; advice to US government, 158; appearance, 197; at Athens Olympics, 182–3, 190, 192, 197; background, 158–9; defection, 159; and Eberly, 162; in England, 159–60; and Haydar, 163; and IFA, 171; and Israel, 192; as president of new national Olympic committee, 166; Radhi on, 204; rumours about Iraqi Sport, 170
Sami (Ammo Baba's son), 82–3
Samuel, Paul Mony, 12
sanctions against Iraq: effect of, 140; and nutrition, 80
Saudi Arabia: against Iraq in Asian Cup, 180; FIFA ranking, 3, 180; football in, 51; Iraqi players in, 23, 217; matches against Iraq, 66, 144, 154, 180
Scandinavia: footballers' backgrounds, 4–5
Schaefer, Winfried, 7
Scotland: FIFA ranking, 3
Seierstad, Asne, 44–5
Seymour, Gerald, 60–1

al-Shaab stadium, 36, 66, 67, 160, 167; occupied by American troops, 19; reconstruction, 160, 213
Shaati, Zawadi, 179, 187
al-Shabab, 52–3
shaving of head: as humiliation, 12, 108, 144
Shawel, Zia, 24
Shias: attendance at matches after invasion, 218; and Ba'ath Party, 92; in boys' football, 80; extremists, 178, 179, 211; football as Shia sport, 37, 80, 84, 93–4, 153, 204; and Iranian revolution, 96; in Iraqi army, 96; as majority party in Iraq, 31; poverty, 57, 80, 84, 93–4, 153, 183, 204; resistance to intervention in Iraq, 31; rivalry with Sunnis in Iraq, 57, 178; Uday and, 76, 84, 103
Shnishel, Radhi, 114, 141; protection of fellow footballers, 145–6
al-Shurta football club (the Police), 34, 49, 117; before Saddam, 52; and Hammoudi, 163, 164; in post-invasion league, 212, 218, 219
al-Sinaa (Industry) football club, 49
Spain: footballers' backgrounds, 4–5; organization of football, 90; role of coaches, 5
sponsorship for Iraqi sport: 128, 169–70; Ammo Baba's team in Gothia Cup, 176; by Alkadhi, 122, 132–4; need for, 168, 169; for sports equipment, 44
sport: and government, 12–13; media coverage, 2
sport in Iraq: after invasion, 157; American attitude to, 160–1; Ba'ath Party control, 164–5; corruption, 32, 52, 93, 112, 145, 170–1; elections, 166; exclusion of those who worked for Saddam, 161; facilities after Saddam, 167; finance after Saddam, 165–6; football, 93, 128, 150, 204, 206, 207, 208; history, 160; importance for Iraqis, 52, 53, 161; iraqsport.com, 50–1; range of sports, 166; and regime change, 161; and Saddam's regime, 158; under control of al-Samarrai, 157, 159, 166–7; *see also* boxing team, Iraq; football in Iraq; wrestling team, Iraq
sports clubs: Baghdad, 51; *see also* al-Rasheed sports club
sports literature, 2
Stange, Bernd, 1, 8, 64–5, 138, 219, 220; accusations against, 7, 42; affection for Iraqi players, 16; Alkadhi on, 134; and Ammo

Baba, 65, 69; appearance, 129; as Iraq coach, 1, 7, 9; at Athens Olympics, 195; autobiography, 129; award from FIFA, 26, 41–2; bodyguard, 16; character, 1, 9, 15, 130; Clark on, 137; as coach in East Germany, 8; coaching abroad, 8–9; contract with IFA, 7, 41, 136, 137; CPA on, 134; criticism in Germany, 6–7, 9; dismissal, 212; fear for own safety in Iraq, 26, 43; financing of Iraqi football team, 22–3; first meeting with author, 129; as footballer, 8; in Germany to train Iraqi team, 19; goals and achievements as Iraq coach, 41–2, 137, 212; on 'Goodwill Tour', 119, 125, 129–30, 135–6; on Iraqi people, 16; on Iraqi success at Olympic Games, 190; lack of consistency, 20–1; on lack of money and support for Iraqi football, 23–4, 25–6, 130; and the media, 7–8; Nabeel on, 132; proposed TV documentary on, 17–18; rebuilding of Iraqi football, 43–4; and Saddam, 6, 42; on Saeed, 128; salary, 22, 41, 130, 137; as Stasi informer, 8; on Jack Straw, 125; on war in Iraq, 15–16
Stange, Dorothea, 9
Stasi (East German secret police), 8
steroids: and athletes in Iraq, 116
Straw, Jack, 125
Students see al-Talaba (Students) football club
suicide bombings, 178, 215
al-Sulaimaniyah football club, 205, 206
'Sunni triangle', 39, 136, 218
Sunnis: Ansar al-Sunna group, 215; and 2005 election, 219; as élite, 57, 92; extremists, 178, 179, 199, 211, 219–20; and football, 84; al-Qaeda, 31, 207, 211; resistance to intervention in Iraq, 31; rivalry with Shias in Iraq, 57, 178
survival under Saddam's regime, 31, 65, 67, 84, 177, 185, 209
Suweira, 178
Syria, 23, 51, 144, 155

al-Taal, Rokan, 149
Tabra, Assil, 150
al-Taey, Abdul Razak, 31
al-Talaba (Students) football club, 21, 38, 49, 50, 51, 53, 95; Haydar in, 112; Ja'far on, 152–3; match against Army club, 96; in post-invasion league, 212, 218
Tashkent, Uzbekistan, 64
al-Tayaran (Airlines) football club, 50, 52
Tehran: four-sided tournament (2003), 17

television: in Iraq, 216; satellite television, 3, 12, 216; sports coverage, 2
television documentary, proposed: negotiations, 17–18, 27
terrorism: and Islam, 211; professionalized, in Iraq, 220
Thamer al-Diwan see al-Diwan, Issam Thamer
Tikrit, 94; Saddam in, 39
al-Tikriti, Abid Hamid Mahmud, 39
torture: of athletes in Iraq, 32–3, 167; Baghdad torture chambers, 98; evidence of, 5–6, 32–3; FIFA investigation, 12, 109, 114; of footballers by Uday, 5–6, 7, 9–12, 98–9, 113, 125, 142; long-term effects, 207; methods, 6, 11–12, 109, 110, 145–6, 148, 152, 155, 167; protection against, 147; results of, 147; of wrestling team, 155; see also punishments
Transport football club see al-Naqil (Transport) football club
Trinidad and Tobago football team, 68, 122, 125
Truce International, 120, 124
Tunisia: Iraqi players in, 140
Turkey, 24, 60, 97
Turkmenistan football team, 180
Tylfah, Khayrallah, 94

Uday Hussein see Hussein, Uday
United Arab Emirates: Iraqi players in, 140, 154; Revie as coach, 5, 95
United States of America see America (USA)
Uraybi, Ghanim, 143–4
Uruguay: defeated by Iraq (2003), 17; FIFA ranking, 17
USA see America (USA)
USA Today: sports coverage, 2
Uzbekistan football team: against Iraq in Asian Cup, 180; defeat of Iraq (2004), 212

volleyball in Iraq, 31, 114
Vulliamy, Ed, 34

Wahab, Tariq Abdul, 102
Wahabbites, 178
Wahid, Aziz Abdul (weightlifter), 160
Wales: FIFA ranking, 3
Wallechinsky, David, 14
Wassila (Ammo Baba's daughter-in-law), 82–3
Watkins, Maurice, 173
Wenger, Arsene, 8
West Bromwich Albion FC, 125

Western governments: support for Saddam,
105
women: girls' team suggested for football
academy, 176; on INOC, 167; in Iraqi
Olympic team for Athens, 172–3; in Iraqi
sport, 166–8; Iraqi Women's Sports
Federation, 167; in sport in the Middle
East, 14; working with foreigners, fate of,
179; *see also* Sabeeh, Dr Iman
World Cup: 1986, Iraq in, 97, 143–4; 2006, 1,
25, 68, 206, 212
wrestling team, Iraqi: Arab Championships,
155–6

Yahia, Latif (Uday's double), 12, 105–6;
background, 106; in exile in England,
213–14; on invasion, 214; on Iraq under
Saddam, 106; refusal to help Western
intelligence, 214; retirement as *fiday*, 108;

on Saddam, 106; tutored to become Uday's
double, 106–7; as Uday's double, 107–8
Yasin, Nabeel (Yamam Nabeel's father), 120,
131
Yassin, Arshed (Saddam's brother-in-law), 149
Yemen: Iraqi footballers in, 140, 154; Iraqi
players ordered to return by Uday, 150
Yugoslavia: comparison with Iraq, 211–12

Zaidang, Moufaq, 83, 86; on Ammo Baba,
86–7
al-Zarqawi, Abu Musab (terrorist), 179, 211
al-Zawraa football club, 23–4, 51, 118, 149,
206; attacks on, 206; before Saddam, 52;
matches against al-Shurta, 34, 117; in post-
invasion league, 212, 218, 219; Radhi as
president, 204, 206; sponsorship by Itsalat,
133; support for players, 149
Zionism: hatred by Arabs, 58